TEACHING

IN COLLEGE

A Resource for College Teachers

Third Edition

Bill J. Frye, Editor

Teaching in College, A Resource for College Teachers
Bill J. Frye, Ph.D.
Editor

Published by:

Info-Tec, Inc.
P.O. Box 40092
Cleveland, OH 44140
216/333-3155
216/933-9285 (fax)

Library of Congress Data
Catalog Card Number: 94-076413
ISBN (softcover) 0-940017-18-0
ISBN (hardcover) 0-940017-19-9

Printed in the United States of America

Acknowledgements

While the contributions of all who helped shape the Third Edition of *Teaching in College* may go unheralded, recognition is gratefully extended to those who were particularly generous in giving their time and expertise.

I am indebted to Don Greive for his forthright conviction that changes in American higher education demanded a new and different *Teaching in College.* Steve Aby, Education Bibliographer provided kind assistance in conducting the preliminary research for my chapters. Eleanor Young, June Stoll and Sharon Latkovich generously contributed vital editorial and technical review and assistance. Patricia E. Ruth and Bonita L. Lusardo kindly allowed their instructional development work to be included as exemplary examples. Deborah Loukota contributed painstaking editorial, layout and typesetting duties. Lastly, the many, many students and faculty who have helped shape my understanding of, and appreciation for, the complexities and realities of modern college and university teaching are gratefully acknowledged.

—Bill J. Frye, Ph.D.
Editor

Table of Contents

Chapter 3

Teaching in Racially and Culturally
Diverse Environments 55

Jaslin U. Salmon, Ph.D.

Chapter 4

Instructional Planning for College Courses 81

Bill J. Frye, Ph.D.

Chapter 5
The Adult Learner 107
Paul Kazmierski, Ph.D.

Chapter 6
Thoughts on Teaching 131
Elizabeth M. Hawthorne, Ph.D.

Chapter 7

Planning Student Evaluation, Constructing Tests and Grading

Bill J. Frye, Ph.D.

Preface

Bill J. Frye, Ph.D.

The third edition of *Teaching in College* responds to the unprecedented attention being given to instructional universities. Myriad changes are combining to assure that the practices of old will not survive into the twenty-first century. Skyrocketing higher education costs, older students seeking employment survival, waves of under-prepared traditional students, an overall student body of unparalleled diversity, a dwindling pool of private and public financial support, and the scorn of some popular writings critical of higher education and its teachers are some of the forces that challenge the traditional practices of American higher education.

Amid the complexities of the modern higher education institution, one arena in which success of the enterprise will be judged is the classroom. Students who enter the classrooms carry with them expectations that are both high and consumer-oriented. This edition of *Teaching in College* offers college and university teachers, both beginning and experienced, guidance that can lead to effective and successful teaching.

In chapter one, Milton D. Cox offers a broad perspective of twenty-first century college and university teaching and a challenge to teachers to discover ways to enhance student learning. Cox's extensive work with the writings and practices of reflective and innovative college and university teachers affords the reader a concise overview of contemporary and emerging college teaching.

Don Greive presents a mosaic of differing and constantly evolving forms of American higher education in chapter two. Historical background punctuated by significant legislation and social forces reveal a wide range of institutional philosophies. Central to each type of college and university is the goal of serving a rapidly changing student clientele.

In the third chapter, Jaslin Salmon combines personal experience with a well-focused literature review to present a compelling case for institutions and faculty to respond to increasingly diverse students. Foremost, Salmon offers recommendations that begin with the board of trustees and administration and culminate in an expansive treatment of professor responsibilities.

Chapter four offers a detailed, example-filled treatment of student-oriented planning from course description to measurable objectives. Relationships between college course content and student goals and objectives are presented through both rationale and example. The cognitive, affective and psychomotor domains are presented through the use of examples illustrating how each is actually used in instructional planning.

Paul Kazmierski presents an examination of selected contemporary learning theories through the use of easily understood examples in chapter five. He also presents major works on adult learner characteristics for guidance in creating a classroom atmosphere that responds to unique adult learner needs and abilities.

In chapter six, Elizabeth Hawthorne offers a down-to-earth perspective on college teaching. Her ideas and observations will prove helpful to many readers.

The final chapter, Planning Student Evaluation, Constructing Tests and Grading, will prove useful for beginning and experienced faculty working to integrate multiple assessment measures. Particular attention is given to developing a course evaluation plan with examples and suggestions for implementing various evaluation methods. Noteworthy within this chapter are examples of objectives and test items for each level of the cognitive domain. Finally, instructions for creating a grade management spreadsheet, test item analysis information and sample college syllabus are included.

Emerging Trends in College Teaching for the 21st Century

Milton D. Cox, Ph.D.

New Year's resolutions are interesting phenomena. Some don't take them seriously, but many of us reflect on the ending year and, looking ahead, choose goals, objectives, and a plan for the new one. Our past experiences and extrapolation of recent trends shape our goals and how we plan to achieve them. The approach of a new decade increases the span of our reflection and the complexity of our analysis tenfold, an increase of a full unit on the Richter scale of time. However, the drama of the coming of a new century offers us a once-in-a-lifetime motivation to pause and plan to achieve our best during the rest of our lives.

As teachers, how can we best reflect on the recent past and prepare ourselves for teaching in the 21st century? What are the emerging trends in college teaching, and how can we put them in a perspective that will help us prepare for teaching in the future? Developments during the past five years make this a challenging and exciting task.

*This chapter is a revision and expansion of the "Message From the Editors," M.D. Cox and L. Richlin, in Volume 4 (1993) of the **Journal on Excellence in College Teaching**.*

Over the last 30 years, the role of teaching in academe has been ambiguous. At both established and developing universities, faculty attitudes and activities came to be shaped by the demands of, and rewards for, discovery scholarship. At two- and four-year colleges, heavy teaching assignments stifled pedagogical innovation. Faculty with an interest in teaching became confused and frustrated by the conflicting messages of mission statements and reward structures. In the narrow confines of discipline, specialization, and department, the community nourished by teaching disappeared; professors isolated their classrooms and were left to pour content into students. Dialogue and collaboration around teaching dwindled. Amazingly, through it all, some faculty as individuals—as loners—maintained their interest in and love for teaching. And a few individuals, programs, and colleges developed and published their teaching innovations.

After national calls for the reform of undergraduate education were made a decade ago, students, parents, and legislators began to apply pressure to reestablish the importance of student learning. More recently, central administrators have begun to change reward structures, although entrenched faculty in some departments cling to the old culture. Nevertheless, university-wide community is beginning to be built around teaching. New disciplinary journals that publish the scholarship of teaching are being started, and established ones are gaining respect. National teaching conferences and journals that provide a forum for the scholarship of teaching are expanding. With these emerging opportunities, faculty who have held their enthusiasm about teaching in check for so many years may now discover, learn about, try, and discuss teaching innovations. Faculty are going public about their interest in teaching and learning. Over the last five years, this pent-up desire has given rise to a rush of ideas and theories for improving the teaching-learning connection, which now can be tried and studied as we move toward the 21st century.

At this point, you may wish to pause and think about how you would define "emerging trends" and what teaching approaches you consider emerging trends in college teaching. Make a list to compare with those that follow. How would you organize your emerging trends into subgroups?

What is an emerging trend in college teaching? It is an approach to, or aspect of, college teaching that has been increasing (or decreasing) in the recent few—five or ten—years; for example, teaching techniques, methods, philosophies, goals, assessments, and curricula. For you, an emerging trend may involve an approach that is new to your discipline, even though it is commonplace in another. It may involve teaching outside the classroom as well as inside.

How does one discern emerging trends? Perhaps you and your colleagues have been noticing and talking about new teaching approaches, hearing about them at conferences and seminars, and reading about them in teaching newsletters and journals.

I have read and listened to faculty voices, including those in the first four volumes of the *Journal on Excellence in College Teaching* and the hundreds of topics volunteered for presentations at the Lilly Conferences on College Teaching. I now report the emerging trends that I see, and cite a few references (by no means complete) to illustrate.

A Perspective

The emerging trends in college teaching reflect a growing realization and acceptance by faculty of the complexity of college teaching and learning. A helpful perspective from which to classify and discuss these trends is to look at this complexity as change in the communication process: the population, paths, levels, methods, and assessment involved in teaching and learning.

Population

Teaching and learning involve, of course, both teachers and students. Each group is becoming more diverse, raising interesting challenges (Poplin, 1992; Simcock and Lokon, 1992; Smith, 1991). We have discovered some things about learning in certain categories, for example, adults (Cross, 1992); women (Clinchy, 1990); new students (Baxter Magolda, 1992); and race (Treisman, 1992). One emerging trend addresses the challenge of teaching in the mixed classroom (remember the one-room schoolhouse)—a class often contains students of varied ages (Bishop-Clark and

Lynch, 1992); different stages of intellectual development (Baxter Magolda, 1992); different learning styles (Grasha, 1990); and diverse cultures (Jenkins and Bainer, 1991). The faculty also is diversifying. Teachers will need to investigate ways their differences can affect faculty collaborative efforts (Austin and Baldwin, 1991) in teaching, mentoring, and developing curriculum.

Communication Paths

In the past, communication between teacher and student has consisted mostly of a few traditional one-way paths.

Figure 1
Traditional Teaching/Learning Feedback

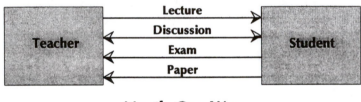

Mostly One Way

Emerging now, however, are many new two-way paths connecting not only teacher and student, but also teacher and teacher and student and student. For example, classroom assessment techniques (Angelo and Cross, 1993) can inform teachers and students immediately of expectations and realities about learning before traditional assessment—exams or papers—takes place. Broader feedback also is an emerging trend; student portfolios can give the teacher a measure of improvement over time, and provide opportunities for students to analyze their own learning (Murnane, 1993). Both continuous quality improvement (Cross, 1993) and cooperative learning (Cooper and Mueck, 1990; Millis, 1991) empower students to take active roles in their learning. Collaboration and peer teaching (Whitman, 1988) connect students as learners. The faculty colleague is accepted increasingly as collaborator in the role of mentor (Boice, 1992) and partner (Katz and Henry, 1988). Also, as a respected literature (Cashin, 1994) on college teaching and learning (Cross, 1990) is developed and read by faculty, it will inform scholarly teaching and then inspire and generate more scholarship, creating an ongoing cycle of discovery and practice in teaching (Richlin, 1993).

Figure 2
Immediate Teaching/Learning Feedback

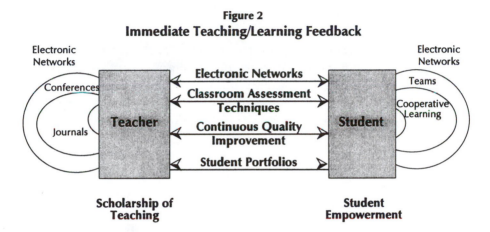

Broader Feedback

Communication Levels

In addition to the increasing number of paths of communication, there are new levels at which communication is taking place to meet emerging teaching and learning goals. In the past, an individual's teaching goals (often not made explicit) have included only the presentation of the content and skills of a discipline. Now interest is emerging in various aspects of student development. In addition to teaching disciplinary content, more faculty are attempting to facilitate student intellectual development (Baxter Magolda, 1992). There is more activity in the design of courses and curriculum to foster interdisciplinary and connected learning (Thomas, 1992). Interest in how to teach critical thinking (Kurfiss, 1988; Nelson, 1993) continues to grow.

Communication Methods

Emerging methods of communication will enable teaching and learning to take place on more paths and at more levels. Technology can enhance the speed, detail, economy, and efficiency of communication, but is tempered by practical and humanistic realities. Electronic networks and journals can engage some teaching and learning styles, but not all. Case studies (Silverman and Welty, 1990), long used in teaching in business schools, are now emerging in other disciplines to connect in-class learning with the reality outside the classroom. In fact, teaching outside the classroom is an emerging trend (Kuh, 1991). Howard Gardner's categorization of multiple intelligences helps teachers foster understanding and creativity in new ways (Lazear, 1992). Active learning methods (Bonwell and Eison, 1991) are emerging as ways to increase students' involvement in their own learning. Capstone courses connect learning both across and within disciplines (Wagenaar, 1993). And there is a reawakening of the role of practice in learning: The idea of traditional internships and co-ops (Linn and Jako, 1992) has been extended to include international (Beidler, 1990) and multicultural experiences. In the coming years, finding ways to merge these with theory in the classroom will be an important endeavor.

Assessment of Communication

Finally, assessment of the effectiveness of these emerging trends will require a much broader range of measurement than has existed in past years. Measuring teaching effectiveness too often has been limited to hearsay or student evaluation, while measuring student learning has been limited to the results of national professional exams (McClymer and Knoles, 1992). Over the last decade, ways of measuring student learning outcomes have been emerging from the assessment movement. Now, multiple methods for assessing teaching effectiveness and student learning are being developed. The use of portfolios, long used in writing and the visual arts, is most promising for demonstrating teaching effectiveness and student learning while honoring the complexity of teaching, individual talents, and style (Froh, Gray, and Lambert, 1993; Seldin, 1993). Classroom research (Cross,

1990) also is emerging as a way to assess how our teaching is enhancing our students' learning. Classroom research is different in procedures and purpose from formal educational research, yet it is moving beyond Cross's initial intention of being limited to one's own students and classroom. As classroom research is shared within departments and disciplines, it informs and provides benchmarks for teaching and learning.

Adopting and Keeping Your Resolutions

One of our "new century resolutions" should be to become better teachers. The emerging trends in college teaching can help us keep this resolution, provided we incorporate them into our planning in a thoughtful and reasonable way. Here are some things to keep in mind as you reflect on the ending century and set teaching goals and objectives for the new.

First, learn more about the teaching approaches that are considered emerging trends. In this chapter, references for your reading are given for most of them. Ask for and arrange seminars in your department and college to get ideas and reports from faculty who are using the new approaches; select presenters who have done classroom research and can provide evidence that the new approaches have increased student learning. Be sure that these sessions involve some microteaching so that the audience can experience the new approach firsthand.

Second, analyze critically the value and appropriateness of these emerging trends with respect to your discipline, courses, students, teaching style, and classroom experience. What is emerging is not necessarily better for you and your students. An interesting exposition in this vein is Fong's (1987) article, "Commonplaces About Teaching: Second Thoughts." Here, Fong describes some commonplaces—popular positions—that seemed false to his classroom experiences; for example, the silent student is an uninvolved learner; discussion is preferable to lecture; students need to acquire skills, not memorize information; and instruction must be geared to student backgrounds and aspirations. Decide which emerging trends are appropriate for you.

Finally, place in context and balance the emerging trends you favor and the successful approaches that have worked for you over the years. Try to blend these approaches into a recipe whose gourmet creation will whet, then satisfy, the appetites of your students. Teaching and learning are complex, and as teachers, we must sample the many flavors—new and old—and determine the ingredients and mixture that best enhance learning.

In conclusion, best wishes for the 21st. May the coming of the new century inspire and energize your teaching.

*Milton D. Cox is university director for teaching effectiveness programs at Miami University in Ohio, where he founded and directs the annual Lilly Conference on College Teaching. He also directs the 1994 Hesburgh Award-winning Alumni Teaching Scholars Program at Miami and is editor-in-chief of the **Journal on Excellence in College Teaching**. He is currently directing Miami's teaching portfolio pilot project. For the past 28 years he has taught mathematics at Miami, designing and teaching courses that celebrate and share with students the beauty of mathematics. Nationally, Cox has developed programs to enable the presentation of undergraduate student papers at national professional meetings. In 1988, he received the C. C. McDuffee Award for Distinguished Service to Pi Mu Epsilon, the National Mathematics Honorary Society.*

References

Angelo, Thomas A. and Cross, K. Patricia, *Classroom Assessment Techniques: A Handbook for College Teachers* (2nd ed.), Jossey-Bass, San Francisco, 1993.

Austin, A.E. and Baldwin, R.G., *Faculty Collaboration: Enhancing the Quality of Scholarship and Teaching* (ASHE-ERIC Higher Education Report No. 7), The George Washington University, School of Education and Human Development, Washington, DC, 1991.

Baxter Magolda, Marcia B., *Knowing and Reasoning in College: Gender-related Patterns in Students' Intellectual Development*, Jossey-Bass, San Francisco, 1992.

Bishop-Clark, C. and Lynch, J., "The Mixed-age Classroom," *College Teaching*, *40*(3), 114-117, 1992.

Beidler, Peter G., "From the Other Side: An American Teacher in China," *Journal on Excellence in College Teaching, 1,* 118-127, 1990.

Boice, Robert, "Lessons Learned About Mentoring," in M.D. Sorcinelli and A.E. Austin, Eds., *New Directions for Teaching and Learning: No. 50, Developing New and Junior Faculty* (pp. 51-61), Jossey-Bass, San Francisco, 1992.

Bonwell, C.C. and Eison, J.A., *Active Learning: Creating Excitement in the Classroom* (ASHE-ERIC Higher Education Report No. 1), The George Washington University, School of Education and Human Development, Washington, DC, 1991.

Cashin, William E. and Clegg, Victoria L., *Periodicals Related to College Teaching* (Idea Paper No. 28), Kansas State University, Center for Faculty Evaluation and Development, Manhattan, KS, January, 1994.

Clinchy, Blythe McVicker, "Issues of Gender in Teaching and Learning," *Journal on Excellence in College Teaching, 1,* 52-67, 1990.

Cooper, J. and Mueck, R., "Student Involvement in Learning: Cooperative Learning and College Instruction," *Journal on Excellence in College Teaching, 1,* 68-76, 1990.

Cross, K. Patricia, "Teaching to Improve Learning," *Journal on Excellence in College Teaching, 1,* 9-22, 1990.

Cross, K. Patricia, *Adults as Learners: Increasing Participation and Facilitating Learning*, Jossey-Bass, San Francisco, 1992.

Cross, K. Patricia, "Involving Faculty in TQM," *Community College Journal*, *63*(4), 16-20, 1993.

Fong, Bobby, "Commonplaces About Teaching: Second Thoughts," *Change*, 28-34, July/August, 1987.

Froh, Robert C., Gray, Peter J., and Lambert, Leo M., "Representing Faculty Work: The Professional Portfolio," in R.M. Diamond and B.E. Adam, eds., *New Directions for Higher Education: No. 81, Recognizing Faculty Work: Reward Systems for the Year 2000* (pp. 97-110), Jossey-Bass, San Francisco, 1993.

Grasha, Tont, "Using Traditional Versus Naturalistic Approaches to Assessing Learning Styles in College Teaching," *Journal on Excellence in College Teaching, 1,* 23-38, 1990.

Jenkins, Carol A. and Bainer, Deborah L., "Common Instructional Problems in the Multi-cultural Classroom," *Journal on Excellence in College Teaching, 2,* 77-88, 1991.

Katz, Joseph and Henry, Mildred, *"Turning Professors into Teachers: A New Approach to Faculty Development and Student Learning,"* ACE/Macmillan, New York, 1988.

Kuh, George D., "Teaching and Learning—After Class," *Journal on Excellence in College Teaching, 2*, 35-51, 1991.

Kurfiss, J.G., *Critical thinking: Theory, Research, Practice, and Possibilities* (ASHE-ERIC Higher Education Report No. 2), Association for the Study of Higher Education, Washington, DC, 1988.

Lazear, DavidG., *Teaching for Multiple Intelligences,* Phi Delta Kappa Educational Foundation, Bloomington, IN, 1992.

Linn, Patricia L. and Jako, Katherine L., "Alternating Currents: Integrating Study and Work in the Undergraduate Curriculum," *Journal on Excellence in College Teaching, 3*, 93-100, 1992.

McClymer, John F. and Knoles, Lucia Z., "Ersatz Learning, Inauthentic Testing," *Journal on Excellence in College Teaching, 3*, 33-50, 1992.

Millis, Barbara J., "Fulfilling the Promise of the 'Seven Principles' Through Cooperative Learning: An Action Agenda for the University Classroom," *Journal on Excellence in College Teaching, 2*, 139-144, 1991.

Murnane, Yvonne, "Good Grading: Student Portfolios—A Primer," *The National Teaching and Learning Forum, 3*(2), 1-4, 1993.

Nelson, Craig E., *Fostering Critical Thinking and Mature Valuing Across the Curriculum,* Paper presented at the 13th Annual Lilly Conference on College Teaching, Miami University, Oxford, OH, November, 1993.

Poplin, Mary S., "We Are Not Who We Thought We Were," *Journal on Excellence in College Teaching, 3*, 69-79, 1992.

Richlin, Laurie, *The Ongoing Cycle of Scholarly Teaching and the Scholarship of Teaching,* Paper presented at the 13th Annual Lilly Conference on College Teaching, Miami University, Oxford, OH, November, 1993.

Seldin, Peter and Associates., *Successful Use of Teaching Portfolio,* Anker, Bolton, MA, 1993.

Silverman, R. and Welty, W.M., "Teaching with Cases," *Journal on Excellence in College Teaching, 1*, 88-97, 1990.

Simcock, Bradford L. and Lokon, Elizabeth J., "Training for Cross-cultural Awareness in the College Classroom," *Journal on Excellence in College Teaching, 3*, 81-92, 1992.

Smith, Daryl G., "The Challenge of Diversity: Alienation in the Academy and its Implications for Faculty," *Journal on Excellence in College Teaching, 2*, 129-137, 1991.

Thomas, Trudelle, "Connected Teaching: An Exploration of the Classroom Enterprise," *Journal on Excellence in College Teaching, 3*, 101-119, 1992.

Treisman, Uri, "Studying Students Studying Calculus: A Look at the Lives of Minority Mathematics Students in College," *College Mathematics Journal, 23*(5), 362-372, 1992.

Wagenaar, Theodore C., "The Capstone Course," *Teaching Sociology, 21*(3), 209-214, 1993.

Whitman, N.A., *Peer Teaching: To Teach is to Learn Twice* (ASHE-ERIC Higher Education Report No. 4), Association for the Study of Higher Education, Washington, DC, 1988.

Colleges In America—The Curriculum and Clientele in Historic Perspective

Donald Greive, Ed.D.

Background

Providing information on the background, historic development, curriculum, philosophy, organization, and clientele of colleges and universities, this chapter is intended to give faculty and others a better greater understanding of the institution(s) in which they are employed.

The Community College

Background

The community college (or junior college as it was called in the early years of its existence) dates from the turn of the century. The junior college, as originally conceived, was significantly different from the comprehensive institution of today. Although the first formal junior college is believed to have been established in

Joliet, Illinois, in 1890, the concept of separating the first two years of a baccalaureate degree was put forth earlier by William Rainey Harper at the University of Chicago. Harper's idea, however, was quite different from the modern community college. He felt that since many students were coming to the university without adequate preparation for university work, the university should place its emphasis on upper division work and should allow the basics to be learned elsewhere. Since at the turn of the century the American secondary school system was not fully developed, it was his perception that a lower division, or "junior college," should be developed to ensure that students entering the university would possess appropriate skills. There is a lack of clarity as to whether the term "junior" was a reflection of the fact that students would enter the university for their junior year or whether it denoted "lesser than" senior college. Regardless, the term "junior college" is generally not used today because it emphasizes to a greater degree the academic studies of the first two years of a baccalaureate program; whereas, the modern "community college" emphasizes comprehensiveness as it relates not only to academic studies but also to career and community service programs.

During the first thirty years of the 1900's, the number of two-year colleges did not increase significantly. They developed slowly, sometimes being formed by the reduction in services of four-year colleges. In a few cases, junior colleges, as described by Harper, were established within universities while other two-year colleges were formed as add-ons to local high schools or as extensions of universities. Due to the depression of the 1930's, community service and adult education programs were added to many public institutions, leading to the adoption of the name "community college." Many of the community programs were evening classes intended for adults who needed training for jobs. Although the purpose and functions of the junior college were not clearly defined during the developmental years, one belief was the concept of transfer and terminal (educational) functions. As far back as 1918, Alexis Lange stated, "Probably the greatest and certainly the most original contribution to be made by the junior college is the creation of means of training for vocations, flying in the middle ground between those of the artisan type and the professionals" (Lange, 1918, p.212). Thus the marriage between the academic junior college, as defined by Harper, and the vocational-technical institution was completed.

The community college, as it is known today, has essentially come into its own since World War II. It is an evolving institution constantly adapting to reflect cultural and economic change. If there was a need for a final impetus for the community college movement, it was provided by Dr. James Conant in his study conducted shortly after World War II. Conant's study concluded that a large part of future enrollment in higher education should be accommodated by junior colleges and that there would be no inconsistency with the ideal of equal educational opportunity if these institutions were to enroll half of the total number of college students. This redistribution of students, he felt, would permit the major universities to concentrate on their proper role as centers of scholarly work, graduate and professional education, and research (McConnell, 1956).

In the decade 1960's, the impact of the comprehensive community college became evident with the evolution of several factors. The first of these was the influx of students who were approaching college age due to the post-World War II baby boom. These potential students could not all be accommodated by the existing colleges and universities. Also during the sixties, it became evident that our highly industrial, technical society needed trained citizens who could function in a productive and efficient manner. The comphrensive community college emerged as the institution equipped to fill those needs. An additional stimulus to enrollment at that time was the acceptance (in many states) of the philosophy that community colleges would be available to all students who felt they could benefit from the services offered. This philosophy, more than any other factor, was to be a catalyst for the important role two-year colleges were to play in the future. The open door philosophy was based upon the assumption that a much larger proportion of our population could benefit by education beyond high school and that students could best show what they could do by being allowed to try. It also required that these efforts take place in an environment where alternative learning experiences were available. This "chance to try" was provided by the community college at minimal cost—financial and social, to the student and to the state (Gleazer, 1977). The open door concept did not necessarily mean that students were to be admitted arbitrarily to any program in the college. Admission to the college simply meant that students could select from the many offerings they felt would benefit or prepare them for further education or for a career. Selection and testing procedures were used many times to make a final determination of student eligibility to enter specific programs.

There is no question that the open door concept of admitting students with diverse abilities, goals, and perceptions impacts the task of faculty teaching in the community college.

The issues of access and retention became a major concern of community colleges during the decade of the 80's and beyond. As noted, the open door concept provided nearly unlimited access to students desiring to enter the community college. With the leveling of enrollments, greater attention was directed toward the concern that the open door access was in fact not appropriately serving thousands of students who became drop-outs. Although major studies addressed the problems of access and retention in many community colleges, a solution to this problem has not yet been reached and remains a concern of faculty in the two-year college.

Also, it was during this period of time that the recognition of the significant role that part-time faculty were playing in the instructional process of the two-year college became evident. In many colleges, 40% to 60% of the credit hours were being taught by part-time faculty. This concern opened a whole new field—the management and development of part-time faculty and support for their instructional activities. It also brought about internal political pressure by full-time faculty organizations to force institutions to increase the commitment to full-time faculty instruction. These two issues, the development and support of part-time faculty and the role of full-time versus part-time faculty, continue as concerns within two-year colleges. Finally, the concern for accountability, as well as instructional quality and the development of academic strategies to deliver instruction, will continue to be factors in the future.

Curriculum—Two Year/Community College

Although many two-year institutions concentrate upon career education or university transfer, most two-year colleges today are moving toward comprehensiveness in their offerings. This implies that two-year college faculty will encounter students who are pursuing one or more of the following goals:

1. To complete the first two years of a transfer or a college parallel program.
2. To complete a two-year career education or terminal program.
3. To complete the first two years of a tech-prep program.
4. To take adult continuing education programs.
5. To enroll in a general education program.
6. To develop competencies and skills necessary to succeed in any of the above and life in general.

In the early days of the community college movement, the transfer program was clearly defined for students planning to transfer to a four-year college or university. Since the 1960's, the transfer program has been modified to accommodate the many students transferring to four-year schools who are receiving credit in general electives that are not labeled "college transfer" by the community college. For that reason, the tendency in two-year colleges has been to offer a general Associate of Arts or Associate in Science degree consisting essentially of requirements for four-year institutions, but emphasizing also the college requirements for the Associate Degree. Therefore, students transferring to a four-year degree program may receive differing evaluation of credit from the receiving institution, depending upon the courses completed and requirements of the receiving institution.

Thus, there has been some confusion historically regarding the "transferability" of courses from two- to four-year colleges. For all practical purposes, however, two-year colleges have a responsibility for offering standard or lower division courses that permit students with two years of completed course work to transfer with junior standing to four-year colleges. In fact, some states have gone so far as to adopt programs of "joint admission" that provide admission with junior standing to the transfer college of the students' choice after successful completion of a prescribed program at the community college (Mercer, 1993). Faculty involved in instruction in these courses find course requirements, work assignments, outside reading, etc., to be the same as that of a four year-college campus. Similar programs have been developed in the career and technical areas. These programs, referred to as two-plus-two and tech-prep, are formal arrangements between two-year colleges and universities that allow students to continue studies toward a B.S. degree in a technical or career field after successfully completing a prescribed program at the community college.

The career education component of the two-year college has found the most difficulty in gaining "respectability." Although some states developed a network of two-year colleges, concentrating upon technical or vocational programs, much of the career component in two-year colleges is an outgrowth of the adult education movement. Some institutions, however, are hesitant to incorporate the career or terminal program for fear of "lowering standards." In 1931, the *Committee on Vocational Education* of the American Association of Junior Colleges came forth with recommendations charging the Association with defining the public image of the junior college as a community institution and indicating that the community college should not imitate the first two years of a four-year college, but should create an effective program of vocational curricula of the semi-professional type (Brick, 1965). With that impetus, plus the need for vocational training during the depression and technical training during World War II, greater emphasis was placed upon the technical curricula of the two-year college.

The post-war years witnessed the accelerating pace of technology and the intensification of the demand for highly trained personnel. With the rise in high technology, the concept of training individuals to meet the nation's technical needs became acceptable. Thus, as two-year colleges matured through the 1960's and 70's, two-year technical-career programs became appropriate and legitimate offerings of the college. Many students who enrolled in community colleges realized the most beneficial part of the program would be to gain marketable skills in a respected and accredited setting rather than to attend arts and humanities courses for which they saw no immediate need. With the rise of accreditation standards and the accreditation of two-year colleges, the stigma of attending a "vocational program" was minimized. Faculty teaching in these institutions today must be alert to the fact that the goals and objectives of the students enrolled in vocational-technical programs are more immediate than those of transfer students.

In many two-year colleges, the number of adults enrolled during evening and weekend hours exceeds the number of regular full-time students. Some colleges call this the continuing education program while others simply refer to it as the evening division. The evening courses usually consist of the same offerings as the day program. However, the adult evening hours reflect a significant change in clientele. Many adults in the evening attend merely for brush-up of previous courses or to take courses for audit or no credit. In other cases, non-credit courses of special interest are offered based upon an expressed interest by a group of individuals in the community. Faculty may find that they will have each of these types of students in the classroom: those seeking a degree, those seeking marketable skills, and those without serious goals and objectives attending college simply for the experience.

In addition to the regular courses presented in evening and off hours, many community colleges have extensive community service programs which combine the separate and diverse communities that make up the college service area. The successful community service program of this type strives to develop close cooperation of citizens and community agencies: educational, cultural, recreational, professional, and industrial. Hence, the community college provides special programs of community services rather than the relatively passive role of classes for adults. The college in this case acts as a catalyst supplying the leadership, coordination, and cooperation necessary to stimulate action programs by appropriate individuals and groups in the community (Harlecher, 1969).

The most recent development in growth of community college curriculum has been in general education programs. After the establishment of the college-parallel transfer program and the career or terminal program, there surfaced a need for individuals to complete a two-year degree applicable to their individual and personal needs. Many of these students were established in their careers without the need to develop new employment competencies or to transfer to four-year colleges. These factors, coupled with the varying policies involved in transferability of courses and stimulated by a general trend toward the development of the "whole person" in both two- and four-year colleges, spawned the general education movement. This movement resulted in the development of associate degree programs in general education.

Individuals enrolled in two-year colleges pursuing such degrees are involved in the development of several competencies. The goals of general education in one institution reflect this concept. *These goals include the development of the fundamental skills of speaking, listening, writing, and reading to the point of effective communication; a knowledge of the major biological, physiological, and social natures of man, including worthwhile use of leisure time and assessment of prejudices on their attitudes and behaviors; the development of students' abilities to analyze and assess their personal values of life and life goals, including an investigation of career choices compatible with their abilities, interests, and opportunities; the setting of appropriate objectives; the development of individual relationships with other persons and groups as well as the knowledge and appreciation of the major accomplishments of the various cultures, philosophies and lifestyles, including a knowledge of major events that shaped United States society; the development of the knowledge of the basic concepts, structures, and functions of natural phenomena, the philosophy of science and principles that are based on scientific inquiry; and analysis of human inquiry and the natural environment* (Lukenbill and McCabe, 1978, pp.43-45). Thus, faculty members must also be alert to the fact that some students who enroll in their classes are pursuing a generalized program of personal growth and development in contrast to emphasizing a strong discipline, academic program, or career enhancement.

Developmental education is the final major program of the community college to be discussed. In the open-door college, there are many students who are not adequately prepared to succeed at college-level work. It is a well-known fact that among those in higher education today there are increasing numbers of students with severe deficiencies in basic communication and computational skills. Since formerly these students did not attend college, most community colleges today assume that the preparation of individuals in basic skills is part of the community college's responsibility. Thus, special "developmental education" programs are incorporated into the curriculum to assist students who have academic deficiencies. Faculty should be aware that many of the students they are teaching are at the same time involved in developing skills to a competency level.

Also important are a broad range of general services provided to students enrolled in community colleges. Faculty in community colleges will find that services such as counseling, tutoring, health services, and faculty advising are readily available to students, and faculty should become acquainted with the processes involved for students to benefit from these services. In addition, many community colleges offer an extensive array of activities including the arts, lectures, film series, tours, trips, media programs, and general community programs.

During the twenty-first century, community colleges will continue to expand educational services with special programs. Such programs may include centers for environmental study, engineering research, and organizational development. Many of these centers and programs will be established independent of the departmental and divisional structure of the college. Faculty serving in the community college in the future need to be aware of the benefit of this very practical type of educational center working side by side with academia. In addition to such an approach, special efforts will be made in the retraining and upgrading of under-employed individuals in the communities surrounding the colleges.

Stabilization of the community college in recent years has had a positive influence upon the curriculum. Rather than constantly addressing the addition of new programs, the emphasis has been placed upon upgrading and improving the quality of existing programs. New programs continue to be added as needed, but are void of the massive explosion of instructional programs that preceded the present decade. This has allowed for a more effective development of teaching strategies and faculty support to the benefit of both students and instructors. In addition, as the college continues its role as liaison with the business community, expectations are raised. Special training programs, custom programs not previously identified in the curriculum, and special business-industrial services will be required of the successful community college. This, of course, presents opportunities for the dynamic and creative college instructor.

In the future, universities will see better qualified college transfer students, somewhat due to the improved status of the community college, but to a larger extent because of financial necessity. There is also the development (already existing in some states) that students planning to attend the state universities will be required to get their first two years of education at the local two-year college. These factors will continue to place upon the college transfer divisions the responsibility for maintaining quality within major and minor programs.

Finally, the *Futures Commission Report,* published by the American Association of Community Colleges (AACJC), outlines sixty-three points that should be of major importance to community colleges in the future. Although it is impossible to list the complete findings, some of the topics directly related to instruction are that good teaching is the hallmark of the community college, restriction of class sizes, establishment of distinguished teaching chairs, the role of faculty members focusing on instructional evaluation as part of their research, campus-wide plan for use of computer technology, incentive programs for use of technology, and exploring new uses of technology (AACJC, 1988).

Faculty Role—Two Year/Community College

Community colleges are known as teaching institutions. Thus, the primary role of faculty is conveying knowledge rather than research or publishing. Individuals who opt to spend their teaching careers in the two-year college will experience significant difference in their roles compared to their university counterparts. The teaching load in the two-year/community college is considerably higher than that at universities. A twelve to seventeen-hour teaching load is not unusual, and in some situations, laboratory courses can add additional clock hours. Faculty in two-year and community colleges will find that greater numbers of students require remedial work and special help.

Also, there will be high expectations concerning the pedagogical skills possessed by faculty in the community college. Faculty will find the community college to be student-centered, with faculty more inclined to "institutional" rather than "discipline" loyalty. They also will be subject to evaluation of their teaching by students, peers, and possibly administration. Some form of accountability in the modern two-year college can be expected. One of the reasons for this is the fact that the two-year and community colleges are more closely associated with the immediate community, thus, political and other pressures will come to bear.

On the other hand, faculty in community colleges will usually find extensive support systems for their teaching endeavors. Most comprehensive community colleges have faculty development programs that incorporate both human and physical resources to assist in the instructional process. The latest in technological support is normally available, and it is not unusual for community colleges to have complete video capability, not only for classroom presentations but also to enable faculty members to view themselves in action.

Addressing the role of community college faculty and related faculty support systems, one community college president states, "Community colleges must have faculty who are good teachers. Good teachers are those who are experts in pedagogy, are experts in their discipline or technical field and therefore know what to teach. They must be current in their teaching field, and they must be enthusiastic about both their teaching and their discipline" (Parilla, 1986, p.3). However, Parilla goes on to state that "teaching, although the most important role of community college faculty, is not devoted exclusively to pedagogical aspirations. As with the university professor, scholarship is necessary to understand the results of basic research, to organize facts and information for quality teaching, and to maintain the currency of one's teaching field. Perhaps most important it is necessary for maintaining enthusiasm for teaching and love for one's academic discipline or technical speciality" (p.4).

The emphasis on scholarship and teaching in the community college in recent years is documented by the fact that many colleges have included in their policy and procedure manuals certain guidelines of expectations of faculty. Following is one such list:

1. *To conduct or complete the scholarship and writing for a paper or publication.*
2. *To prepare or complete a work of scholarly synthesis or opinion.*

3. *To participate in a performing arts activity, such as directing a professional community play or conducting an orchestra.*
4. *To create or complete an artistic work, such as a painting or musical composition.*
5. *To perform discipline-related work in a public or private setting as a non-paid consultant or intern.*
6. *To hold a major office in a discipline-related local, state, or national professional organization.*
7. *To develop knowledge of state-of-the-art developments in the technology areas by participating in non-paid work in a public or private setting.*
8. *To update teaching and professional competence through the reading of an extensive bibliography of works at the cutting edge of the discipline, as part of a pre-planned program.*

Reprinted with permission from Montgomery College, Rockville MD

A recent major study supports the expectations of faculty described in the preceding list. The Carnegie Foundation for The Advancement of Teaching, found that in 1989, 77% of two-year college faculty stated they were primarily interested in teaching rather than research, and 92% agreed that effective teaching should be the primary criterion for promotion. There were, however, nearly one-third who were involved in other types of scholarly activities and desired to be evaluated for it (Carnegie, 1989). Thus, it is evident that teaching in the community college, both full- and part-time, has evolved into a much more complex and demanding role than could have been imagined a decade or two ago.

Administrative Organization—Two Year/ Community College

The academic organization of most community colleges reflects the comprehensiveness of the institution and the desire to address student needs. The line organization will normally consist of a department or division chairperson and/or an assistant dean, a dean of instruction, and/or a dean of career and technical programs. This line organization usually reports directly to the president in a single campus operation, or it may report to central leadership in a multi-campus college. All activities involving curriculum and instruction will be addressed through this organizational line. In addition, most institutions have a similar organization to address community and student services. Finally, and directly related to faculty involvement, most community colleges have an office responsible for administrative details of the evening and part-time program and support of adjunct faculty. Thus, in most two-year institutions, faculty members should have dual support systems to assist them in their instructional tasks. Figures 1 and 2 show typical organizational arrangements for a multi-campus community college and an independent two-year college.

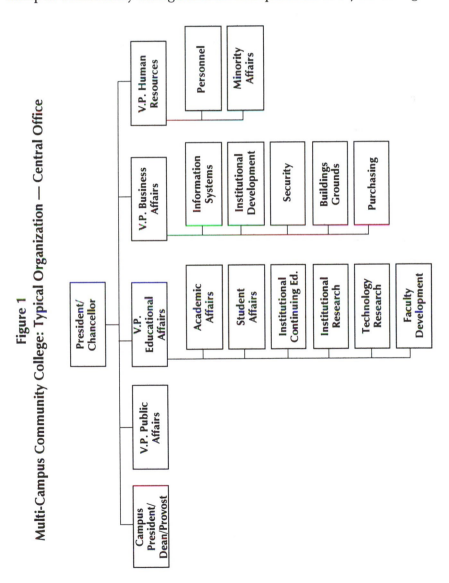

Figure 1
Multi-Campus Community College: Typical Organization — Central Office

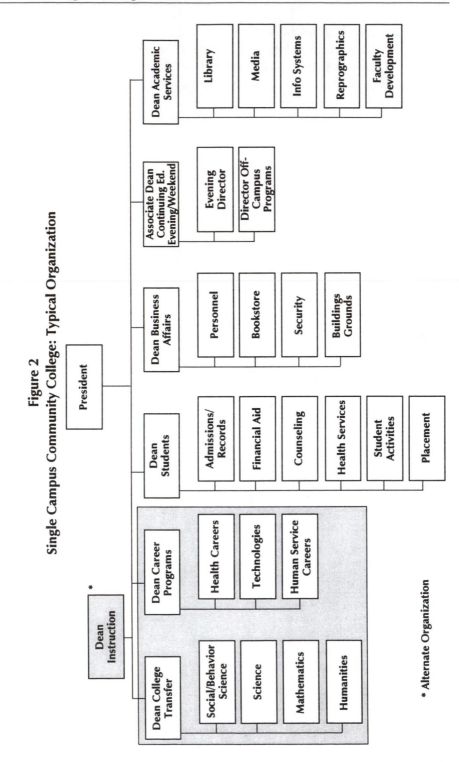

Figure 2
Single Campus Community College: Typical Organization

* Alternate Organization

The Public University

The earliest colleges in the United States were small, colonial institutions founded by religious denominations. In fact, many of the larger liberal arts colleges in colonial times were influenced by churches. For example, originally the trustees of Yale were required to be ministers of the gospel, and Columbia was ruled by the Archbishop of Canterbury, the Rector of Trinity Church, four ministers of non-conformist congregations, and two government officials (Hutchins, 1956).

Colleges for the first 150 years of American history changed very little from the dictates of the church. After the Revolutionary War, as the population grew and sects multiplied, many additional denominational colleges sprang up. The college of the first half of the nineteenth century was a creature of a relatively simple agrarian community, a community of subtle ways and of ancient certainties. It existed as an instrument for class or religious purposes. During the next one hundred years, however, church colleges found themselves increasingly surrounded by new institutions effectively addressing the questions of intellectual and popular purpose. By the time of the Civil War, there were more than two hundred denominational colleges in the United States. In addition, there were seventeen colleges and universities that were founded by the states (Rudolph, 1962).

In 1862, a significant act of legislation, the Morrill Act, (also known as the Land-Grant Act), permanently changed the college scene. The Morrill Act authorized federal grants of land to each state "for the endowment, support, and maintenance of at least one college where the leading object shall be, without excluding other scientific classical studies, and including military tactics, to teach such branches of learning as are related to agriculture and mechanics arts, in such a manner as the legislatures of the states may respectively prescribe, in order to promote the liberal and practical education of industrial classes in the several pursuits and professions in life" (Hutchins, 1956). This legislation provided federal support, raised by the sale of land, recognized these previously excluded occupations, and introduced state-supported colleges.

Laboratories were established in colleges and universities. Libraries were enlarged and collections made accessible to students. Modern languages were given a greater place in the curriculum. English was welcome, and American history, economics, and political science were taught. Universities, as they developed, even added new colleges such as business, engineering, etc. They were also organized into departments and divisions, and administrative staff was necessary. Shortly thereafter, the newly founded land-grant colleges, which began as trade schools, won the struggle for status by elevating the specialized training to the level of the professional. Thus, colleges were in the business not of preparing farmers and mechanics, but of preparing engineers, not of preparing cooks and seamstresses, but of preparing home economists, and not as practical farmers of the land, but as agricultural scientists (McConnell, 1962). The introduction of this federal support for colleges would leave a significant imprint upon all institutions of higher education.

The next significant impact upon colleges and universities was the development of the public school system. The passage of legislation in several states authorizing taxation to support public schools created a need for teachers in secondary schools. The training of teachers was introduced into the college curriculum in the latter half of the nineteenth century. This was also stimulated by the expansion of agricultural/mechanical colleges since their roles directly related to teaching in public education. Many early colleges had been separate institutions intended specifically for training teachers. They were first called "normal" schools, later "teachers" colleges, and still later "state" colleges. It was simply a matter of time until these colleges broadened their courses of study to attract other students (Hutchins, 1956).

By 1890, the leading universities of the Midwest had come to depend almost entirely upon secondary schools for their students. In 1895, only 17% of the students entering colleges were graduates of college preparatory departments, and already 41% were graduates of public high schools. The public high school had made going to college a possibility for a greater number of young Americans and had provided great reservoirs for both the developing state universities and the older institutions which learned how to tap this new source of students (Rudolph, 1962).

In the first decade of the 1900's there was a realization that the state university concept could be broadened beyond teacher training and agricultural enhancements. In a bid for public support, colleges and universities expanded their offerings to include engineering departments and the use of commercial and mechanical devices to solve industrial problems. Universities went so far as to specify that they were preparing young men for careers in public service. In Wisconsin, the development of a concept, later called the Wisconsin Idea, stated that university service rested on the conviction that informed intelligence, when applied to the problems of modern society, could make democracy work more effectively. They even went so far as to direct research in universities toward the solution of state problems (Rudolph, 1962).

The passage in 1917 of the Smith-Hughes Act expanded the intent of the Morrill Act considerably to "pay the salaries of teachers, supervisors, and directors of agricultural subjects, to pay the salaries of teachers of trades, home economics, industrial subjects, to prepare teachers for these subjects, to study problems connected with the teaching of the same, and to pay for the administration of the law" (Good, 1962, pp.303-305). This act affected significantly the curriculum of many state universities.

Colleges and universities had not completely recovered from the impact of the Morrill and Smith-Hughes Acts and the public education movement, when they were to absorb another significant development affecting the curriculum. There was, at the beginning of the twentieth century, a trend toward education of the individual for the purpose of relating the work of the college to the apparent life needs of the students. In the 1920's, this became known as the general education movement. This movement produced many new courses that emphasized intellectual and spiritual traditions and experiences of man over the old stress on military and political events. To some degree it was a reaction to the excessively implemented elective systems with uncontrolled individualism that had arisen earlier (Rudolph, 1962).

Not only did the colleges of the 1920's and 30's experience significant change due to the general education movement but also to the rise in extra-curricular activities. The movement of inter-collegiate athletics gained momentum. Students began to take a more participatory role in the development of club activities, student newspapers, and student government. This led to a period of unrest on college campuses that lasted throughout the thirties. Concurrent with this evolution was the work of John Dewey, who insisted that education and experience were one and the same thing. Dewey was concerned over the disjunction between education and society. All of these factors led to extensive experimentation by faculty, students, and administration. Such experimentation led to unique approaches to the education of students, including study of one subject at a time; co-op education; general education; core curricula; separation of upper division and lower division study; and vocational, technical, and professional training, often at the expense of the humanities and liberal arts.

If there was an element necessary to liberalize the curriculum and finalize the break from the traditional disciplines, it was provided by the *Harvard Report On General Education In A Free Society* in 1945. This study, conducted by the faculty at Harvard University, concluded that the chief concern of American education was "the infusion of the liberal and humane tradition into our entire education system" (Good, 1962, p.490). The committee took this to mean training in effective thinking, clear communication, making relevant judgments, and discrimination among values. Courses described to meet these goals were identified as the general education component. In many cases these courses took the place of the old distribution requirements of previous years (Good, 1962).

The impact of *The Harvard Report* provided a change that was irreversible. For the first time, universities and liberal arts colleges began to look at the humane tradition and the entire educational system. The general education goals in most cases reflected a considerable change in courses and course work (Good, 1962). This movement became full grown after World War II.

At approximately the same time, colleges and universities were required to absorb another impact. This was provided by Public Law 346, passed in 1944, and otherwise known as the G.I. Bill of Rights. This bill provided veterans returning from World War II the opportunity to attend college with federal financial assistance, an opportunity to which they responded in large numbers. In the year 1947 alone, there were more than a million veterans enrolled in college, affecting not only curriculum offerings and teaching strategies, but a whole new institutional concern about housing, expanded facilities and more numerous and different classes. Many of the demands that were put forth by this group of students, even as the colleges became stabilized at a later date, were put into effect (Good, 1962).

The influx of more than three million veterans, many of whom would not have taken part in higher education under the old system, not only impacted the social and academic role of the college, it introduced a significant role on the part of the federal government in the involvement of financing education for individuals. This involvement by the federal government did not cease with veterans but permanently affected the make-up of the college constituency. The effect on the faculty was to realize that considerable change was forthcoming in terms of who was being taught in higher education (Rudolph, 1962).

If there remained any doubt about institutions of higher education being agents for social change as well as agents for the maintenance of the traditions and philosophies of the past, it was probably removed by the developments of the fifties and sixties, in which extensive campus unrest was experienced.

During this time, the impact of broadening the curriculum to include the general education of the citizenry, as well as the disciplines and the professions, led to the rapid development of four-year public colleges into multi-purpose institutions. Additionally, it aided the expansion of the junior college system. This made it feasible for the principal state universities to (1) recognize research, both in the basic disciplines and in their professions, as a primary function; (2) confine their educational programs primarily to advanced undergraduate, graduate, and professional fields with strong emphasis on scholarly and theoretical foundations; and (3) admit only students thought to be capable of a high level of intellectual attainment. Thus, the broadening of the base of higher education in the United States did not reduce the need for, and the probability of, many institutions remaining selective in terms of the clientele they served.

The modern university has expanded its role considerably within the past decade. Even mission statements indicate the evolution of the role of the major university. Typical statements include a recognition of the commitment to educate its students in skills necessary for the pursuit of a career. Some major universities have even gone to the point of accepting students on a conditional admission basis if they feel the students have questionable background to succeed at the university level.

The greatest change probably has been in the structural/ organizational make-up of the university system. Recently, many major universities have opted for the establishment of regional or even branch campuses. Some of this growth is economic and even political; however, it is also simply the desire to serve students in outlying areas who could not attend in residence at the home university. This phenomenon has also led to the establishment of extensive continuing education and adult programs which address an entirely new clientele. Some universities have even opted for the development of evening and weekend programs to serve students who cannot attend the traditional day classes. Lifelong learning centers, including non-credit courses and programs dedicated to the public and corporate sector, have been developed and presented. Numerous centers for special activities, involving corporate, financial, environmental, and social concerns, have been established. Some of these are institutionally supported, although many are supported by outside grants obtained under the auspices of the university.

Universities must also continue to find ways to better serve a changing student clientele. Older, consumer-oriented, part-time students are fast becoming the dominant student. These students are often highly selective when choosing a university and specific classes, and they are likely to hold high expectations for classroom instruction.

Faculty Role—College and University

There is no question that the university professor's role has maintained its traditional nature more closely than any other in higher education. With the establishment of the university based upon the German model in the late 1800's, Johns Hopkins University is credited with combining the roles of teaching and research, thus establishing a new profession called the university professor. With universities concentrating on their goals of producing knowledge and presenting knowledge through research, the objectives were clear and easily maintained. This tradition led to a university and college system which prided itself in providing faculty with reduced teaching loads, usually from six to nine hours a semester and providing appropriate opportunity for the investigation of this expansion of knowledge. Along with these conditions it was expected that university professors would have the time to provide individual mentoring to their students so that they too might flourish as seekers of additional knowledge. Today, the university retains its historic demands upon faculty concerning publication of noted research and ideas. Faculty entering the academic ranks of university teaching will find that those expectations still exist. In addition, and in contrast to community college faculty, there is expected a considerable loyalty to the discipline in which one teaches contrasted to the loyalty to the institution or to the community.

Although many universities have developed the concept of an operational teaching-learning center, faculty development programs are often lacking. In fact, one study has shown that beginning faculty in a four-year college, over a period of two or three years, experienced considerable surprise and distress over the lack of support and the inattention to teaching shown by the established faculty of the institution that they joined. Concerned help for new faculty was almost nonexistent and much of the faculty interchange with the new faculty in the early months was related to colleague behavior and politics (Boice, 1991).

In the more established universities, however, a realization of the role of the new faculty member is surfacing by overt efforts to support and help prepare teaching assistants (TAs). Many institutions, in an effort to improve the effectiveness of TAs, have established programs designed specifically for that purpose. These programs might include working with mentors, developing a close and continuing working relationship with gifted teachers, providing opportunity for observation/consultation and discussions about the nature of teaching, and support in efforts for the integration and application of good teaching practices (Boyer, 1990).

In addition, there is a movement presently taking place in university circles examining the merits of applying an expanded definition of scholarship in terms of the expectation for faculty performance. Boyer and others have argued that faculty evaluations have given too much emphasis to the discovery of new knowledge and too little emphasis to other scholarly contributions (El-Khawas, 1992).

A recent major study states: "In the dynamic endeavor of teaching all the analogies, metaphors, and images that build bridges between the teachers' understanding and the students' learning, pedagogical procedures should be implemented, carefully planned and continuously examined" (Boyer, 1990, p.12). To accommodate this approach, it is suggested that one such technique would be the establishment of the creative contract, an arrangement by which faculty members would define professional goals in three to five year periods, possibly shifting from one principal scholarly focus to another. This would provide variation from the continuous year after year devotion to one's specific scholarship area. It would bring teaching and research into better balance, and, if implemented, universities should extend special status and salary incentives to those professors who devote most of their time to teaching and who are particularly effective in the classroom. Thus, the recognition of the teaching role at the university level is becoming an actuality (Boyer, 1990).

In summary, as one looks at the evolving dynamic role of the university professor, it appears appropriate to examine a statement recently published by Toffler: "As an educator in the United States today, one can face this info-age as a challenge and as an opportunity to accomplish the following: teach different ideas, teach the thinking or scientific discovery process, teach diffusion of ideas, teach the logical synthesis of ideas, teach the use of imagery for comprehension of intangible concepts, teach open-ended thinking with experimentation and innovation" (Toffler, 1990, p.10).

Administrative Organization—College and University

The administrative organization of the college and university system reflects the fact that institutions can no longer confine their efforts to campus teaching of academic subjects. Colleges and universities carry out research, render services to students and to the public, on and off campus, and teach many occupational and career subjects as well as academic ones. Presently, the higher education system of public four-year colleges consists not only of universities and small colleges but also state colleges, technical schools, proprietary schools, and women's colleges. Normal schools became teacher colleges, and these have been turned into state colleges with diversified programs of which teacher training is only a part. Public higher education institutions, although a minority in number, are maintaining their strength, and some of the larger private institutions continue to control a large portion of the enrollment of college students. However, as one moves to the western section of the country, there is predominately greater enrollment in public institutions. But academic standards vary within different institutions. Some institutions will not accept applicants who do not rank in the upper one-third of their graduating class. Other institutions honor the open-door policy.

The organization of the large modern university, as a result of the development of separate departments and professional schools, has taken on the characteristics of the assemblage of several independently functioning colleges within a large university complex. In many such institutions, each college (for example: dentistry, engineering, or social work) might publish its own catalog describing requirements, curriculum, resources, objectives, graduation requirements, academic information, and even student application instructions and activities. These separate catalogs very often make little reference to the central authority of the total university. The organization of such colleges within the university will usually include the dean of the college, with staff consisting of associate deans or directors, and a complete administrative organization of support for their college offerings. Each of the schools or the academic departments within the college may then have a leadership position with the title of director or department chair. The implication in this situation is that most academic activities that relate to the instructional assignment will be viewed on a college or department basis rather than a university basis.

The large university will usually be governed by a Board of Trustees, frequently business people, very often political appointments, and the president of the organization will be the executive officer of the board rather than a member of the faculty. This board is a policy-making body and does not normally concern itself with administrative detail. Figure 3 shows the organization of a typical university.

Figure 3
Public University: Typical Organization

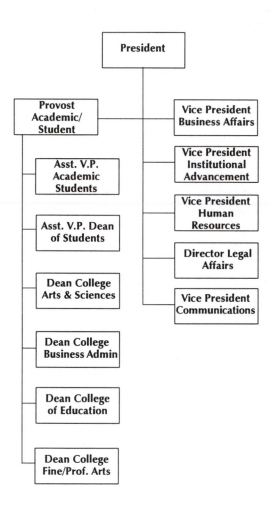

The Private Church Related Liberal Arts College/University

Background

Private church-related institutions comprise about half the colleges and universities in the United States. Although their religious affiliations may differ, their philosophies are similar as is indicated in their goal statements. A review of the philosophy statements of Protestant institutions indicates their goals as follows:

1. To foster a concern for the worth and dignity of each individual.
2. To emphasize spiritual as well as intellectual development.
3. To cultivate an appreciation of cultural heritage.
4. To instill values for a rich and productive life.
5. To create a spirit of community.
6. To value academic excellence.
7. To encourage service to society.
8. To expand the students' goal of awareness.
9. To promote a view of life-long learning as a process.
10. To support the teacher and the student in their pursuit of truth.
11. To provide an understanding of the inter-relationship among the humanities, fine arts, and sciences (Dunkel, 1989, p.30).

Catholic liberal arts colleges reflect a similar approach. They aim to help students achieve a living synthesis of faith and culture within their own persons. Catholic liberal arts colleges seek to produce graduates who are

1. Liberally educated, benefiting from a core curriculum designed to educate the whole person.
2. Academically and professionally competent in their disciplines.
3. Able to make value-centered, ethically-based judgments.
4. Articulate, possessing oral and written communication skills.

5. Socially conscious, especially of the pressing contemporary need to work for peace and justice.
6. Possess the inner resources, values, and experience in social involvement needed to become effective leaders for change in their personal, social, and civic lives (Burdenski, 1989, p.38).

Protestant church-related liberal arts colleges date to the earliest founding years of our country. In colonial America eight of these colleges were established before 1780. These highly respected institutions continue today as Harvard, Yale, Princeton, Dartmouth, Brown, Rutgers, Columbia, and William and Mary (Wicke, 1964). In early America there were no institutions, other than churches, which were organizationally strong enough to offer higher education. The British colonists used the English university as their model for establishing colleges in the United States.

In contrast, almost all the U.S. Catholic colleges started in the nineteenth century were founded by European members of religious orders and congregations. Such orders were groups of either men or women who accepted the teaching of Christ as their inspiration and guide of their lives. Georgetown University was founded in 1789 and is this country's oldest Catholic institution of higher education. By 1850, forty-two Catholic colleges had been founded but only twelve of those original colleges still exist. With the massive immigration of the mid-nineteenth century, the founding of Catholic colleges accelerated. The single decade of the 1850's saw forty two new Catholic colleges founded, and between 1860 and 1920, 156 Catholic colleges were established (Gleason, 1967).

Originally, fierce competition for funding and survival of colleges existed even among the same denominations. These differences no longer prevail in church-related colleges. Today there is a healthier attitude of cooperation. As the twentieth century in higher education concludes, the emphasis is toward building on the strengths of established colleges and providing an educational environment which benefits society in a variety of ways (Dunkel, 1989).

Curriculum—Church Related Liberal Arts College/ University

Church-related liberal arts colleges and universities offer a broad curriculum. Nearly all such colleges have a "core" requirement of course work. This "core" assures that all students receive a broad fundamental background to enable them to be successful in their succeeding studies, whether they be the fine arts, science, theology, business or other studies. It is important to the liberal arts college that students also spend considerable time in understanding the traditions and values of the culture in which they live. In light of this concern, these colleges will have requirements in religion and possibly philosophy. In addition, students are allowed a wide variety of choices for elective coursework.

Liberal arts colleges offer majors in many fields of study. A student can choose a major which allows a concentration of courses selected from a particular department. Usually the requirements for the major have been determined by the faculty from the department, and there is little cause for altering them. At the present time, however, some colleges encourage student participation in the design of a unique major, tailored to the student's career goals and interests. A major that blends several departmental areas of study is not haphazardly decided. Although such a system permits some individuality on the part of the student, there are guidelines to be adhered to and checkpoints along the way to assure that academic standards are fulfilled (Dunkel, 1989).

Faculty Role—Church-Related Liberal Arts College/ University

Generally, private college teachers are appointed on the strength of their credentials (graduate degrees earned) and on evidence of their expertise and knowledge in a specific subject area. Most liberal arts colleges attempt to maintain small class sizes and pride themselves in providing more individual student/ teacher interaction. Faculty in liberal arts colleges should expect considerable emphasis upon student advisement responsibilities.

Teaching assistants are non-existent and it is expected that faculty will take advantage of opportunities to improve teaching competencies through self and professional development opportunities. The number one responsibility, without a doubt, is teaching and student guidance. This "student-centered" environment removes the pressure of "publish or perish" and community responsibility to a considerable degree.

Administrative Organization—Church Related Liberal Arts College/University

Most liberal arts colleges are governed by a Board of Trustees. In the Protestant college such members may be from the church, alumni, or business. Policy is unusually established by the Board and carried out by the president, who is appointed by the Board. In Catholic liberal arts colleges, the management may be based upon the type of establishment of the college: orders, congregations, dioceses, or lay. Although many such colleges are established by religious communities, they are chartered by the state and lay boards. The functions of the individual administrative units are not unlike those of the typical public institution. Figures 4 and 5 show some typical organizations for private liberal arts colleges.

Figure 4
Church-Related Colleges: Typical Organization

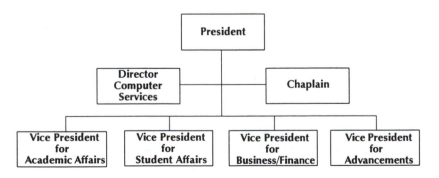

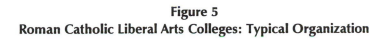

Figure 5
Roman Catholic Liberal Arts Colleges: Typical Organization

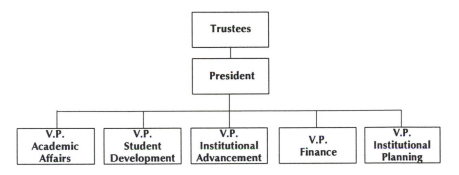

The Private Proprietary Career College*

Role and Purpose

A detailed analysis of the private proprietary-career school movement in the United States is much too diverse and complex to attempt in a publication of this type. Probably the first institutions of higher education in the United States were proprietary schools. As America grew from an agrarian culture into an industrial society where special skills were needed to perform tasks, proprietary schools responded by providing needed training. In fact, it was the mid-nineteenth century before public colleges and universities attempted to address the vocational and technical needs of public school students. During this time, private proprietary schools provided the training for business and vocational occupations necessary for the development of the country.

In the early 1900's, proprietary schools and colleges led all other institutions in the education of individuals desiring to learn business skills. In fact, many of the early entrepreneurs of our nation learned their "bookkeeping" in proprietary schools. The proprietary business school became especially important with the use of the typewriter. The training of thousands of individuals in the use of this new technology revolutionized the business world.

---

*Preferred name by many proprietary schools commencing in the 1980's.

Although this is only one example of the functional and immediate applicability of private proprietary education, it exemplifies the role that proprietary schools would play in the coming years.

Unlike other institutions, private proprietary schools have no difficulty delineating their role in higher education. Typical of the indication of such purposes is that made by one state association in its recent membership directory:

> *Subject specialization allows the school to devote all its energies to one goal: Make all its courses relevant to the student's career objective. In addition, the school offers a staff of teachers who have significant experience and training in their field of specialization. A top priority of a private career school is to prepare people with skills they need to enter a career field. The school's placement of adequately prepared graduates is critical to its success.* (OCPC, 1981, p.5).

The private proprietary vocational school in recent years has taken on greater meaning despite the rapid growth in other institutions such as community colleges. As stated in another recent publication, "The promising future of the schools is based upon two major conditions: first, only about one-fourth of all high school students are enrolled in vocational education programs; second, less than twenty-five percent of all high school students ultimately complete a four year college program." (Belitsky, 1969, p.1).

Philosophy

The philosophy of private career schools is significantly different than that of other institutions of higher education. Conflicting teaching theories and philosophical approaches are seldom a problem. Motivation of students has been minimized simply because students enrolling in private career colleges have a definite goal in mind. The traditional issues of distribution and concentration of coursework is not a major problem. Students entering career education generally have similar goals in mind—to obtain skills, to upgrade themselves, and to obtain employment.

Career colleges pride themselves on the fact that they are success-oriented. Their very existence depends upon the success of the students, both in the classroom and in the work world after leaving the college. Career schools feel that they start with the student, not the subject, to build the results. It is the students who always come first.

Essentially the philosophy of the independent private career school is that in the long term it will adjust to the student, or it will not survive. Career schools are profit-making organizations and must satisfy their customers by delivering a product that is acceptable not only to the individuals attending but also to the culture in which the individuals live. No other institution of higher education is faced with that challenge. At the same time, career schools serve the role of a humane conveyer of learning— to make certain that students with high potential have that potential developed into proper training leading to a useful role in society.

A formal statement of philosophy of private schools is quoted from a recent publication: "To help make self-evident to the student that he possesses mental intelligent potential; to provide enough dexterity (physical) and know-how (mental) tools to give vent to his intelligence and potential; to integrate instructional theory with practice in a manner to make through demonstration and reinforcing the understanding initiated by structuring continued relationship in the world of work." (Katz, 1973, p.26).

The philosophy of private proprietary schools has not changed significantly from one such school's catalog at the turn of the century:

> *The student's stay with us is made so pleasant and profitable a part of his life that he forever afterwards looks back at pleasant remembrances of college days because when a student enrolls at this college he becomes one of us, his interest is ours, his success is ours. We encourage him in his work, help him out of his student difficulties, exercise care onto his associates, and keep in touch with his parents and guardians at all times. We do this knowing it is for his good, realizing that his parents have placed him in our responsibility.* (Bliss, 1912, p.4).

In summary, the philosophy of private career schools is very simple; they must serve their clientele, serve them meaningfully and serve them well, in a humane manner, or they will not survive. Thus, the sometimes confused, public image of the fly-by-night proprietary school is not a major problem. Such institutions simply will not stay in existence.

The Students

The teaching role in private career colleges is very demanding. The students in attendance are as diverse as any in higher education. Career schools will reflect the culture in which they function and the needs of that social/economic setting. The students will vary considerably in academic background, from older high school drop-outs to high school graduates, GED recepients to college transfer. Career school students are typically more highly motivated than the average higher education student, simply because of their desire to achieve and obtain employment. Their expectations of faculty are also probably higher than the typical college student. Instructors should be cognizant of the fact that career school students will expect faculty to be up to date in every aspect of the employment field they plan to enter and in the instruction related to that career field. Faculty members working in schools that cannot afford to employ all the latest state-of-the-art equipment should take it upon themselves to subscribe to journals in their fields and to utilize such information in the classroom. They should also visit and maintain liaison with places of employment. Students expect faculty to be able to perform all the tasks and to execute all the principles they teach. Private school faculty members must be capable of providing a professional example that is usually not required of faculty of other institutions of higher education.

A fundamental error on the part of the general population concerning the image of proprietary and trade schools has been a problem for those working in the field. Traditionally, it was felt by many individuals that those who attend career schools were low in ability and could not achieve in other more formal training institutions. Nothing could be farther from the truth. Even during the initial founding of the schools, many of the technical skills learned were equal to, or were a greater challenge than, the bookwork learned elsewhere. In more recent years, one need read only a journal announcement of the programs presented by proprietary schools to realize the cognitive abilities required. Not only do many proprietary school students attain degrees at both the Associate and Bachelors level but they are also studying the elements of computers, electronics, interior design, cosmetology, and numerous other highly sophisticated occupational skills.

There is another significant difference between the relationship of faculty members in a private career school and other institutions of higher education. Many such schools, especially those of a vocational nature, wish their instructors to view students as their clients and to remember the important financial responsibility that is dependent upon a client. Student referrals from former students are vital to enrolling new students, and it is important that all students leave the institution with a positive image.

Faculty of these schools will also find that students usually encounter the same problems as students attending other institutions of higher education. Generally, it has been found that students leave career schools for the typical reasons: financial, personal and family problems; full-time employment; and lack of ability or motivation.

It is generally assumed that students in private career schools are entering to begin training that will ultimately lead to a job. Many times the students are already employed in a related area. It is the intent of the career schools that students may learn one set of skills that belong to a more complicated set if they wish. But in the event the student is not equipped to move on to these types of experiences, he or she should leave the institution with a marketable skill at the level suited to the student.

Organization

The organization of private career schools and colleges is not as easily described as other institutions of higher education. The structure of private proprietary schools and colleges will vary depending on the type of school and the location. In recent years, there has been a rise in corporate career schools. These institutions tend to take on the mode of a corporate structure, which is usually a division head, a controller, and other administrative officers with similar titles. In other cases career schools will model themselves much like a community college; they will hire a president, director or dean, and administrators who will then be appropriately assigned to oversee student affairs, financial affairs and academic affairs. With the great increase in financial aid funding in recent years, administrators in that area may also be employed. On the other hand, individual or partnership owned schools may employ a director and other individuals to assist in the administrative tasks of the school.

Many faculty members in private career schools will find their institution recognized by the National Association of Trade and Technical Schools (NATTS). This organization evaluates schools as an agent of accreditation.

When determining accreditation for an institution, the following questions are posed:

A. Does the school clearly state its objectives and demonstrate an overall ability to meet them?

B. Does it have a qualified administrative staff and faculty?

C. Does it have fair and proper admissions and enrollment practices in terms of educational benefits to the students?

D. Does it provide educationally sound and up-to-date courses and methods of instruction?

E. Does it demonstrate satisfactory student progress and success including acceptance of graduates by employers?

F. Is it fair and truthful in all advertising, promotional and other presentations?

G. Does it reflect financial business soundness of operation?

H. Does it provide and maintain adequate physical facilities, classrooms, and laboratories?

I. Does it provide student and administrative accounting? (NATTS, 1985, p.42.)

Following is an organizational chart of a typical private-career college.

Figure 6
Private Proprietary Career College: Typical Organization

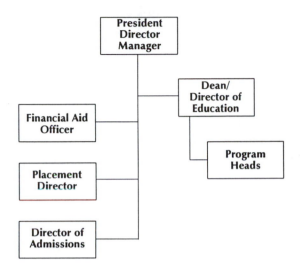

The Changing Student Clientele in Higher Education—The Multicultural Classroom

During the past two decades the greatest change in higher education is not the curriculum or faculty—it is the make-up of the student body. This change has resulted in a college classroom that more accurately mirrors the general population. Differences in the numbers of males and females enrolled has diminished. Between 1976 and 1990, the college student body became more heterogeneous. Minority students increased from 15% to 19% and non-resident aliens from 2% to 3% of the total enrollment. In 1990, blacks made up 9% of the enrollment, Hispanics 6%, Asians 4% and American Indians 1%. At two-year colleges the proportions were higher (Travaglini, 1992). Age is also a changing factor. Enrollment of students aged twenty-five and older continues to grow. Six in ten institutions reported such enrollment increases, as well as increases in part-time enrollments (El-Khawas, 1992).

These changing demographics have left an impact upon institutions probably not realized since the G.I. Bill. Colleges and universities have found it necessary to retool to adjust to this phenomenon. Many institutions have responded by implementing some form of diversity or multicultural education. These efforts have impacted the role of faculty in all types of colleges and universities. Today about three-fourths of all campuses with general education requirements have integrated multicultural materials into general courses. Eighty-six percent of independent institutions and 83% of public four-year institutions have done so. Many institutions incorporate such material in the major field of study (El-Khawas, 1992).

How does this diversity affect college teaching? The following paragraphs describe the challenge. Another chapter in this volume details implications and information for the classroom teacher.

Diversity may include not only people of differing race, ethnic origin, gender and age, but also those of differing physical and learning ability, sexual identity, lifestyle, religion, and others. Multicultural education should provide multiple learning environments that match the academic, social, and linguistic needs of students. The goal of multicultural education is to create a campus atmosphere that maximizes the academic achievement of **all** students. It is an "attempt to bring into the educational mainstream those students who, historically, have been left out" (Cortes, 1990, p.3).

During the past few decades, the **purpose** of multicultural education has shifted from attempting to instill cultural sensitivity, (or making educators culturally aware), from providing access or educational opportunity to its present goals of

1. **Equalizing learning outcomes**, thus, providing an equally high quality of education to all students.
2. Teaching **multicultural competencies** for effective participation in a diverse work environment.
3. **Teaching competencies for living effectively** and in a multicultural world (Bidwell, 1993).

The primary areas in which faculty can make a difference are in helping students enhance their awareness and appreciation of differences; in curriculum development; and in modifying teaching strategies to match diverse students' learning styles (Bidwell, 1993).

It is obvious that in the coming decades, the student clientele will play an ever-increasing role in helping shape the mission of higher education. The demands of this evolution will require faculty not only to be aware of this environment, but to be an active participant in affecting a successful teaching/learning experience.

Conclusion

This chapter reviewed the major historic developments in higher education and their effect upon the curriculum, clientele, and faculty. Although most of the changes did not come about in dramatic fashion, they nonetheless left a lasting legacy on colleges and universities. Most of the events described herein have one thing in common; they were brought about by legislative change and court decisions, both at the federal and state level. The reader is referred to Appendix 2.1 for that documentation. The listing shown there, however, does not end this evolutionary process. In the latter part of this chapter changes in the social, ethnic, and demographic characteristics of the students were presented. Although it is too early to document, it is possible that these characteristics were also influenced by legislation and court decisions. The comparatively recent action of equal employment, Title IX, student financial assistance, as well as litigation concerning student rights, are a reflection of that concept. It is almost certain that the future will bring additional activity of this kind.

Donald Greive is a former Dean of Academic, Evening and Part-Time Services at a community college. He has served as teacher trainer at two major universities, has been an adjunct faculty mamber at a liberal arts college, state university, and community college. He is presently an active part-time faculty member.

References

AACJC, *Summary of Recommendations of the Commission on the Future of Community Colleges*, Futures Commission Brief, Washington, D.C., 1988.

Belitsky, A. Harvey, (2) *Private Vocational Schools and Their Students, Limited Objectives, Unlimited Opportunities*, Schenkman Publishing Co, Inc., Cambridge, MA., 1969.

Bidwell, Sheri E., "Multi-Cultural Education: A Focus Paper," Columbus State Community College, Columbus OH, 1993.

Bliss College, (College Catalog), Columbus, OH, 1912.

Boice, Robert, "New Faculty as Teachers," *Journal of Higher Education, 62,* 155, March/April 1991.

Boyer, Ernest L., "The Scholarship of Teaching From Scholarship Reconsidered: Priorities of the Professoriate," *College Teaching, 39,* 1, (Highlights of the Carnegie Report): Carnegie Foundation for the Advancement of Teaching Lawrenceville, N.J., 1990.

Brick, Michael, *Forum And Focus for the Junior College Movement*, The American Association of Junior Colleges, Teacher's College Press, Teacher's College Columbia University, New York, 1965.

Burdenski, Helen M., S.N.D. *Teaching in College-A Resource for College Teachers*, Info-Tec Inc., Cleveland OH, 1989.

Carnegie Foundation for the Advancement of Teaching, *The Conditions of the Professoriate: Attitudes and Trends*, ERIC Document #ED312963, April 1989.

Cortes, Carlos E., "Multicultural Education A Curricular Basic for Our Multiethnic Future," *Doubts & Certainties*, 4, March/April 1990.

Dunkel, Peggy, *Teaching In College-A Resource For College Teachers*, Info-Tec Inc., Cleveland, OH, 1989.

El-Khawas, Elaine, *Campus Trends, 1992, 82*, American Council on Education, Washington, D.C., July 1992.

Gleason, Philip, "American Catholic Higher Education: A Historical Perspective," in *The Shape of Catholic Higher Education*, Robert Hassenger, Ed., Chicago, The University of Chicago Press, 1967.

Gleazer, Edmund J., Jr., "The Future of the Community College," *Intellect, 106,* 152-154, October 1977.

Good, H. G., *A History of American Education*, The Macmillan Company, New York, 1962.

Harlecher, Ervin L., *The Community Dimension of the Community College*, Prentice-Hall Inc., Englewood Cliffs, New Jersey, 1969.

Hutchins, Robert M., *Some Observations on American Education*, Cambridge University Press, London, 1956.

Katz, H.H., *A State of the Art Study on the Independent Private School Industry in the State of Illinois*, State of Illinois, Advisory Council of Vocational Education, Springfield, IL, 1973.

Lange, Alexis, "The Junior College: What Matter of Child Shall This Be?" *School and Society*, VII, 211-216, Feb. 23, 1918.

Lukenbill, J. D. and McCabe, R. H., *General Education in a Changing Society*, Kendall/Hunt, Dubuque, IA, 1978.

McConnell, T.R., *A General Pattern for American Public Higher Education*, McGraw-Hill Book Company, Inc., New York, 1962.

Mercer, Joyce, "Admission at 2 Levels," *The Chronicle of Higher Education,* December 8, 1993.

NATTS, *Trade and Technical Careers and Training,* National Association of Trade and Technical Schools, Washington, D.C., 1985-86.

Ohio Council of Private Colleges—1981—Membership Directory, Ohio Council of Private Colleges and Schools, Columbus, OH, 1981.

Parilla, Robert E., "Gladly Would They Learn and Gladly Teach," *Southern Association of Community and Junior Colleges Occasional Paper, 4,* 1, January, 1986.

Rudolph, Frederick, *The American College and University, A History,* Alfred A. Knopf, New York, 1962.

Toffler, Alvin, *Power Shift,* Bantam Books, New York, 1990.

Travaglini, Mark, ed., U.S. Department of Education, National Center for Education Statistics. *The Condition of Education, 1992,* Washington, D.C. 1992.

Wicke, Myron F., *The Church-Related College,* The Center for Applied Research in Education, Inc., Washington, D.C., 1964.

Teaching in Racially and Culturally Diverse Environments

Jaslin U. Salmon, Ph.D.

Introduction

According to the U.S. Bureau of the Census, between 1970 and 1991 the nation experienced a dramatic increase in the number and proportion of minorities attending college. In 1970, blacks constituted 8% of college enrollment, Hispanics 3% and females 43%. By 1991, the proportions had increased to 11% black, 6% Hispanic and 54% female. An examination of the statistics for Americans who had completed at least a baccalaureate degree reveals a similar trend. In 1970, of those who had completed at least the baccalaureate degree, 8.1% were women, 4.4% blacks, and 4.5% Hispanics. The 1991 proportions showed significant improvement, increasing to 18.8% women, 11.5% blacks and 9.7% Hispanics (*Statistical Abstract of the U.S.A.*, 1993). Predictions are that the racial and cultural mix of the American society will continue to grow, and concomitantly, the racial and cultural diversity of institutions of higher learning will increase.

As institutions of higher learning become more racially and culturally diverse, it becomes imperative that college teachers develop a greater understanding of the importance of taking a multicultural approach to education. Many educators have argued that teaching African-Americans and whites, for example, about the contributions of people of color to human civilization and to the United States will foster greater respect for people of color today, as well as present a more accurate picture of human endeavor and achievement (Mabry, 1991). This author concurs with this view and encourages such an approach.

The author acknowledges that it is difficult, if not impossible, to give adequate coverage in one chapter to the topic being considered; therefore, the aim here is limited to presenting a theoretical as well as a practical approach to multicultural education. Additionally, it is intended to present and elucidate the nature of the challenges facing college teachers and the educational establishment, as they seek to cope with this increasing diversity.

The term racial diversity is used in reference to racial (color) differences. In its broadest sense, cultural diversity is associated with differences due to culture, gender, ethnicity, socio-economic status, sexual orientation, age, etc. Although the discussion throughout the chapter can be easily applied to all facets of diversity, by design the focus is on race, gender, culture and ethnicity.

Basic Assumptions

The discourse contained in this chapter is best understood when examined in conjunction with the following basic assumptions:

1. The American society has always been racially and culturally diverse, but over-emphasis on the mythical "melting pot" has resulted in minimal attention to the intergroup conflicts that have always been a part of the society.

2. Although the American society is racially and culturally diverse, societal policies and practices provide ample evidence that such diversity is not highly valued.

3. The college or university is a reflection of the larger society, and as such, its performance on racial and cultural matters is not significantly different from that of the larger society.

Racism and Ethnocentrism in Academia

Over the past few years, the mass media have been focusing attention on the increasing racial tensions and conflicts on college and university campuses across the nation. These conflicts, usually involving whites and nonwhites (particularly blacks), have served to remind those in charge of these institutions that the problems of racism and ethnocentrism are not yet solved, as was commonly assumed during the decade of the 1980s. *The Journal of Blacks in Higher Education* (Autumn, 1993) catalogs a series of incidents on campuses across the nation, which in the view of the *Journal* editors, depicts the tension that presently characterizes institutions of higher education. The following are a few such examples.

At Bethel College in Minnesota, a man was arrested for threatening a black professor and his wife with violence; it is alleged that the man told the professor that "Hitler had the right idea" (p.106). At Central Michigan University in Michigan after a basketball game, the coach reportedly said, "I wish we had more niggers on this team." The coach was fired after a public outcry. A former student body president accused the Princeton University administration of civil rights violations for failing to prevent racial incidents; the student also claimed to have been harassed by campus police. A report on racism commissioned by the Pennsylvania State Universities identified 286 hate crimes that occurred on the 52 campuses. Marcus Mabry (1991) reported that at Arizona State University, four black coeds encountered a flier on the door of a dorm room with the heading, "Simplified Form of a Job Application—Form for Minority Applicants" (p.94). Clearly, the flier was used to express the racist view that minorities are intellectually inferior.

Although tensions and conflicts centered around race get the most attention, tensions related to cultural diversity have also increased significantly.

Quite unfortunately, institutions of higher learning which are supposed to enlighten are instead being accused of perpetuating racism and ethnocentrism (Gollnick and Chinn, 1980; Steel, 1992; Warren, 1992). Racism and ethnocentrism permeate all facets of college life. Although the dorm is thought to be an intellectual sanctuary where students can remain cloistered in pursuit of academic excellence, they have become a menace for students of color, for female students, and for students who are culturally different. In a special report in *The Black Collegian* (1991), Marcus Mabry presented a grim picture of racism on campus. Incidents in the dorm ranged from verbal abuse to physical attacks. Such acts are distressing for students, but they are doubly distressing for their parents, many of whom were college students in the turbulent days of the 1960s and experienced similar indignities, but had hoped that their children would have been spared such conditions.

Racism and ethnocentrism are also manifested among the ranks of the faculty. When President Kennedy signed Executive Order 110925 in 1961, calling for affirmative-action efforts in education and other fields, there were very few black faculty members in predominantly white institutions (Wilson, 1993). Despite some improvement, the proportion of minorities in faculty positions at institutions of higher learning is still small. Table 1 shows the racial make-up of faculty at all institutions of higher education in the United States in 1991:

TABLE 1

Racial makeup of Faculty at All Institutions of Higher Education in the United States (1991)

Job Title	Race				
	White	Black	Hispanic	Asian	Other
Professor	91.5%	2.5%	1.4%	4.5%	0.1%
Associate Professor	89.1%	4.2%	1.8%	4.6%	0.3%
Assistant Professor	84.3%	6.0%	2.6%	6.9%	0.2%
Instructor	86.5%	6.7%	3.2%	3.0%	0.6%

Source: Journal of Blacks in Higher Education, Autumn, 1993 #1

It is obvious that minorities are found mainly in the lower ranks, but the picture becomes even more gloomy when one realizes that approximately half of all black college professors in the United States teach at historically black colleges, and they are included in the statistics given above. Patricia Larke (1992) contends that demographic reports consistently show that the number of minority students at predominantly white institutions is increasing, while the number and proportion of minority teachers is decreasing. In predominantly white institutions, the odds that a student will see a non-white face at the front of the classroom are about 50 to 1 (*Journal of Blacks in Higher Education,* 1991). By contrast, the faculty at historically black institutions of higher education still averages 35 percent white (Wilson, 1993).

The effects of practices based on race and gender are also evident when one looks at salaries. *The Journal of Blacks In Higher Education* (1993) indicates that in 1991, the median income of white faculty was approximately fifty-thousand dollars, while the median salary for black male, white female and black female faculty was only approximately forty-five, forty, and thirty-nine thousand dollars respectively.

Racism and ethnocentrism extend to the classroom as well. During my twenty-five years of teaching and consulting at various levels in higher education, one of the most frequent complaints I have heard from both minority students and students who are culturally different is that their professors tend to say things and present material that disparages those who are racially and culturally different. In some cases, students complain that they are ignored in class and when they seek assistance they do not get it. Katz and Henry (1988) contend that faculty have found it difficult to respond to changes in the racial composition of the student body, student attitudes and student expectations.

If one accepts the notion that one of the functions of modern educational institutions is to prepare students to cope in the "real world," then why is it, according to Alan Wagner (1992), education authorities and institutions are finding it so hard to deliver an education that can take into practical account in the classroom, not only local and national interests but also the origins of students?

Advocates of multiculturalism claim that educational institutions have adopted an assimilationist ideology as a national goal, and as such are bent on transmitting that model in all their endeavors (Gollnick and Chinn, 1980; Craft, 1984; Slayer, 1992). Donald Warren (1992) is even more emphatic when he asserts that some educators have squandered student potential by using ethnocentric approaches to teaching and learning.

The assimilationist model is based on the notion that for society to be held together, the various groups must work to get rid of the social and cultural differences which set them apart, and in the end they will become blended into the dominant group. It is obvious that this model does not reflect the reality of the American society. The American society has always been racially and culturally diverse, and at no point in our history was there an assimilation in which the various groups completely relinquished their identity. Educators should not see themselves as existing merely to preserve the status quo as it relates to diversity, because in defending the status quo, they serve as apologists for the racism, sexism and ethnocentrism that have become entrenched elements of the American culture.

If institutions of higher learning are to serve their constituents adequately, they must come to the realization that preserving the racial and cultural heritage of those who are different, and preserving the unity of the American society, are not mutually exclusive. Carlos Cortes uses the national motto, "E Pluribus Unum: Out of Many One," to bolster his defense of a multicultural and multiracial society. Cortes states, "pure Unum is as impossible, as pure Pluribus is untenable, because history has forged the United States into a land of diverse races, religions, ethnicities, and cultures" (Cortes, 1991, p.13). In his view, assimilation connotes eradicating differences, and this is not only undesirable, it is impossible.

Unfortunately, one response of the academic world to the call for multiculturalism is to become more strident and vocal in its attacks on what is called "political correctness." The term "politically correct" is patently barren; it is used cynically and derisively to denigrate those individuals or ideas with whom or with which one disagrees, and adds nothing to intellectual discourse. One of the most distressing developments on campus is the fact that, under the guise of academic freedom, many faculty members have launched an all-out attack on the movement for a more racially and culturally diverse curriculum and environment, in order to protect the dominant culture (Schoem, et al, 1993).

Certainly, colleges and universities have historically played an important role in educating members of society, and there is good reason to believe that they will continue to play that role. The question is whether these institutions will acknowledge and fulfill their obligations to those who are racially and culturally different. Colleges and universities are confronted with the challenge of becoming either the cradle for racial and cultural tolerance and coexistence, or of serving as fertile ground for racial intolerance and ethnocentrism. Given the realities of the society, the choice is clear: faculty, administrators, support staff, students and boards must commit themselves to protecting the social and cultural integrity of minorities as vigorously as they defend the social and cultural integrity of the majority.

Theoretical Framework

Review of the literature reveals that discussion of teaching in diverse environments typically takes place under three main topics—multiculturalism, intercultural education and multicultural education. These three concepts are used interchangeably and will be similarly used throughout this chapter. Multiculturalism, also referred to as cultural pluralism, is a generic concept which refers to a general orientation toward, and acceptance of, social and cultural differences. Intercultural education is defined as the process by which an individual transcends his or her culture in an attempt to understand and appreciate how persons of other cultures view and interpret life and reality (Walsh, 1973). Jack Levy (1980, p.65), quoting the National Council for the Accreditation of Teacher Education says,

> *Multicultural education is preparation for the social, political, and economic realities that individuals experience in culturally diverse and complex human encounters. These realities have both national and international dimensions. This preparation provides a process by which an individual develops competencies for perceiving, believing, evaluating and behaving in differential cultural settings.*

If the college teacher is to be maximally successful, he or she must develop a conceptual framework that accommodates the realities of a diverse society and campus. Implicit in the previous statement is the contention that such a conceptual framework is not now a standard dimension of the college teacher's intellectual orientation. Certainly there are those faculty members who have a well-developed and internalized multicultural conceptual framework, but they are far too few. Too often, professors think about these matters only when faced with a crisis, or when someone in authority conducts the obligatory faculty workshop on the topic Valuing Racial and Cultural Diversity.

This author believes that the overwhelming majority of college professors are committed to the quest for excellence in teaching. However, true excellence in teaching can never be realized if, concomitantly, "valuing diversity" is not a fundamental element. The term "valuing" connotes to think highly of; to esteem; to prize. The word "valuing", carries with it the notion of continuity. "Diversity" implies difference or variety. Therefore, valuing racial and cultural diversity demands that we think highly of, and that we esteem or prize, racial and cultural differences. As stated earlier, the term cultural diversity in its broadest sense includes, among others, differences based on culture, gender, sexual orientation, age, nationality, religion and social class. Valuing diversity requires that we recognize and accept the intrinsic worth of cultures and races that are different from our own. Valuing diversity requires rejection of the view that minority groups must give up their ethnic identity in order to be American (Gollnick and Chinn, 1980).

As an intellectual orientation, valuing diversity involves a belief system—a belief system that rejects ethnocentrism. Ethnocentrism is the belief that one's culture, one's way of doing things is the best. Each individual has cultural and behavioral preferences, but these need not be construed as necessarily better or worse than any other choice. If educators value diversity, their thinking must transcend the myths, stereotypes and prejudices that have been transmitted from childhood and through the educational system. It is imperative that educators recognize that these myths, stereotypes and prejudices may become so imbedded in their intellect that they continue to exist under more palatable labels or co-exist with more progressive orientations.

The tragedy lies in the fact that the host of these negative orientations may be oblivious of their existence, and their presence may even elude the notice of students and employers. Their negative effects, however, will be manifested in teaching and other relationships with students and peers.

The incorporation of these negative beliefs is not peculiar to the majority faculty member. Faculty members who are racially and culturally different may also internalize many of these negative views about themselves and other minorities. If the minority educator fails to recognize the effect of the dominant culture on his or her belief system, that minority may pose an even more ominous threat to the education of minorities than whites, because he or she is viewed as a role model. It must not be assumed that the minority educator will automatically value diversity. Both the majority and minority educator must consciously and deliberately develop an intellectual orientation to valuing diversity.

The educator who perceives his or her role as merely to reinforce and defend the dominant culture, or to protect the interest of the middle-class, leaves the impression that he or she does not value diversity. Cultural pluralism is not based on assimilation, rather it is a posture which maintains that there is more than one legitimate way of being human without paying the penalties of second-class citizenship. Teaching in a racially and culturally diverse environment, requires that teachers recognize the inherent dignity in the cultures of students they teach. Valuing diversity demands seeing differences for what they are. According to Walsh (1973), cultural differences are facts of life just like air, water and fire are facts of life. It is what we think about these differences, our attitudes and feelings toward them, and what we decide to do about them that determine whether there will be positive or negative outcomes. The challenge that valuing diversity poses is that each generation must update its knowledge of diversity within the society, and incorporate this into educational endeavors (Craft, 1984).

Probably, the greatest obstacle to valuing diversity is "dichotomous thinking." Dichotomous thinking is defined by this author as a bi-polar mode of conceptualizing and presenting one's point of view. For example, a student is either right or wrong; a student either knows the material or doesn't know it. If there are two different perspectives on an issue, then one has to be right and the other wrong; one is either for us or against us; one is either part of the solution or part of the problem, etc. These may be emotionally satisfying expressions, but they have little or no intellectual value. One cannot value diversity and continue to think dichotomously. Valuing diversity requires that educators consciously and deliberately reorient their thinking, and their language ought to reflect that change in thinking.

Institutional Responsibility

It would be grossly misleading to leave the impression that professors are solely responsible for developing and maintaining an environment that is hospitable to diversity. The institution through its board, president and administrative team must set the tone. The board has the responsibility to set policies that demonstrate that the institution values diversity, and it must demand that the president and his or her administrative team implement these policies. Administrators must provide real leadership on issues of diversity. The strategic plan that guides administrative decisions ought to be infused throughout with diversity concerns. Carlos Cortes (1991) articulates this point best when he states that goals, structure and operation of American educational institutions must be oriented to multiculturalism. Job descriptions of employees ought to include responsibilities related to diversity, and one major element of performance evaluation ought to be the extent to which the employee carries out these responsibilities.

It is not enough for the institution to establish such programs as women's studies, ethnic studies or native American studies. These programs deserve institutional support, but multicultural education extends far beyond these parameters (Levy, 1980). If the institution relinquishes the responsibility for multicultural education to these special programs, it will help to create the impression that multicultural education is only for students who belong to these different groups. All students, regardless of the demographic make-up of the school, community, state or region need multicultural education which engages the full spectrum of the country's racial and cultural diversity (Cortes, 1990).

The leaders of the institution of higher learning must commit resources to institutional multicultural objectives. These objectives cannot be the personal agenda of any one individual; they must be institutionalized, thereby becoming the prerogative of every segment of the college or university. If a multicultural orientation is to become a reality, and if the change is to persist, institutional leaders will have to recognize that attempts to establish a more inclusive curriculum and teaching environment do push against the traditional academic environment; therefore, they are considered a threat to established notions of academic excellence (Schoem, et al, 1993). Institutional policies and practices must be coordinated to ensure that multicultural education includes the following:

1. Staffing patterns that reflect pluralism
2. Curricula that are appropriate, flexible, unbiased, and that incorporate the contributions of all cultural and racial groups
3. The languages and cultures of others seen as different, not deficient
4. Materials that are inclusive and free of bias, omissions and stereotypes (Grant, 1977).

When those who are from groups that are diverse arrive on campus, they expect to find a place that is hospitable; but instead they often find that the institution revolves almost exclusively around the cultural norms of the majority. They find themselves like strangers in a new land. College life requires adjustment for all students; but for those who are different, the adjustments affect far more areas of campus life, and it appears that as soon as they have made one adjustment the rules change. For minorities, college life may exacerbate the feeling of alienation and marginality that people from non-dominant groups experience in the society.

This author vividly recalls sitting in a history class in the middle sixties, listening to his white professor lauding the bravery and revolutionary spirit of the white colonists who fought valiantly against the oppressive rule of the mother country, Great Britain. The sixties, of course, were filled with revolutionary fervor among blacks, women and native Americans, who were fighting against racist and sexist oppression within this country.

Being the only person of color in the class, I seized the opportunity to help my fellow students and the professor understand the civil rights and women's rights movements; I pointed out the similarity between the effort to get rid of British oppression and the effort to get rid of racist and sexist oppression in this country. Much to my chagrin, instead of helping the class to deal with the comparison at an intellectual level, the professor challenged and condemned my statement, pointing out that blacks and women were trying to destroy the society, but the white colonists had been trying to build a society. This kind of response is not unique; it is the kind of response that permeates many facets of campus life. The message is clear: what is happening to people who are different can be dismissed in the most cavalier manner. It is the extent to which this attitude permeates institutions of higher learning that creates a feeling of alienation among students who are racially and culturally different.

When these students look at institutional hiring and promotional practices, as well as the resistance against changes that will make the curricula more inclusive, they see entrenched racism, sexism and ethnocentrism.

Encountering Difference and Teaching With a Difference

The faculty member is in a unique position to influence the education and, ultimately, the lives of students. It is reasonable to assume that college teachers aspire to attain success and excellence in teaching. However, it must be recognized that attaining success and excellence when teaching for multicultural education is inherently more demanding than when teaching in a more traditional manner. In a multicultural environment, educators must discover the sensitive points of contact between their worlds and those of their students (Warren, 1992). However, whether one teaches in a multicultural or monocultural situation, the instructional approach should have a multicultural focus (Grant, 1977; Thomas, 1984). A multicultural approach to teaching is centered around two simple, but basic, rationales: first, it attempts to join the streams of many groups to create a common pool of goals, traditions, and languages, thereby making it possible for each group to thrive and contribute in its own way (Ramsey, 1987); secondly, the approach is predicated on the fundamental belief that all people must be accorded respect, regardless of their social, ethnic, racial, cultural and religious backgrounds (Grant, 1977).

The Teacher as a Product of Culture

The faculty member is a product of his or her culture; therefore, it is to be expected that he or she will think and act in ways that reflect that culture. Culture is defined as all modes of thought and production that are handed down from generation to generation through speech, gestures, writing and building; it is the totality of life's experiences handed down from one generation to the next (Kornblum, 1991). It is virtually impossible for someone to grow up in a society without acquiring culture; therefore, the statement, "He has no culture" is not valid. Culture is made up of norms, which are the rules and regulations that govern social life. Another important element of culture is values, which may be defined as the measure of goodness or desirability.

Certainly there are commonalities between cultures that are different, but the fact that individuals or groups come from different cultures unavoidably means that there are some significant differences in their norms, values and standards of conduct. Educational institutions provide the context where the American culture formally introduces its members to the skills, attitudes, information, knowledge and values that will make it possible to preserve and enhance the culture (Walsh, 1973). The college professor, along with all educators, has an obligation to ensure that not just one culture, but all cultures, are enhanced and preserved. Therefore, in order to educate all American students about diversity, the approach must be multicultural education; and the process must be continuous, integrated, multi-ethnic and multi-disciplinary (Cortes, 1990).

Educators need to be constantly mindful of the fact that as products of this culture they have been socialized and educated to down-play differences. This tendency is often manifested when, in reference to a mixed class, one says, or hears a colleague say,

"In my class I don't see black, white, Hispanic or native American students; I see students." Verbal or psychological negation of the differences will not make them disappear. A fundamental ingredient in the development of an intergroup or multicultural attitude is the ability to recognize difference (Thomas, 1984). Failure to see and acknowledge the differences means not understanding those who are different in terms of their own cultures.

Educators have been trained to see and deal with students in terms of white, middle-class, Anglo-Saxon values and beliefs. This orientation is inadequate for serving a diverse student population or providing multicultural education. Monte Slayer (1992) suggests that this problem can be solved by first recognizing one's mindset and then focusing on the next step, which is the development of multicultural appreciation through multicultural learning. Walsh (1973) points out that an observer, in this case a professor, with a particular cultural background might fail to see important aspects of another culture because he or she is not looking for them; they are outside his or her range of interests or mental vision. On the other hand, the professor might attach undue importance to minor indicators because they fit his or her prejudices or misconceptions.

The educator is not immune to societal influences; therefore, he or she is likely to bring to the classroom many of the negative perceptions of people who are different, as derived from media portrayals. Patricia Ramsey (1987) posits that everyone approachs social situations with expectations and preformed ideas about people. These expectations and ideas shape one's perceptions and responses, which in turn affect the actions of those with whom one interacts. Unfortunately, perceptions of people who are different tend to be negative. Some people may have succeeded in ridding themselves of these stereotypical and negative perceptions, but others may be unaware that they still harbor them; and still others, in an attempt to remove cognitive dissonance, may deny their existence. Whatever the situation, educators must engage in constant introspection to ensure that students are not judged by the racist, sexist and ethnocentric standards that are so intricately interwoven into the fabric of the culture.

The Student

The student is not a passive entity in the teaching and learning environment. Similar to the educator, each student is also a product of his or her culture; therefore, he or she brings to the campus learned characteristics that may either aid or impede the attainment of objectives. For example, given the history of racism and sexism in the society, the student may bring to the classroom a certain amount of distrust for his or her professor who is of a different race or gender. One of the frequent complaints made by educators is that minority students on campus typically segregate themselves in the classroom and in the communal areas. Such a complaint fails to note that white students of similar ethnic backgrounds also stick together. Given the fact that the society is highly segregated, one should expect the same pattern to manifest itself on campus. Furthermore, the more people have in common, the greater the tendency to associate together. Studies of American students have shown that ethnic preference begins at an early age, and same race preference increases with age (Cohen and Manion, 1983).

Students of color will, undoubtedly, accuse white professors of racism, and one can expect those charges to increase as the numbers of non-white students increase. It is important that the white professor does not over-react to such charges because over-reaction is usually a defensive posture, and defensiveness comes across as, "How dare that little black, or brown, boy or gal accuse me of being racist?" When there is a charge of racism, the professor should carefully and retrospectively examine his or her behavior to see if he or she did something that contributed to the perception. If so, an effort must be launched to make the necessary changes as well as to mend the relationship. If the professor finds no contributing behavior, he or she has to accept the charge as an occupational hazard, and move on. Female students often face a tremendous amount of sexism on campus; such behavior is, today, often much more blatant than racism. Charges of sexism should be handled in much the same way as charges of racism. However, the professor must always be cognizant of the fact that although one may abhor racism and sexism, one may inadvertently behave in racist and sexist ways.

Models for Change: Empowering the Teacher

Nowhere is the challenge posed by racial and cultural diversity greater than in the classroom. To reiterate a point that was made earlier, a fundamental premise of this chapter is the notion that whether teaching in a multicultural or monocultural situation, one's approach to education should have a multicultural focus. For the faculty member, developing and maintaining a multicultural focus is a most difficult task for several reasons. In the first place, it may involve much discomfort and even psychological pain (Slayer, 1992). The discomfort and pain exist for many teachers because race is treated as a taboo topic; the condition becomes even worse when there are students of color in the classroom (Wood, 1978). Secondly, a multicultural focus is threatening to many faculty because it forces them to see that their insights and knowledge are limited and that they have studied the world from a very narrow perspective (Schoem et al; 1993). Thirdly, the approach is difficult because it forces the faculty member to face his or her prejudices, insecurities and ignorance. Despite the difficulties, a multicultural approach to education is achievable. However, the process will be gradual, especially if the prior attitude was negative (Slayer, 1992). If the faculty member is to be empowered to use a multicultural approach to education, he or she must pay special attention to the preparation of syllabi, the choice of textbooks, and classroom deportment, management and presentation.

Preparing the Course Syllabus

Prior to preparing the syllabus, the professor should develop an intellectual rationale that is student-centered (Butler and Schmitz, 1992). Such a rationale should take into account the social and cultural realities of students. Combatting racial and cultural insensitivity should be among the primary objectives, and it should be explicitly stated. In other words, the faculty's educational philosophy should include accepting, respecting and appreciating racial and cultural differences. Having developed an intellectual rationale, the educator ought to prepare a syllabus that is centered around the rationale. Since most texts are written from a narrow perspective, the teacher is obliged to take extra precautions to ensure that he or she includes topics that reflect the racial and cultural diversity of the society and the world. In preparing a course, the college teacher might ask what skills and facts he or she wishes students to develop (Katz and Henry, 1988); valuing diversity ought to be one.

A few examples will help to elucidate the point being made about preparing a syllabus. One teacher of literature who wanted to broaden her approach to American literature found herself asking the question, "What is American literature?" In answer to the question she said, "As I consider revising this syllabus, I realize I need to include Native American, Asian American, Hispanic American along with African American works" (Butler and Schmitz, 1992, p.40).

A colleague told how, as a student, she registered for a course in world literature, only to find that all the literary works listed in the syllabus were by writers of European descent. She found it preposterous that the professor did not see the educational value of including African-American authors, or authors from Latin America, the Caribbean, Africa, or Asia, and she told him so. His response was defensive and he ended up ignoring her point.

A common remark by some professors is that their subject cannot be taught from a multicultural perspective. That is an empty excuse because every course can be taught from a multicultural perspective. A science course can include scientific discoveries and research by individuals who are racially and culturally diverse. Since history books are usually written from the perspective of the majority, and until recently with mostly negative references to minorities and women, a history course can be so designed as to present a more balanced view of the accomplishments of minorities and women. A multicultural approach should not merely be confined to a small segment of the course, but in as much as is possible, should be infused throughout the course. Claude Steel (1992) wrote, "The particulars of black life and culture — art, literature, political and social perspective, music — must be presented in the mainstream curriculum of American schooling, not just consigned to special days, weeks or even months of the year, or to special-topic courses and programs aimed essentially at blacks" (p.78). He went on to point out that the problem is not what is taught, but rather what is not taught.

A multicultural approach will initially require a greater investment of time, but it will produce students who are better educated and better prepared to cope with a diverse world.

Choosing Textbooks

An educator who values diversity will take special care to ensure that textbooks and other materials selected demonstrate sensitivity to diversity. Listed below are some guidelines that should help in making a proper selection:

1. Look for books that do not treat racial and cultural minorities stereotypically. For example, are women usually presented as stupid, weak and emotional? Are blacks typically portrayed as happy-go-lucky, lazy, criminal, drug dealers?

2. Avoid books and other materials that resort to caricature and ridicule. If minority characters are used, they should be presented as genuine individuals.

3. Illustrations should not present minorities and women only in subservient roles.

4. Being white or male should not be projected as the only ideal.

5. Material conveying the impression that those who are racially and culturally different must possess extraordinary qualities to gain approval or acceptance ought to be approached critically or avoided.

It is conceivable that a professor could choose a bad text and use it to stimulate discussion, but the risks of such a practice may outweigh the benefits. In the final analysis, when choosing textbooks and other materials, the aim should be to help students develop socially-unifying knowledge, understanding, beliefs, values and loyalties, as well as helping them to acquire the skills that will improve their chances of success in a diverse world (Cortes, 1990; Fletcher, 1968).

Classroom Deportment, Management and Presentation

The general deportment of a faculty member in the classroom may have even greater significance than his or her verbal pronouncements. This is possible because most communication is non-verbal and occurs with less awareness on the part of the communicator. When a student wearing a culturally unique outfit enters the classroom, the facial expression of a professor conveys a powerful and lasting message to the rest of the class. When lecturing, the professor can easily convey a message that he or she intends to "exclude" students who are racially and culturally different. This can happen when, inadvertently, the standing position or eye contact of the faculty leaves the impression that comments are being addressed only to a particular group of students or section of the class. The human tendency is to gravitate to those who are like us or who we think are sympathetic to our position. To avoid this outcome the teacher can consciously move around the room, which will have the added benefit of providing a stimulus that can keep students awake. From the first day of the semester or term, the professor should project a demeanor that says, "I am culturally sensitive and I respect cross-cultural differences as well as similarities."

One of the most difficult tasks for the college teacher is management of a class of diverse students. When a student disparages another student's taste in dress, food or music in the course of classroom discussion, the challenge is how to express disapproval without at the same time discouraging discussion or causing harm to the errant student's sense of self. To remain silent in such a situation is to give tacit support to the behavior. Black students often complain that on many occasions when they raise their hands in class, white professors pass them by and call on white students. This is interpreted as blatant racism. Female students also complain of sexism when they are similarly passed over. Experience suggests that many of the complaints are well founded. Whether such behavior is intentional or unintentional is quite irrelevant, because the effects are devastatingly negative in either case. The teacher has the obligation to change the behavior that is creating the problem. He or she can quite readily rectify the situation by deliberately monitoring his or her behavior to ensure that he or she does not selectively call on students.

Another problem area is when the professor devalues or ignores significant performance by a minority or female student. This can occur because the professor has been conditioned not to expect quality work from minorities or females. A South African colleague of mine who studied in this country told how as a student in an English class, she received a "B" on successive papers, but there were no marks to indicate what was unsatisfactory. When she challenged the grade and asked for an explanation, the professor told her that because English was not her native tongue, there was no way she could earn an "A" in his class. Of course the professor displayed his ignorance, because English is one of the official languages of South Africa. This attitude is not peculiar to the college setting. Claude Steel, in a 1992 issue of the *Atlantic,* recounts the story of a third-grade youngster who produced the best art work in his class but was ignored, while lesser works of other students were lauded and showcased. The situation was observed by a white parent who had been visiting the class on a regular basis. She concluded that the only logical explanation for the teacher's behavior was race. The student with the exceptional art work was black.

The difficulty involved in classroom management is even more obvious when one realizes that to pay too much attention to the student who is racially or culturally different is as problematic as ignoring him or her. For example, to look to the female or black student to be the instant expert when discussing gender or racial discrimination comes across as patronizing. It is a tight rope but the professor has no alternative but to walk it. The case of an Hispanic young man further dramatizes the difficulty one encounters when using a multicultural approach. The young man's name is Jorge and the professor, wanting to show cross-cultural appreciation, calls him Jorge as it is pronounced in Spanish. The student quickly corrects the professor by saying, "My name is George, not Jorge." The professor ought to be commended and should not feel embarrassed. The young man's reaction is not unusual; it illustrates several issues:

1. The high status of Anglicized names.

2. The repudiation of his Spanish name reflects the frequency of mispronunciation or Anglicization by others;

3. Some people distance themselves from their background so as to be accepted by the majority (Ramsey, 1987).

A world of high speed communication and transportation is a constant reminder of the heterogeneity of the world and the American society. The college professor does a disservice to students and his or her profession if he or she ignores the diversity of the world and society in making classroom presentations. Nothing should be taught unthinkingly and uncritically; cultural assumptions must be placed in their social and historical context, and ethnic or racial stereotypes should provide a basis for open discussion (Craft, 1984). It is important that the examples used to clarify points, during lecture, are racially and culturally diverse. A very common problem is that the examples chosen for women and minorities are usually negative. When seeking to help students reach their educational potential, it is necessary to understand that the differences that students bring to the classroom means that they may also be different in intellectual ability and the way they learn (Gollnick and Chinn, 1980; Katz and Henry, 1988).

The challenge, then, is to recognize that no one method of teaching is best for all students. As a matter of fact, it is incumbent on the professor to utilize multiple strategies in light of the diversity in college classrooms. In order to present an unbiased view of difference, first the educator has to view difference as an asset (Walsh, 1973; Warren, 1992). Despite the fact that each professor has personal positions on academic or philosophical issues, he or she is obligated to present all sides of the issues and allow students to arrive at their own conclusions. One does not have to subscribe to a position in order to present a strong intellectual defense of that position; however, one is well advised to present, also, the drawbacks of that position.

What is important is that what the professor teaches and how he or she teaches it, is done through a multicultural approach and utilizes critical analysis throughout the course. Katz and Henry

(1988) best summarize the teacher's responsibility when they state that "the essence of good teaching is the greatest possible individualization of the teacher's responses to students" (p.4). In order to achieve this result, it is necessary to know something about the backgrounds and aspirations of one's students.

It is easier to continue along the traditional educational path than to initiate change. However, the professor who refuses to make the necessary changes, runs the risk of not adequately serving students, and in so doing jeopardizes the realization of his or her commitment to the impartial search for, and imparting of, knowledge.

Avoiding Common Pitfalls

All students possess certain vulnerabilities, but those who are racially and culturally different possess some additional ones. This reality imposes on the faculty member the responsibility to discover ways to enhance the relationship with those who are racially and culturally different, as well as to recognize those behaviors that should be avoided. The following are some specific suggestions about things to avoid and some suggestions for constructive behaviors:

1. Often professors have difficulty pronouncing names , and in those situations they sometimes succumb to the American tradition of shortening names by calling the individual a shortened form of his or her name. Under no circumstance should a student be given a "preferred name."

2. Do not assume that a minority student knows a lot about his or her group.

3. Even if no member of a particular group is in a class, avoid talking negatively about that group.

4. Do not tell or tolerate racist, sexist or ethnic jokes because they do damage and, even when told with an innocent intent, they can be misunderstood.

5. When alluding to racial and cultural differences, do not imply a negative.

6. Do not leave the impression that all blacks live in ghettoes, that all Hispanics are illegal aliens, that all native Americans are drunkards or that all women are money grabbers.

7. Every effort must be made to ensure that stereotypical characterizations are not made of either those who are different or those who are similar.

Here are some things that can enhance relationships with students who are different:

1. The professor must become aware of his or her own prejudices, insecurities and ignorance. It is not advisable to go around admitting them to everyone, but one must admit them to oneself.

2. It is crucial that the professor determines whether his or her personal values and standards are being used as the sole basis for judging students. The operative word in the preceding statement is SOLE.

3. The faculty member must become knowledgeable about the groups he or she serves.

4. Each individual possesses his or her own insecurities; therefore, the educator must constantly evaluate his or her perceptions of others to ensure that his or her perceptions are not based on personal insecurities.

5. Every effort must be made to ensure that the information one has is a reliable basis for judgements.

Summary

This has been an attempt to examine the realities and challenges of teaching in a racially and culturally diverse environment. Because of the difficulty entailed in dealing with so broad a topic in so brief a space, a conscious decision was made to focus on diversity related to race, gender, culture and ethnicity.

Faculty members in institutions of higher learning are encountering an increasingly diverse student body; therefore, their approach to teaching must be different. The author contends, however, that even in a homogeneous environment there is a need to take a multicultural approach to education.

It can be said that there is a climate of racism, sexism and ethnocentrism in academia and that these conditions jeopardize the effectiveness of teachers and the social and academic well-being of students. It is suggested that the best approach for resolving these problems, is multicultural education. This approach is predicated on the assumption that faculty, administrators and the governing board all share a commitment to "valuing diversity."

The faculty member plays a most crucial role in the lives of students; therefore, he or she must endeavor to teach with a difference and in so doing make a difference. All the players on the academic stage bring to their respective roles positive and negative attitudes and perceptions concerning each other. However, the way each actor perceives people who are racially and culturally different tends to be uniformly negative. In carrying out his or her duties, the faculty member has an obligation to consciously and deliberately reorient his or her thinking so as to eliminate any negative disposition toward students. The professor can demonstrate a willingness to change by taking a multicultural approach in preparing course syllabi, choosing text-books, and classroom deportment, management and presentation.

Jaslin U. Salmon is a Professor of Sociology at Triton College in Illinois. He received his B.A. from Olivet Nazarene University, M.A. from Ball State University and Ph.D. from the University of Illinois, Chicago.

As a consultant he has worked extensively with institutions of higher education on issues of diversity. He is the author of one book and numerous articles and is presently completing another book. He is the co-producer and a co-author respectively of a videotape and manual entitled, "Succeeding in Racially and Culturally Diverse Environment."

References

Butler, Johnella, and Schmitz, Betty, "Ethnic Studies, Women's Studies and Multiculturalism," *Change, 24,* (1) 36, Jan./Feb. 1992.

Cohen, Louis, and Manion, Lawrence, *Multicultural Classrooms: Perspectives for Teachers,* Croom Helm, London, 1983.

Cortes, Carlos E., "E Pluribus Unum: Out of Many One," in *California Perspectives,* California Tomorrow, 1990.

Cortes, Carlos E., "Multicultural Education: A Curricular Basic For Our Multiethnic Future," *Doubts and Certainties,* (7/8), Mar.Apr. 1990.

Cortes, Carlos E., "Pluribus and Unum: The quest for community amid diversity," *Change, 23,* (5), 16, Sept./Oct. 1992.

Craft, Maurice, "Education for Diversity" in *Education and Cultural Pluralism,* Craft, Maurice, ed., Taylor and Francis Printers Ltd., Basingstoke, 1984.

Fletcher, B.A., "The Aims of University Teaching," in *University Teaching in Transition,* Layton, David, ed., Oliver and Boyd, Edinburgh, 1968.

Gollnick, Donna M. and Chinn, Philip C., "Multiculturalism In Contemporary Education," *Journal of The School of Education/Indiana Univ., 56* (1), Winter 1980.

Grant, Carl A., "The Teacher and Multicultural Education: Some Personal Reflections," in *In Praise of Diversity: A Resource Book For Multicultural Education,* Gold, Milton J. et al., eds., Teacher Corps, Washington, D.C. 1977.

Katz, Joseph and Henry, Mildred, *Turning Professors Into Teachers,* Macmillan Publishing Co., New York, 1988.

Kornblum, William, *Sociology in a Changing World,* Harcourt Brace Jovanovich Inc., New York, 1991.

Larke, Patricia J., "Effective Multicultural Teachers: Meeting the Challenge of Diverse Classrooms." *Equity and Excellence, 25* (2-4), 133, Winter 1992.

Levy, Jack, "Multicultural Education and Intercultural Communication: A Family Affair," in *Journal of The School of Education/Indiana Univ., 56* (11), Winter 1980.

Mabry, Marcus, "Confronting Campus Racism: What You Can Do to Fight a Growing Menace," *The Black Collegian, 22* (1), 78, Sept./Oct., 1991.

Ramsey, Patricia G., *Teaching and Learning in a Diverse World,* Teachers College Press, New York and London, 1987.

Schoem, David et al., eds., *Multicultural Teaching in the University,* Praeger Publishers, Westport, Ct. 1993.

Slayer, Monte, "Educators and Cultural Diversity: A Six-stage Model of Cultural Versatility," *Education, 112* (4), 506, Summer 1992.

Statistical Abstract of the U.S.A., Bernan Press, Lanham, Md., 1993.

Steel, Claude M., Race And The Schooling of Black Americans, *Atlantic Monthly, 68,* April 1992.

The Journal of Blacks In Higher Education, No. 1, Autumn 1993.

Thomas, Ken, "Intercultural Relations in the Classroom," in *Education and Cultural Pluralism,* Craft, Maurice, ed., Taylor and Francis Printers, Ltd., Basingstoke, 1984.

Wagner, Alan, "Teaching in a Multicultural Environment," *OECD Observer, 178,* 29, Oct./Nov. 1992.

Walsh, John E., *Intercultural Education in the Communication of Man,* An East-West Center Book, The Univ. Press of Hawaii, Honolulu, 1973.

Warren, Donald, "Teachers For The Real World," *Education, 112* (3), 324, Spring 1992.

Wilson, Reginald, "Why the Shortage of Black Professors?" *The Journal of Blacks in Higher Education, 1*, 25, Autumn 1993.

Wood, Dean D., *Multicultural Canada: A Teacher's Guide to Ethnic Studies*, The Ontario Institute for Studies in Education, Toronto, 1970.

Instructional Planning for College Courses

Bill J. Frye, Ph.D.

Forward

This chapter presents a rationale and systematic process for deriving student goals and objectives from course content. The chapter seeks to influence college teachers to view their instructional task as not simply the teaching of content, but of using content to shape predetermined, desired student knowledge, attitudes, and skills. If this sounds suspiciously like the work of a behaviorist, you are correct. It is however noted that the behaviorist writing this chapter is borne not by the work of Pavlov and Skinner but by the cries of students.

After many years of listening to college students who aspired to become college teachers, certain lessons were learned by this behaviorist. Uppermost, he learned that some college teachers occupy considerable class time by reading the text to students. Others show no patience with students who dare interrupt their

The writer gratefully acknowledges the contributions of Patricia E. Ruth and Bonita L. Lusardo who have kindly consented to allowing their instructional development work to be included in this chapter.

content performances with questions. And some feel little or no responsibility for student achievement, choosing instead to find satisfaction in having covered all of the chapters in the prescribed quarter or semester.

Student goals and objectives are the means for looking at college courses in terms of what students learn, not just what instructors say. Writing these goals and objectives is what behaviorists and other student-oriented instructors do.

Introduction

How college teachers prepare for class says much about how they view their teaching responsibility. A *content-oriented instructor's* planning may be as simple as highlighting sections of the text to be read to the class, perhaps adding some marginal notes for discussion points. The priority is on covering the content and *the text is the instructional plan.*

Student-oriented instructors spend planning time writing objectives that specify what the student should know and value about the topic. Achieving these stated student outcomes is the instructional priority. In this example *the text is an instructional tool* and as such is used differently. Students would be given the objectives with relevant text sections identified **before** the class meeting, with class time devoted to activities and methodologies that clarify and expand upon the text. This often leads to class time being committed to achieving application and higher level student objectives.

In the above comparison, two things become evident. First, the content-oriented instructor who relies on reading the text to classes might argue that giving students text objectives in advance would leave little incentive to come to class. No doubt many students would reach the same conclusion, having outgrown the delights of having a teacher read to them somewhere around the third grade. Secondly, while the content-oriented instructor's planning **ends** with the text, the student-oriented instructor's planning **begins** with the text. A student orientation is clearly much more demanding in terms of instructor creativity and time.

Did Socrates use objectives?

Not all college instructors agree with objectives and student-oriented teaching. Some feel that "Teaching . . . is a performing art" (Cronin, 1992, p.150) and cannot be encumbered by "inputs and outputs, learners as products, behavioral objectives, . . . and the like" (Apps, 1991, pp.17-18). In arguing for the "artful strategies" (p.18) approach to teaching, Apps posits as myth that "What teachers do is directly tied to what learners learn" (pp.17-18). A student-oriented instructor would counter that any teaching, artful or otherwise, has no purpose other that student learning. Examining how teaching would be evaluated from these two contrasting viewpoints proves interesting.

A content-oriented instructor who delivers an artful performance would consider the lesson a success—irrespective of what the students learn. Failure to understand the material is the student's problem, not the instructor's. The measure of success is how well the instructor performs. Thus an artful and erudite performance that yields confusion for the student may still be judged a success.

In contrast, a student-oriented instructor who delivers an artful performance would measure its success or failure on the basis of student learning. The performance is judged a success if the students learn the material, a failure if they do not. This instructor would likely have written student objectives from which learning could be assessed, thus providing a clear, student-based, objective measure of the lesson's effectiveness. Conversely, the content-oriented instructor's success criterion is more subjective, as is the case of many art forms.

Although content-oriented instructors may speak of goals or objectives for a lesson, such objectives are often no more than some vague mental notion about what they, the instructors, will do for 50 minutes. Angelo and Cross (1993) observe that "College teachers tend to define their instructional goals in terms of course content" (p.8). Thus, the content-oriented instructor might feel that "Going over Chapters 3 and 4" represents a proper instructional objective.

Goals and objectives are written to and for the learner and should "inform students where all the reading and studying are leading" (Erickson and Strommer, 1991, p.83). Well stated, unambiguous objectives direct student learning in the classroom and, even more importantly, during studies outside the classroom. While details may vary, many writers support the position that *objectives should be behaviorally stated, measurable, given before instruction, and the source for student testing and evaluation* (Angelo and Cross, 1993; Davis, 1993; Kellough, 1990; Lucas, 1989; Newble and Cannon, 1989; Brown and Atkins, 1988).

Content-oriented teaching likely results from "a failure to recognize the crucial principle that intellectual competence and pedagogic competence are two very different things" (Cahn, 1978, p.ix). Devoting great time, energy and travel dollars pursuing further study in one's discipline or field is commonplace; yet "a college teacher may go on for years without ever realizing his [teaching] incompetence" (Cahn, p.x). In describing one such person, Cahn observed that "like most other college instructors, he had never spent even a moment of his academic career learning how to teach" (p.x).

In seeking to account for the continued content orientation by so many instructors, Weimer (1990) identified three faulty assumptions often made by college faculty: 1) "If you know it, you can teach it"; 2) "Good teachers are born"; and 3) "Faculty teach content" (pp.4-9). These three beliefs are the hallmarks of content-oriented teaching and have endured for centuries.

Will teaching in higher education improve? Some practices may not. Today's still popular lecture stems from a period when only the instructors had books—handwritten ones at that, and surrounded themselves with hushed students dutifully writing down what was read to them. Centuries of evolution have changed little about the college lecture. About the only advances students can claim are 1) better seating, 2) books that are already filled with print, and 3) a colorful array of highlighters.

On the other hand, a number of unprecedented conditions are emerging that suggest change and improvement may be in the offing.

A New Era in College Teaching

The twenty-first century may witness a renaissance in higher education. Runaway tuition costs of the 1980s and 1990s have heightened student demands for a quality product in return for their increased higher education dollars. Popular writings accusing waste and abuse (***Profscam, Imposters in the Temple***) have been taken seriously by some of the reading public and some legislators. An upward spike in computing power, coupled with a downturn in prices, have ushered in opportunities for sophisticated multimedia instructional development. An increasing pool of older students, bringing serious needs and high expectations, will not suffer incompetent teaching lightly. And lastly, ***Scholarship Reconsidered: Priorities for the Professoriate*** (Boyer, 1990), a publication by the Carnegie Foundation for the Advancement of Teaching appears to be gaining attention.

While two-year colleges have historically placed a high value on quality teaching, only recently have some universities taken seriously the task of rewarding quality teaching on a par with research and service. ***Scholarship Reconsidered*** asserts that although universities have long contended that teaching, research and publication are the three expectations of faculty, "Almost all colleges pay lip service to the trilogy . . ., but when . . . making judgments about professional performance, the three rarely are assigned equal merit" (pp.15-16). Research and publication have been the real avenues for tenure, promotion, and salary advancement—with teaching ranking a distant third. Some colleges have responded by initiating teacher recognition awards and prizes to give considerable public flare to teaching, yet, at the same time, ignoring the more lasting issue of upgrading teaching in tenure, promotion and salary rewards.

Scholarship Reconsidered appears to hold promise for actually changing the way higher education defines the relative worth of teaching. Diamond and Adam (1993) cite the work of twenty colleges and universities as well as numerous professional associations that have taken up the challenge, "to rethink the nature of scholarship, to redefine faculty work, and to redesign the reward system used to recognize professional effort and achievement" (p.2). Recognizing and rewarding teaching skill on a par with research and publication is a vital first step toward achieving student-oriented teaching on an institutional scale.

A Course Planning Paradigm

Whether a beginning faculty member struggling with four or five new classes or an experienced professor seeking to improve existing courses, following a planning paradigm or model offers several advantages:

1. Using a visual, global picture of the planning process illustrates how each part relates to the whole.
2. Knowing the desired interim and final products of a complicated procedure provides a means for evaluating each phase of the work.
3. Altering a complicated procedure by changing the model assures that all subsequent work follows the revised plan.
4. Following a known paradigm allows work to be accomplished at any phase and still conform to the expectations of the whole.

But what model to use? Professional literature abounds with course level planning models. Many texts present theoretical planning models calling for pre-assessment and individualized instruction and evaluation plans. Good models indeed, but difficult to follow when facing a 16-hour teaching load. State coordinating agencies, in-service speakers, college professors, etc., all seem compelled to bring forth slightly different models and vocabularies.

Instructional planners should choose a paradigm that agrees with the institutional expectations, is consistent with contemporary learning theory, can be applied in practice, and supports the instructor's view of instructional planning.

The model (Figure 1) that follows (Frye, 1985, 1987; Greive, 1989) is a guide for systematically examining course content in terms of desired student outcomes. Its product is simple: College course content is justifiable only to the extent that it satisfies or builds toward stated student goals and objectives.

What began as an academic paradigm drawn from the work of Bloom, et al. (1956), evolved through several years of use in a university class for prospective and practicing college teachers. The model reached maturity only after years of use with two-year college faculty who used it to guide the development of goals and objectives for courses they were teaching. Many institutions and instructors have found the model to be a workable guide for developing the types of goals and objectives that lead to student-oriented teaching.

The terms "goals" and "objectives" have widely varied meanings within the educational literature. To avoid the inevitable conflict with other definitions, this chapter simply uses **Level I**, **Level II**, and **Level III**, and generally refers to non-measurable outcomes as **goals** and measurable as **objectives**. As illustrated by the model that follows (Figure 1), **Level I** refers to non-measurable student outcomes written from course catalog descriptions. **Level II** refers to non-measurable outcomes written from instructional unit content. **Level III** refers to **measurable** student outcomes written for lesson/discussion plans and from which unit test items are written.

Figure 1
Instructional Planning Model

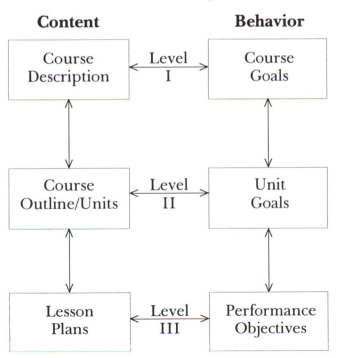

Level I: Establishing Course Parameters

Figure 2
Establishing Course Parameters

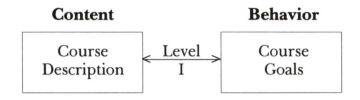

Level I planning (Figure 2) begins with an existing course description. Admittedly, many students and college instructors pay little attention to course descriptions. However, *college catalog course descriptions are a public statement of what a college purports a student will study in each course.* Course descriptions are also subject to existing consumer protection laws. Courts have found some colleges guilty of advertising (via college bulletin) and accepting money (tuition) from consumers (students) who discovered that all that was promised was not delivered (taught).

Adding to the importance of the course description is the fact that institutions determine the acceptability of transfer credit on the basis of the catalog course description. Although a course description often contains prerequisite and fee information, the parts that are of greatest concern for Level I planning are the stated **content** and **activities.**

Level I goals describe the broad student outcomes from the course description **content** and **activities.** In the following example, a course description from a legal assistant program has been broken down to identify each content and/or activity element:

INTRODUCTION TO LEGAL ASSISTING

An introductory course designed to provide an overview of legal assisting. The course includes the role of the paralegal, the legal system, basic legal concepts, and the fundamentals of legal research, legal writing and common skills and duties of the paralegal. 3 credit hours.

Breakdown of course description:
1. overview of legal assisting
2. role of paralegal, legal system, basic legal concepts
3. fundamentals of legal research, legal writing
4. common skills and duties of the paralegal

Each of the above represents a portion of the content identified in the course description. **All** content elements from the description should be identified. For each content element, one or more Level I goals should be written. Level I goals provide a student-oriented view of the description and are, to the extent possible, written in student terms.

The following are examples of how each part of the course description was interpreted into Level I goals:

Sample Level I Goals

INTRODUCTION TO LEGAL ASSISTING:

Content: Overview of legal assisting

Level I Goal: *Become familiar with the role of the legal assistant, including ethical considerations, and the organization of the modern law office.

Content: Role of paralegal, legal system, basic legal concepts

Level I Goal: Understand the organization of the legal system and case and statutory laws.

Level I Goal: Understand basic legal concepts, including the litigation and adjudication process of the courts.

Content: Fundamentals of legal research, legal writing

Level I Goal: Become familiar with the common skills and duties needed by the legal assistant during the investigative and legal research phases of cases.

To avoid repetition, all goals and objectives begin with the unstated "The student shall . . . ."

Content: Common skills and duties of the paralegal

Level I Goal: Become familiar with the common skills and duties needed by the legal assistant for trial and administrative hearings, including legal writing skills.

Another example—Level I goals from an electronics course:

BASIC ELECTRONICS 133

An introduction to electricity and solid state electronics. Basic electrical terms, units, symbols, schematics and code. Fundamentals of alternating and direct current. Ohm's law application, inductance/capacitance theory. Test equipment applied.

Content: Introduction to electricity and solid state electronics

Level I Goal: Develop a basic knowledge of electricity and solid state electronics, employing proper safety and first aid methods.

Content: Basic electrical terms, units, symbols, schematics and code

Level I Goal: Be familiar with basic electrical terms, units, symbols, schematics and resistor color code, applying this to unit of measurement or symbol of electron flow.

Content: Fundamentals of alternating and direct current, Ohm's law application, inductance/capacitance theory

Level I Goal: Demonstrate correct usage of Ohm's Law applied to series and parallel networks.

Level I Goal: Understand the characteristics of inductance and capacitance theory in electronic circuits.

Content: Test equipment applied.

Level I Goal: Use various electronic testing equipment for multiple troubleshooting situations.

The first criterion for a completed set of Level I goals is that they agree precisely with the course description. The second criterion is that they accurately represent what the student studies in the course. In achieving the second criterion, an instructional planner faced with a meager or outdated description may write Level I goals that extend beyond the published course description. When this occurs, the catalog course description should be updated to agree with the Level I goals and the current substance of the course. Two-year colleges concerned with course transferability bear particular responsibility for maintaining descriptions that are both accurate and detailed.

Additional examples of course descriptions and Level I goals are included in Appendix 4.1 (BASIC Programming course) and Appendix 4.2 (Respiratory Care Physics course).

Level II: Course Scope, Sequence and Units

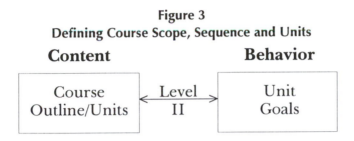

Figure 3
Defining Course Scope, Sequence and Units

Every approved college course begins with a course content outline. Outlines typically evolve through minor changes, deletions and additions as time and instructors change. Institutional practices determine the extent to which such changes are formalized or are simply allowed to meander with the preferences of individual instructors. *While multiple instructors for the same course may employ vastly different teaching methodologies, all should be following the same course content outline.*

For content-oriented instructors the text table of contents **is** the outline. However, student-oriented planners devote considerable energy to building a sound content outline. A good outline supports the course description and Level I goals, presents the content in the same order it will be taught, and gives extensive subordinate heading detail. Once finished, a well-developed course content outline serves both the instructor and the students much as a roadmap serves the traveler. Whether the instructor is given a detailed outline that must be followed, or a brief overall outline from which subordinate heading details must be developed, the course content outline specifies the breadth (scope) and order (sequence) of what will be taught. An examination of the sample course content outlines in Appendix 4.3 (pp.212, 219) and Appendix 4.4 (pp.221-231) illustrate the attention skilled instructional planners give to the details of their course content outline.

Instructional Units

Instructional units are divisions of the content outline that divide the course into teachable parcels. Instructional units are determined by identifying the points in the content outline that meet three criteria:

1) Conceptually consistent content

2) Length suited to level of the learner

3) Evaluation/feedback

Conceptually consistent

Arguably all content in a course outline is conceptually consistent. That is, to be included in a particular course, surely all of the outline headings and sub-headings are related. However, when dividing an outline into instructional units, natural content divisions are sought. This criterion seeks to group together those parts of the outline which have the greatest learning commonality. By so doing, difficulties in transfer of learning and understanding content relationships should be lessened.

Length suited to level of the learner

Beginning or less skilled college students may benefit from short units—perhaps five throughout a quarter and eight in a semester. For a quarter system, this translates into a new unit every two weeks. As the sophistication of the student increases, the amount of material constituting a given unit may also increase. Graduate students can be expected to remain focused on broad expansive relationships over a longer period of time than a typical college freshman. Similarly, experienced and successful college students should be fairly self-directed and less dependent upon frequent content breaks. For a new instructor, determining unit length is particularly difficult. Without benefit of prior experience in teaching a particular course, anticipating topics that will prove troublesome for students becomes little more than an educated guess for the instructor.

Evaluation/feedback

The third criterion for determining an instructional unit is the point in the content where student evaluation should occur. Test results provide valuable knowledge of progress for the student as well as teaching feedback for the instructor.

The unit test point establishes a content juncture at which student understanding is assessed. Thus, if students are having difficulty with the material, the problem can be identified and addressed before progressing to the next unit. Complex material may dictate frequent testing intervals, while less rigorous content may allow for a longer testing interval.

Typically, after applying the three criteria, a quarter course may yield three or four instructional units. The sample outline in Appendix 4.3 is broken into five units—probably because it is an introductory course with diverse content coverage. The outline in Appendix 4.4 has three units covering fairly complex material, suggesting that this is a course undertaken by advanced students.

Level II Unit Goals

For each identified unit, a set of Level II unit goals should be written. Similar in form to a Level I, unit goals **identify** desired learner outcomes for each unit. These outcome statements should be categorized as cognitive (Bloom, 1956, Appendix 4.5), affective (Krathwohl, 1964, Appendix 4.6) or psychomotor (Simpson, 1965) and should be supportive of the Level I objectives already written.

All Level I goals must be supported by one or more unit goals. After all unit goals are written, a well-developed course will often show Level II goals from different units supporting a common Level I objective. Such interweaving between Levels I and II may be expected, and is regarded as a sign of course planning integrity. If any Level I objective is **not** supported by one or more Level II goals, then a serious planning omission has occurred. Under no circumstances should a Level I objective go unsupported. Such a planning breach can lead to gaps between the course description (the source for Level I objectives) and material covered in the instructional units.

When writing unit goals, simply ask the question, "For this unit, what do I want the students to **know,** to **value,** and be able to **do?**" Each answer forms a unit or Level II goal. Since Level II goals only **identify** desired learner outcomes, non-observable verbs such as **know** and **understand** may be used. Additionally, it is **not** necessary to include a criterion or statement as to how the behavior will be measured. Several examples of Level II unit goals follow:

Sample Level II Unit Goals

Unit: Human Relations

Cognitive Goal: Recognize the major social, cultural and environmental forces which affect the development of human relations.

Affective Goal: Appreciate the effect of proper listening skills in effective communications.

Psychomotor Goal: Use a variety of appropriate non-verbal behaviors.

Unit: Allied Health

Cognitive Goal: Understand the various types of medical records and information they typically contain.

Affective Goal: Appreciate the role of public health agencies in American culture

Psychomotor Goal: Take and record patient vital signs.

Unit: Programming Fundamentals

Cognitive Goal: Know the BASIC commands and the function of each.

Affective Goal: Appreciate the need for proper handling of data storage media.

Psychomotor Goal: Use conventional keyboarding techniques for alpha and numeric data entry.

Unit: Composition

Cognitive Goal: Know the rules for verb and pronoun agreement.

Affective Goal: Value proper grammar in written and oral communications.

Psychomotor Goal: Sketch a scene representing the central theme of a personal experience paper.

The above examples are offered as illustrations of how goals for each domain may be worded. It is important to point out that a set of unit goals will nearly always be comprised of more than three statements. And while all units should have several cognitive and one or more affective goals, psychomotor goals are usually found only in laboratory courses.

The following is a complete set of Level II goals for a unit from a Physics for Respiratory Care course. Note the high number of affective goals, typical of most medical-related courses:

Set of Level II Goals—Physics for Respiratory Care

UNIT: Heat Transfer, Humidification and Electricity

1. Know the first law of thermodynamics and its relationship to human metabolism (cognitive).

2. Understand what is involved in the process of metabolism and how it relates to physically compromised patients (cognitive).

3. Appreciate the importance of heat transfer as it pertains to therapy and equipment (affective).

4. Know the characteristics of humidity and how it can be applied through respiratory equipment to alter a deficit (cognitive).

5. Know the laws and principles of operation for various analyzers used in the field of respiratory therapy (cognitive).

6. Understand the relationship between electrical current and the flow of gases as it pertains to analyzers (cognitive).

7. Appreciate the two basic protection mechanisms necessary for safe operation of electrical devices (affective).

8. Recognize the importance of choosing the correct analyzer and monitor in a critical setting (affective).

The following examples illustrate the relationship between Level I and Level II goals:

Level I Goal: Understand basic legal concepts, including the litigation and adjudication process of the courts.

Level II: Know the types of remedies for breach of contract in property law (cognitive).

Level II: Understand the legal structures in corporate law and administrative law (cognitive).

Level II: Appreciate the need to litigate and adjudicate an unsettled dispute in civil and criminal law (affective).

Level II: Know the basic stages involved in a civil litigation action (cognitive).

Level II: Know the various procedures involved in an administrative hearing (cognitive).

Appendix 4.7 offers an example of unit content, a Level I goal, and resultant Level II Unit Goals. What is not revealed by the example is the considerable interplay between the Level II goals and the unit content. This symbiotic relationship between outcome and content is perhaps best illustrated by examining the **process** for writing Level II goals.

Starting with an examination of the unit content, the instructional planner begins writing desired student goals. For example, the student cognitive goal of *"Know[ing] the various types of trial documents the legal assistant is expected to prepare"* should lead the planner to reexamine the content outline to assure that all such documents are listed. If additional documents are deemed important by the planner, then they should be added to the unit content. Similarly, a goal such as *"Identify[ing] the elements of a trial notebook"* might be a legitimate expectation yet have no supporting content in the unit outline. In this case, the content would be added to the outline. Lastly, content that supports no goal is a candidate for removal from the outline.

In addition to the considerable interplay between unit content and unit goals, the planner must also be mindful of the Level I goals. Implementation of the planning model calls for all Level I goals to be supported by one or more unit goals. If a unit goal does not, in fact, support any stated Level I goal, the planner must assess the impact of instruction that goes beyond the course description. While minor infractions of this planning rule are no cause for alarm, *one must keep in mind the importance of making certain the course delivers what the course description promises.*

Level II goals are **not** typically given to students. Rather, they are planning statements for instructor and/or departmental use. They offer assurance that important cognitive, affective and psychomotor goals direct the learning outcomes from each unit. Another reason for not including Level II unit goals in a student syllabus relates to how the goals are supported at Level III.

Level II and III Relationship

Figure 4
Relationship Between Unit Goals (II) and Measurable Objectives (III)

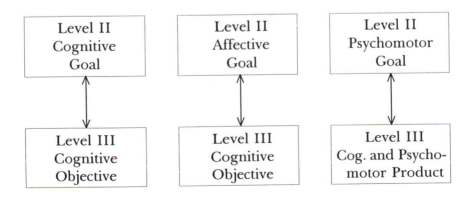

A cognitive Level II unit goal is supported by cognitive Level III performance objectives. Less obvious is the method for supporting affective and psychomotor goals. In the case of affective goals, **direct** measures of the affective domain are generally not feasible. For example, a desired employment value may not reveal itself until after the student has graduated and started working—in many cases, years after taking the class where the value was taught. At other times one also suspects that some students may hold an appreciation for the intricate workings of a free enterprise economy or impressionistic painting just long enough to finish the course. Although the levels of the affective domain are important in understanding the stages of value development, they do not readily lend themselves to being specified by performance objectives.

The recommended method for supporting affective goals is with cognitive Level III objectives that logically build the attitude or value. The following example illustrates this relationship:

Level II Affective Goal: Appreciate the uses of a legal assistant during trial.

> *Level III Cognitive Obj:* From class discussion and handout, list the 5 primary responsibilities of the legal assistant when acting as "second chair" during trial, no errors.

> *Level III Cognitive Obj:* From text and class lecture, describe at least 4 advantages of using a legal assistant as a "second chair" rather than using a secretary, no errors.

In the above example, the goal of "Appreciate[ing] the uses of a legal assistant during trial" is supported by one Level III objective calling for memorization of "5 primary responsibilities" and one requiring a description of "advantages." If a student can fully meet the two Level III objectives, will the appreciation then exist? Maybe. Maybe not. The point is that the actual value (or its absence) cannot be directly assessed. An instructor could provide the student with both Level III objectives, teach the relating information, then test and confirm objective attainment and still not know if the value exists. If additional objectives requiring higher cognitive stages and direct student experiences in real courtrooms were required, could the instructor then confirm the existence of the appreciation? Not really.

Using cognitive Level III objectives to support affective Level II goals is based on the premise that all values are learned. Well-designed, high level cognitive objectives and learning experiences can and do instill values. The problem arises when attempting to measure the value.

An instructional planner can never objectively confirm the existence of a value. However, objectives that require high level cognitive processing and reality-based experiential learning methods can greatly increase the probability of achieving student values. Although a content-oriented instructor may simply tell a class what values they should have, the student-oriented instructor must plan and deliver a cognitive argument so convincing that students freely embrace the value as their own.

Simpson's (1965) psychomotor domain presents important information about the stages of motor skill development. The recommended method for implementing the psychomotor domain involves supporting Level II psychomotor goals with both psychomotor product and cognitive Level III objectives. A psychomotor product objective specifies a skill level, such as playing nine holes of golf in sixty or fewer strokes or landing twelve of twenty serves inside the service lines. A Level III objective requiring a student to correctly label all characters and symbols on a standard keyboard is a cognitive behavior. A Level III objective requiring the student to type 30 wpm with no more than four errors is a psychomotor product objective. *The psychomotor skill cannot be performed without the cognitive knowledge.*

All psychomotor skills have a **knowledge** base. Whether hitting a golf ball or taking a blood sample, knowledge about how to do the skill is vital to correct psychomotor performance. However, as anyone who has attempted to play golf knows, knowledge alone does not a skill make. For psychomotor skills it is important that the instructional planner analyze, teach, and test the cognitive steps that a student will use when attempting to reconstruct a skill at some time in the future. Emphasizing the cognitive reconstruction of a motor skill is important for college students who may possess a desired psychomotor skill near completion of a class, but may not be required to perform the skill again until beginning employment—perhaps years later.

Level III: Measurable Outcomes and Lesson Plans

Figure 5
Defining Daily Presentations and Specifying Student Outcomes

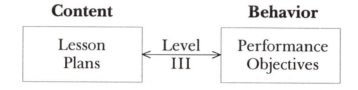

Level I goals are drawn from content and activities identified in a course description—the content side of the model. Unit goals (II) are written from the unit outline, also on the content side. Conversely, Level III starts with the behavior side of the model by specifying desired student competencies that satisfy the Level II goals. Written Level III objectives direct the development of lesson plans that will lead the learner to achievement of the objectives.

The components of a Level III performance objective are universally accepted. An observable behavior or performance, a criterion or stated level of acceptable performance, and the conditions or givens that may affect the performance are the three required parts. This chapter will not attempt to improve upon the landmark work by Robert Mager (1984) in detailing how to develop the parts into measurable performance objectives.

Interestingly, while the constituents of a good performance objective are not disputed, the name by which such a statement is known is quite a different matter. In the nearly thirty years since the standards for a performance objective have been established, they have been referred to by the following array of terms:

- Behavioral objectives
- Daily objectives
- Learner outcomes
- Performance objectives

- Specific level objectives
- Terminal behaviors/objectives/performance

The name used to refer to student outcomes is of no great concern. What really matters is whether or not an objective is written with adequate clarity that it can be understood by students. For an objective to fulfill the purpose of giving specific direction to student learning beyond the classroom, it must be stated in a clear, concise, and non-ambiguous manner. If an instructor has to explain what an objective means then it is not well written. When writing objectives, the challenge is to write with such clarity that a student studying at home knows what is expected.

The following examples of Level III performance objectives are offered, along with the Level II unit goal that they support:

Unit: Human Relations

Cognitive Goal: Recognize the major social, cultural and environmental forces which affect the development of human relations.

> *Performance Objective:* Cite the seven human relation skills which develop through typical childhood play as stated during class discussion
>> *Performance:* cite
>> *Conditions:* none
>> *Criterion:* seven human relation skills stated during class discussion

> *Performance Objective:* Given a written description of a conversation between two people, identify all examples of crossed transactions.
>> *Performance:* identify
>> *Conditions:* given a written description of a conversation
>> *Criterion:* all examples of crossed transactions

> *Performance Objective:* Name the three symptoms found in cases of extreme environmental deprivation in children, using examples from the text.
>> *Performance:* name
>> *Conditions:* none
>> *Criterion:* three symptoms, using text examples

Performance Objective: Given a list of human behaviors, write the country in which they are culturally acceptable, from notes, no errors.

> *Performance:* write
> *Conditions:* a list of human behaviors
> *Criterion:* country in which they are culturally
>   acceptable, from notes, no errors

Affective Goal: Appreciate the effect of proper listening skills in effective communications.

Performance Objective: From text and lecture notes, state the three recommended behaviors for developing effective listening skills.

> *Performance:* state
> *Conditions:* none
> *Criterion:* three recommended behaviors, from text and
>   lecture notes

Performance Objective: Using text and class notes, select the six adverse effects which poor listening skills have upon your conversation.

> *Performance:* select
> *Conditions:* text and class notes
> *Criterion:* the six adverse effects

Performance Objective: From the film "Is Anybody Listening?" write the four recommended methods for gathering feedback from your listeners.

> *Performance:* write
> *Conditions:* "Is Anybody Listening?"
> *Criterion:* the four recommended methods for
>   gathering feedback

Unit: Allied Health

Cognitive Goal: Understand the various types of medical records and information they typically contain.

Performance Objective: From completed health records, mark all missing information and all incorrect entries; 100% accuracy required.

> *Performance:* mark
> *Conditions:* completed health records
> *Criterion:* all missing information and all incorrect
> entries, 100% accuracy

Performance Objective: On the handout "Records and the Law," number the six required information categories; no errors or omissions.

> *Performance:* number
> *Conditions:* "Records and the Law" handout
> *Criterion:* the six required categories, no errors
> or omissions

Performance Objective: List the four major diseases, from text and class notes, which the use of medical records has helped in finding cures; .

> *Performance:* list
> *Conditions:* none
> *Criterion:* four major diseases from text and class notes

Performance Objective: State the medical incidents which must be reported to legal authorities upon treatment; from text, no omissions.

> *Performance:* state
> *Conditions:* none
> *Criterion:* incidents which must be reported; from text,
> no omissions

Additional examples of Level III objectives may be found in Appendix 4.8.

Authorities might differ on several of the above examples, some arguing that parts of the criterion should be included in the conditions, or that certain conditions should be part of the criterion. Such differences of opinion can make for interesting academic discussions, but the true test of a good performance objective is whether or not a student can understand what is expected.

Once written, performance objectives serve the instructor by directing what must be included in the lesson plans. They also serve the instructor as the singularly acceptable source for test items (see Chapter 7, Table of Specifications). Lastly, performance objectives enable the student to focus studies on known outcomes.

Objective Hierarchy

An objective hierarchy is a means for viewing all three levels of goals and objectives and their relationships. Appendix 4.9 contains all Level I and Level II goals for the INTRODUCTION TO LEGAL ASSISTING course used in earlier examples. Also included are the Level III objectives for one unit. Relationships between each of the three levels are clearly evidenced by arraying all goals and objectives in this manner. The hierarchy also provides a student-oriented view of the total course.

Goals and Objectives in Lesson Plans

A lesson plan includes whatever materials and notes a college or university instructor needs to conduct one class meeting. Unlike public schools, the format for higher education lesson plans is generally left to the discretion of the instructor, and can be markedly different from one class to another. For a class that closely parallels an instructor's experience and expertise, the notes may be fairly sparse. Conversely, for classes in which the material is highly detailed, or somewhat new to the instructor, the lesson plan may be quite lengthy. Finally, the lesson plans must be designed to suit each individual instructor.

Although no single lesson plan design is suggested, an examination of how one instructor integrated the Level II goals and Level III objectives into the body the plans may be instructive. Appendix 4.10 contains sample lesson plans for classroom and laboratory instruction. The goals and objectives appear in the notes adjacent to the materials and activities that support them. Constructing lesson plans in this manner, with the measurable objectives inserted into the plans as the notes are developed, help assure that the instruction stays on target with the intended objective. Also, with the Level III objectives included in the plan along with the discussion notes, instructors can readily ask questions to receive ongoing feedback on student progress toward attainment of the objectives.

Conclusion

Beginning instructors should find this chapter useful as a guide for their instructional planning. The time demands on beginning college instructors are too great to allow each teaching of a course to be another exercise in emergency planning. Starting with a viable overall plan will allow improvements and refinements with each successive teaching of a class.

Experienced college teachers wishing to improve their instructional effectiveness are urged to try the model with one course. Pick a difficult course, one that causes the students the most problems. Well-written Level III objectives and tests that have all items linked to the objectives should lead to a marked gain in student achievement levels.

Using goals and objectives to achieve student-oriented instruction demands considerable work. However, improved student performance seems reason enough to make the effort.

Dr. Bill J. Frye is an Associate Professor at the University of Akron, where he teaches technical education curriculum and instructional design and development. He has been an active consultant to many higher education institutions.

Dr. Frye received his B.S. and M.S. degrees from Indiana State University, and his Ph.D. from Ohio State University. He is noted for his work in the areas of competency-based instructional development and the non-traditional learner.

References

Anderson, Martin, *Imposters in the Temple*, Simon and Schuster, New York, 1992.

Angelo, Thomas A., and Cross, K. Patricia, *Classroom Assessment Techniques; A Handbook for College Teachers*, Second Edition, Jossey-Bass, San Francisco, 1993.

Apps, Jerold W., *Mastering the Teaching of Adults*, Kreiger Publishing, Jalabar, Florida, 1991.

Bloom, Benjamin S., ed., et al., *Taxonomy of Educational Objectives, Handbook I: Cognitive Domain*, David McKay, New York, 1956.

Boyer, Ernest L., *Scholarship Reconsidered: Priorities for the Professoriate*, Carnegie Foundation for the Advancement of Teaching, Princeton, N.J., 1990.

Brown, George and Atkins, Madeleine, *Effective Teaching in Higher Education*, Methuen and Co., New York, 1988.

Cahn, Steven M., ed., *Scholars Who Teach: The Art of College Teaching*, Nelson-Hall, Chicago, 1978.

Cronin, Thomas E., "On Celebrating College Teaching," *Journal on Excellence in College Teaching*, 3, Miami University, Oxford, Ohio, 1992.

Davis, James R., *Better Teaching, More Learning-Strategies for Success in Postsecondary Settings*, American Council on Education, Oryx Press, Phoenix, 1993.

Diamond, Robert M. and Adam, Bronwyn E., *Recognizing Faculty Work: Reward Systems for the Year 2000*, Jossey-Bass, San Francisco, 1993.

Erickson, Bette LaSere and Strommer, Diane Weltner, *Teaching College Freshmen*, Jossey-Bass, San Francisco, 1991.

Frye, Bill J., *Competency Based Instructional Planning and Objective Writer* (software), ETAA, Inc., Akron, Ohio, 1985, 1987.

Greive, Donald, ed., *Teaching in College: A Resource for College Teachers*, rev. ed., Info-Tec, Inc., Cleveland, 1989.

Kellough, Richard D., *A Resource Guide for Effective Teaching in Postsecondary Education: Planning for Competence*, University Press of America, Lanham, Maryland, 1990.

Krathwohl, David R., Bloom, Benjamin S., and Masia, Bertram B., *Taxonomy of Educational Objectives, Handbook II: Affective Domain*, David McKay, New York, 1964.

Lucas, Ann F., ed., *The Department Chairperson's Role in Enhancing College Teaching*, New Directions for Teaching and Learning, *No. 37*, Jossey-Bass, San Francisco, 1989.

Mager, Robert F., *Preparing Instructional Objectives*, rev. 2nd. ed., David S. Lake Publishers, Belmont, California, 1984.

Newble, David and Cannon, Robert, *A Handbook for Teachers in Universities and Colleges*, St. Martin's Press, New York, 1989.

Simpson, Elizabeth J., *The Classification of Educational Objectives*, (Abstract Contract Number: OE 5-85-104), University of Illinois, Urbana, 1965-1966.

Sykes, C.J., *Profscam: Professors and the Demise of Higher Education*, St. Martin's Press, New York, 1988.

Weimer, Mary Ellen, *Improving College Teaching*, Jossey-Bass, San Francisco, 1990.

The Adult Learner

Paul Kazmierski, Ph.D.

While formal adult education in the United States can be traced historically to Benjamin Franklin's Junto and extensions in the Lyceum and Chautauqua movements of the nineteenth century, not much attention has been given to understanding how adults learn in formal or non-formal settings. Professional educators, psychologists, and even geneticists have provided voluminous theories and models about how young people gather information and use it in their formal development, but little time has been spent looking at older people.

The concern for how adults learn in a formal school setting has only recently evolved, since the ratio of individuals above the age of twenty-five was formerly lower than that of those below that age. Educators of adults also assumed that the teaching methodology for adults should be similar to that used with children, with only modifications for the adult experience.

Significant increases in adult formal schooling combined with educators' heightened awareness of real differences in the learning patterns of mature students has stimulated researchers and observers of this "neglected species" (Knowles, 1973) to develop a body of theories and models of adult learning useful in the teaching process (Cross, 1981; Knox, 1977; Perlumutter and Hall, 1992).

This chapter will explore some of this research on how adult students learn, their capacities, their styles, and to some extent their personal and social needs as they interface the classroom. Some new research on multiple intelligence theory will also be explored.

Trends Toward Older and More Diverse Students

In 1990 the educational level of the adult population continued to rise, following a general trend of level-plane in 1985. Over three-quarters (78.4%) of all adults age 25 or older reported completing at least four years of high school, the highest level measured in the history of the survey (U.S. Bureau of the Census, 1990, p.526).

Is this another bulge of the times, or is there a marked increase in educational attainment? (Yes, there is an increase says the Bureau (p.527).) With high school completion, the figures for completion of four or more years of college are one-in-five adults (21.4%) age 25 or above. The figures indicate that there is an increase.

But is this enough? Not according to Joseph Boyett and Henry Coon in *Workplace 2000* (1991), who said that

> there will be no places for the functionally illiterate (in workplace 2000). In fact, there may be no place for anyone without at least some level of college education. (p.276)

Another issue facing educators of adult learners is that the American workplace is rapidly becoming more diverse and vocal. Pollsters say that from now until the end of the century, 88% of workforce growth will come from women, African-Americans, and people of Hispanic or Asian origin. White men are the fastest growing group retiring from the workforce (Cook, 1993).

With the statistics giving projections of current and future trends, the higher education provider (full- and part-time) must review the educational delivery system. Teaching approaches, material use, and even the traditional classroom must be reviewed in light of the characteristics of a new "educational consumer."

Adult Learner Characteristics: Preliminary Assumptions

One of the first assumptions "traditional" educators formulate about adult learners is that age must take its toll. They believe learners above the age of twenty-three will not be **able** to master facts, read textbooks, or recite as well as the eighteen-year-old. After all, everyone knows brain cells die after the peak traditional years of formal schooling.

But in fact, almost any adult, according to research summaries, **is able** to learn almost any subject, given sufficient time and attention (Knox, 1977; Trough, 1978). Brain cell erosion, while occurring constantly in the human species, doesn't have a profound effect on the learning process until senility is well under way, i.e. late sixties.

A second assumption by educators, and frequently by adult learners themselves, is that adult intellectual functioning is reflective of early formal school experience. They often believe that if an adult learner did poorly in early schooling, he/she will do poorly in post-secondary studies. The educators and adult learners unfortunately ignore the successful informal learning since their youthful days.

Early in 1970, a Canadian researcher, Allen Trough, decided that there was more to learning than ever happened inside a classroom. He devised definitions of "adult learners" and "adult learning projects." An adult learner was defined as any adult who engaged in deliberate, systematic, and successful attempts to acquire a new skill or new knowledge. The attempt, the "adult learning project," had to take at least seven hours. With his definitions in hand, Trough conducted a series of surveys of randomly selected adults. He found that the typical adult conducts five learning projects each year, and that each project takes approximately **100** hours (Trough, 1978). Similar investigations, summarized by Cross (1978), indicate that between 79 and 98 percent of Americans participate in early learning projects each year, although only 12 to 31 percent are officially enrolled in some sort of accredited course of study.

As a result, most adult learners and educators should base the intellectual function on the successes of "learning projects" rather than earlier formal schooling successes or failures.

Another assumption is that human intelligence, as well as adult intelligence, is best gauged by a single number, an intelligence quotient or I.Q. The assumption further states that if the I.Q. is lower than 100 (average) one cannot participate in the intellectually demanding learning of post-secondary school. Thus, some reason that adults who delay college probably weren't encouraged to be in the "college track" in high school because their recorded I.Q. wasn't in the "magic range" of 100-110.

The fallacy of both of these arguments has been demonstrated by two researched facts. The first fact is that increases in college graduation figures by adult learners suggest that they must have had high or average IQ's but probably were not encouraged (for whatever reasons) as high school students.

The second researched fact was reported by Howard Gardner, head of the Project on Human Potential at Harvard. He has suggested that human intelligence is not a singular operation measured by I.Q. tests, but a multiple of intelligences that can best be described as competencies. Gardner cites at least seven intelligences (linguistic, musical, logical/mathematical, spatial, body/kinesthetic, personal, and symbols - further developed later in this chapter) (Gardner 1983, 1993). It seems a reasonable opinion to state that high schools were not teaching to the intellectual strengths of adults when they were secondary students; therefore, those adults were not successful academically and got the message that they shouldn't pursue other levels of learning.

It is established in research, therefore, that adults can learn and have intellectual functions that vary by "individual differences" just as the traditional postsecondary student varies. But what are these variations? How does an individual think? What are some factors that may vary more for adults? What role does maturity and personality play in the process of adult learning?

An Information Processing Model of Thinking and Learning

How humans become aware of information and deal with it has been, and will continue to be, an issue of great speculation and research. But psychologists, unlike natural science researchers, will never devise the ultimate explanation. The model below is perhaps one reasonable view that might be useful in explaining how humans, including adults, receive and process the stimuli of the world.

Figure 1
Simplified Model of Thinking and Learning

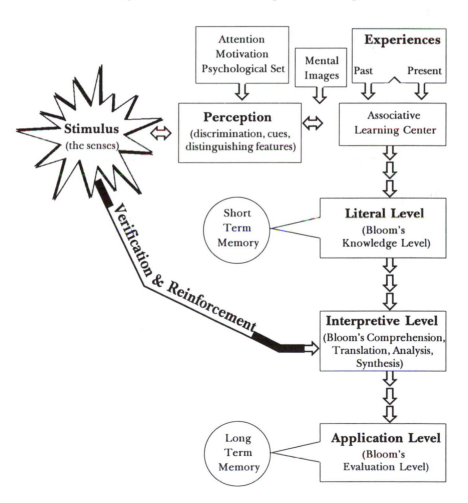

1. Information Reception (Stimulus Reception)

At any one moment a conscious human is bombarded with thousands of stimuli. Heat, light, sound, odor, etc., are continually appealing to our senses. Observations of human response have suggested that we decide to deal with only one, or possibly two, stimuli at any one time. Figure 1 depicts what stimulus we accept is based on the next structure or category, perception or translation.

2. Information Translation (Perception and Associative Learning)

This phase of human information processing, in addition to being the second phase, is also the most complex. As illustrated in Figure 1, it consists of a number of rather abstract terms. Before describing the process, it might be worthwhile to define the terms.

Perception is generally considered a total modification or mediating activity. It consists of discriminating the stimulus from other stimuli, determining its distinguishing features as opposed to others, and recognizing the important cues of the stimulus to verify its characteristics. An example is perceiving **these** and **those** and recognizing the **th** cues and distinguishing between **e** and **o**.

Attention is one of the mechanisms that determines which stimuli we will receive and perceive. Attending to an object is perhaps one of the most important elements in all of information processing.

Motivation, or the felt need to receive and perceive the stimuli, is another factor that determines which of the thousands of stimuli we want to process.

Psychological Set is a perceptual mechanic that suggests we want to deal with some data because we have a prior condition to do so, or want to.

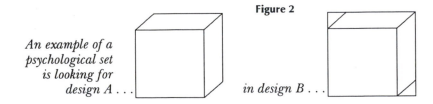

Figure 2

An example of a psychological set is looking for design A . . .   *in design B . . .*

In Figure 2, design **A** gives us a set, so we can receive the stimulus of design **B** and find design **A** embedded.

To give another example of the way the three operations of perception function, suppose we are driving to some destination. We see many objects on the way, but we are attending to the road, so we will be safe. Suddenly we are hungry (a motivation), so in addition to seeing the highway we now look for signs for restaurants (change in attention and use of our psychological set of where there are signs of restaurants we can find food).

Mental Images is how we convert the percept. For example, we might read the words "electric chair" and formulate a mental picture of such an object. The auditory sounds of "electric chair" may also serve as a mental image. Individuals who are deaf may use signs or finger spelling as their mental images for printed and perceived words.

The **Associative Learning Center** is the final phase of the perceptual process. It consists of relating the modified stimulus to some present or past experience that has been stored.

In summary, the translation structure consists of 1) directing what stimuli are to be received based on attention, motivation and psychological set; 2) distinguishing the stimuli from some other stimuli; 3) converting it into a mental image and relating the perception or modified stimuli to past experience.

3. Information Cognition (Cognition and Storage)

If an association or relationship to experience is made in the associative learning center (an actual place in the cortex of the brain), the percept or modified stimulus is not ready for usage and storage in what is frequently referred to as cognition. Cognition is simply defined as comprehending.

According to a number of psychological theorists there are various levels in a hierarchical system of cognitive processes. Benjamin Bloom, of the University of Chicago, has suggested six levels in his famous *Taxonomy of Educational Objectives: The Cognitive Domain* (1956). For purposes of the model, however, this writer prefers to discuss three levels of understanding.

At the first level of knowing or cognition, information is processed at the **literal** level. This means that the learner could repeat the message in a literal or paraphrased way. If the learner were asked to recite the information, it could be given back generally the same way it went into the cognitive area.

If the information has been combined with other data, either by the learner or by the environment presenting the information (teacher, book, etc.), the information may be stored at the **interpretive** level. If asked to recall, the learner could give the information back with some manipulation or interpretation.

The third level of storage is called the **application** level. Here the learner has applied the data in some new way or demonstrates the material as applied.

There are a number of interesting phenomena concerning the cognitive process. One of the most fascinating is the phenomenon of how information is stored and retrieved. Simply stated, if information is processed only at the literal level of understanding, it is subject to a human problem called **short term memory.** Short term memory suggests that information cannot be retrieved or recalled after a brief period of time has elapsed. This is generally the way we forget things very quickly. An example of this is seen in the fact that unless you have processed the material in this chapter beyond the literal level you have **already** forgotten 25 to 50 percent of the facts.

If the concepts have been reinforced, verified, repeated or used, they are stored in **long term memory** from which they are easily accessed.

Adults, as well as all other humans, vary in how efficiently and how quickly information is processed and learned. They also vary in terms of experience (or psychological set), motivation, and storage. Research has summarized some of these variances.

Short-term memory, for moderate amounts of meaningful material and with adequate opportunity to process information to this cognitive (literal) level, tends to be relatively stable during most of adulthood. Older adults, however, experience some increasing loss in the ability to register information in memory. This is especially so when they try to store new information and recall stored information at the same time. Older adults become more cautious and make errors due to forgetting (omission) instead of mistakes due to commission (Knox, 1980).

Long term memory is retained even better with age, and the small amount that is forgotten can usually be regained by practice (Eisdorfer and Lauton, 1973). Especially for older adults, learning and remembering also entail reconstruction of past experience (Meacham, 1977). In other words, older adults frequently try to restructure new materials or information to fit it in with past learning and see if there are relationships.

According to the model of thinking just described, learning is facilitated by reinforcement, which encourages the learner to persist in the learning activity and to master learning tasks. One form of reinforcement is practice. Older adults typically require more practice to master new **verbal** materials (Knowles, 1970). Adults also will study and practice mainly to reduce discrepancies or ambiguities between current and desired proficiencies (Knox, 1980).

In the area of associative learning, adults have a broad range of past experiences. This does tend to facilitate new learning, but it also tends to interfere because a type of dissonance may occur between new and old learning (Knox, 1977). When old learning interferes, it may take longer to master a learning task since interfering information must be first unlearned.

New learning for adults has to be incorporated into an existing framework of learning and experience. Adults need to know how new knowledge relates to their own thoughts and experiences.

In maturity, the greatest decline in learning ability occurs for tasks that are abstract, fast-paced, unusual and complex. Adult learners need many more concrete concepts to serve as pegs for some of the more unusual ideas typically presented in college-level courses.

Whole-Mind Learning

In learning course content, the model of thinking and learning discussed above varies with learners, based on their own unique psychological set, attention patterns, and so on. But learners can learn content as well as generalize the learning process, which some call learning-to-learn. Candy (1990) states that learning to learn "occurs both prior to and coincidental with learning endeavors." Joyce and Weil (1986) also emphasize that these same dimensions exist in the way material is taught and learned: "The process of the method itself is also learned by the student as he or she practices learning in particular ways" (p.403).

It could be stated that models of teaching and learning must be based on the ways learners inquire into a content as well as mastery of that content. Or stated another way, learners should take away, in a content teaching situation, newer approaches to learning that content in the future.

In facilitating a learning situation, i.e., teaching adults, learning-to-learn should be approached with the whole mind. The process and content of learning-to-learn involves both mind and body techniques. Some of the more common techniques, very useful with adult learners, include guided imagery, meditation, metaphors, and relaxation training.

In this author's classes, relaxation techniques are used as breaks in class, before taking exams, and when starting new content. Guided imagery is also used by the author in setting goals for learning, thinking through what the learners want, what achieving their goals will look, sound, or feel like.

Thinking in images—visualizing, fantasizing, is a cognitive process with which we are all familiar. For many, fantasizing is a spontaneous event that occurs throughout the day with little conscious awareness or direction given to the process. In the thinking-learning process described earlier, the mental-image formulation that occurs after perception and before associative learning can be expanded and enhanced if the adult classroom gives acceptance to it being part of their learning activities.

Actively having adult learners attempt to visualize parts of the course content, and report their visualizations (or even associations that are visualized) helps develop the learning-how-to-learn functions through imagery, conscious and unconscious, mind processes can communicate and enrich the learning quality. The body and the mind have mutual sharing (Yabroff, 1992).

Meditation is a very old procedure that seeks a shift in awareness from an externally-oriented active awareness to a receptive, internal center. In other words, meditation can limit the external stimulus and permit the internal focus (the associative learning center) to highlight and develop more associations. This shift from external to internal is useful when a person is faced with only one alternative to a problem. Internal focus helps create more solutions in a distractive-free environment.

A well-publicized contemporary form of meditation, Transcendental Meditation (TM), serves as the basis for a learning technique developed by Herbert Benson (1975). Known as the Relaxation Responses, the techniques are as follows:

1. Locate a quiet place free from distractions.
2. Choose a word or phrase on which to focus (for example, relax, love, peace, one); the word is not as important as the person's response to it.
3. Sit or lie in as comfortable a way as possible.
4. Close your eyes and take several deep breaths to relax the body.
5. Breath normally, become aware of each breath, repeat the word with each exhalation.
6. Ignore distractions. Don't fight interfering thoughts. Let them drift in or out of your awareness.
7. Continue the exercise for ten to fifteen minutes daily. When it is finished, remain quiet and allow your mind to readjust to normal awareness slowly.

Relaxation Responses are a practical and easily learned application that can relieve stress and permit a freer flow of ideas.

When metaphors are used in the learning setting, learners, (particularly adults) center on an analysis of the words of the metaphor and the possible experiences they have had to help them learn from the metaphor.

One metaphor this author uses in teaching some research process follows:

Student: Professor, did Carl Jung do scientific research as the basis for his theories?

Professor: No, he did clinical studies, then drew conclusions from his observations.

Student: But a scientific study that does some kind of experiment is much stronger in supporting theories.

Professor: One swallow doesn't make a summer.

Student: What does that mean?

Professor: Can you visualize a swallow (a bird); summer; then apply your thoughts of it to clinical studies and research studies . . .; that's right . . . rely on your intuition!

Guiding adult learners to see new solutions by internalizing with metaphors is a further enhancement of the learning-to-learn process.

Relaxation is another whole mind learning approach that is based on the model of thinking and learning, cited earlier. The state of relaxation involves total functioning of our information gathering, translation, and cognition by having the body achieve a stress free state. This stress free state is not an automatic process, but can be developed by some simple training.

Progressive relaxation was developed in the 1920's by Edmund Jacobson (Padus, Gottlieb and Bucklin, 1986). Under mental stress, the body becomes tense, which in turn puts more stress on the mind. Progressive relaxation breaks the cycle by forcing the consciousness to recognize the actual feeling of physical tension and relaxation. Starting with one hand, the trainee clinches the fist and holds that for six seconds, then slowly relaxes the hand. By doing so, the person learns to identify the differences between the two states. The training concludes with a personal statement of, "I am calm." The trainee is then directed to remember how relaxation feels and compares it to the former stressed state. training in progressive relaxation must be practiced by the person on a regular basis so it can be employed at will.

While the whole-mind learning paradigm is useful to all individuals in a learning process, adult learners will do better. Younger individuals may benefit from these activities, but adult learners seem to react in a greater developmental sense.

Seven Ways of Knowing

The traditional sense of intelligence is that some individuals have certain underlying abilities that are genetic in nature and are developed in a rich environment. In other words, nature-nurture accounts for one's intelligence, or Intelligence Quotient (IQ).

It has also been subscribed to by researchers and educators that one's intelligence is fixed and cannot be changed by training or even genetic engineering (perhaps that will change).

There have been numerous research studies, most notably by Howard Gardner of the Harvard Project Zero (Gardner, 1983). These studies suggest that intelligence is neither fixed nor stable and that it has a number of dimensions. According to Gardner, there are at least seven intelligences and all can be developed (Lazear, 1991).

The seven ways of knowing are verbal/linguistic, logical/mathematical, visual/spatial, body kinesthetic, musical/rhythmic, interpersonal, and intrapersonal.

When solving a problem or learning a concept, all of our intelligences work in a well-integrated way. Some of our intelligences are better developed than others; consequently, some problems may be more difficult to solve.

1. Verbal/linguistic intelligence generally is responsible for language which includes written and spoken words, humor, memory and recall, and activities that are praised in classrooms.

2. Logical/mathematical intelligence deals with abstract patterns, inductive and deductive reasoning, relationships and connections, scientific reasoning, and activities that are recognized in science and mathematics classrooms.

3. Visual/spatial intelligence is responsible for mental image formulation (cited earlier), space manipulation, graphic representations, and keen visual-perceptual abilities from different angles.

4. Body/kinesthetic intelligence is movement of the body, mimetic abilities, improved body functioning activities, lauded by film and drama critics.

5. Musical/rhythmic intelligence is having a highly sensitive ability for sounds, music, rhythmic productions, good tonality, etc.

6. Interpersonal intelligence is effective use of verbal/nonverbal communication, ability to work in groups, determining others, intentions, and creating synergy with other people.

7. The final intelligence is intrapersonal intelligence, which is the ability to concentrate, have an awareness of feelings, and have a transpersonal sense of self.

While reading these seven, it probably became evident that all seven are useful in adult learning classrooms, but only the first two are rewarded. For further information on these concepts, the reader is referred to *Seven Ways of Knowing* and *Teaching the Seven Ways of Knowing.*

Learning Styles

The process of thinking follows a general pattern of perceiving, translating and then storing information. As stated earlier, adults have variations in some of these psychological processes, but in global terms. They do, however, vary in the way or manner of perceiving, thinking, remembering and problem-solving. In addition to reviewing the research data stated, the adult educator would do well to study the concept of **learning style.**

Basically, the theory of learning style states that we all have characteristic "styles" for gathering, organizing and evaluating information. Some people have dominant styles with consistent ways of selecting and judging data while others are more "bipolar," or flexible, and use a repertoire of approaches based on the circumstances. Some people prefer to learn a skill by manipulating concrete objects, some by listening, some by reading a manual, and some by interacting with others. In brief, people have unique and characteristic ways of using their minds. Learning style, therefore, is "information processing habits which represent the learner's typical modes of perceiving, thinking, remembering, and problem-solving. They are stable, relatively enduring consistencies in the manner and form of cognition (thinking or comprehending) (Messick, 1970).

This human difference in learning is not described in the same ways that intelligence, achievement, and personality are described. In these earlier concepts, individuals are "rated" high to low or normal to deviant. Learning style differences state just that—differences. Learners who gather information by interacting are not deviant from learners who select information from reading or listening, just different.

People vary on a continuum. So far there have been about twenty of these cognitive style continuums established in research reports. A brief description of a few of the more important ones follows.

Dimensions of Cognitive Styles

1. Field Independent versus Field Sensitive (Witken, 1976). This cognitive style continuum has been the most researched and suggests that some people deal with their environments analytically and some more globally. The field independent or analytic learner is usually more oriented to areas like science and math. Field sensitive, or thematic learners, do better in the humanities and social sciences. Field independent learners operate better when isolated from other learners, while field sensitive styles need interaction and collaborative activities.

2. Reflectiveness versus Impulsivity (Kagan, 1965). This dimension deals with the speed or tempo with which problems are selected and information processed. This model suggests that the individual with a predominantly impulsive style will select the first response that occurs and the predominantly reflective individual will ponder the possibilities before deciding. Reflective learners are slower to respond on timed tests but do better in testing situations that allow for contemplation. Impulsive learners finish tests but quicker, have a higher error rate. They learn better in pressured environments that demand quick reaction time.

3. Bipolar functioning using types of learners (Lawrence, 1984). Swiss psychotherapist Carl Jung presented a theory (Jung, 1921) of individual functioning that has been interpreted by Isabel Myers (1980) in the development of the **Myers-Briggs Type Indicator,** a psychological instrument that has become quite popular in the past two decades. The theory suggests that all individuals have preferences for where they place their energy, how they gather information, how they make decisions, and what their preference is for lifestyle. Jung (1921) and Myers (1980) state that each of these four preferences are on a continuum, and where we prefer to be would indicate our learning style (Jensen, 1987).

The first dimension is an Extraversion-Introversion continuum, in which learners rely on some form of activity in the learning process (Jung spelled the words extraversion and introversion). Extraverts prefer to rely on a great deal of activity, with people, in learning. They think best when talking, learn well in groups and have difficulty doing concentrated reading over a period of time. Extraverts prefer to act, then, maybe reflect. Introverts need quiet time for concentration. They seem more comfortable with teacher talk or lecture-based learning. Introverts think or reflect on the learning task, then, maybe, act.

Gathering information is the second dimension. The two preferences are sensing and intuition. While Jung (1921) and Myers (1980) state all individuals use both manners of information gathering, we actually prefer one. Sensing individuals tend to focus on concrete, hands-on, present data. They master facts and details and need to use them. Intuitive learners, on the other hand, will seek general impressions or global concepts. They like to look at the possibilities of ideas. Sensing learners are skill, or procedure-oriented. They complete tasks and practice them. Intuitives dislike routine or structured activities. They seek opportunities to let their intuitions roam freely. Intuitives love concepts and theories.

The third dimension is decision making. Thinking types are making decisions with objective data, a logical, "bottom-line" style. Feeling decision makers prefer to make judgements by subjective data, a value orientation. Thinking types perform best when they have performance criteria. They wish to look at where their learning will lead in a systematic way. In contrast, feeling types need to know that what they learn can be put to work for people, or service or that it meets their values. Thinking and feeling types solve problems differently. Thinking types establish rules or use syllogistic reasoning. Feeling types solve problems by values and people-centered ways.

The final dimension of type theory is the life style preference. Judgement types on this continuum are individuals who prefer efficiency, closure and task-orientation. Perceptive types prefer spontaneity, quality, and more information before closure. In learning, judging types gauge their progress in school by their accomplishments or tasks done. They enjoy goals, deadlines, and structure within the environment. Perceptive types are curious and frequently overcommit themselves. They delay closure until the eleventh hour and want to spend more time on conceptualization.

All individuals have different styles or approaches to organizing information and solving problems. As all of us obtain more schooling, there is a tendency to become more field independent or analytical. We prefer to do more of our own interpretations of information (as opposed to field sensitive learners who would want to "bounce" ideas with others). Initially, adult learners want some socialization in their college learning, as a type of security. As more courses are completed with success, and the adult's ego is stronger, field independent behavior dominates the style of learning.

Personal Factors

Personality has always been a consideration in learning and it is equally so for the adult learner. Personality development continues throughout adulthood (Birren and Schare, 1977; Williams and Werths, 1965) and an understanding of some general personality constructs and trends during adulthood can enable adult educators to assist students to function within the formal learning environment.

The first area of personality information is the concept of life-cycle shifts in self-concept, decision making, attitudes, moral development and adaptation. Various researchers (Levinson, 1974; Gould, 1972; and Neugarten, 1969) as well as researching journalists (Sheehy, 1974) have given us a perspective on these changes. Rita Weathersby (1978) of the Whittemore School in New Hampshire has done an outstanding job in summarizing these cycles for the use of adult educators as displayed in Figure 3.

Figure 3

Brief Characterizations of Adult Life Phases

Life Phase	Major Psychic Tasks	Marker Events	Characteristic Stance
Leaving the Family (16 or 18 to 20-24)	Separate self from family; reduce dependence on familial support and authority; develop new home base; regard self as an adult.	Leave home, new roles and more autonomous living arrangements; college, travel, army, job. Initial decisions about what to study, career, love affairs.	A balance between "being in" and "moving out."
Getting into the Adult World (early 20's to 27-29)	Explore available possibilities of adult world to arrive at initial vision of oneself as an adult. Fashion an initial life structure; develop the capacity for intimacy; create a dream; find a mentor.	Provisional commitment to occupation and first stages of a career; being hired; first job; adjusting to work world; quitting, being fired; unemployment; moving; marriage; decision to have a child; child goes to school; purchase of a home; community activities; organizational roles.	"Doing what one should." Living and building for the future; transiency is an alternative track.
Age 30 Transition (late 20's; early 30's)	Reexamine life structure and present commitments; make desired changes, particularly to incorporate deeper strivings put aside in the 20's.	Change occupation or directions within an occupation; go back to school; love affair; separation; divorce; first marriage; re-marriage.	"What is life all about now that I'm doing what I should? What do I want out of life?"
Settling Down (early 30's)	Make deeper commitments; invest more of self in work, family and valued interests; for men and career women, become a junior member of one's occupational tribe; set a timetable for shaping one's life vision into concrete long-term goals; parenting.	Death of parents; pursue work, family interests; children old enough for mother to return to school.	Concern to establish order and stability in life, and with "making it," with setting long-range goals and meeting them.

Life Phase	Major Psychic Tasks	Marker Events	Characteristic Stance
Becoming one's own person (35-39; or 39-42)	Becoming serious member of occupational group; prune dependent ties to boss, critics, colleagues, spouse, mentor. Seek independence and affirmation by society in most valued role. For women whose first career is in the home, a growing comfort with family responsibilities and independence to seek valued interests and activities.	Crucial promotion, recognition; break with mentor.	Suspended animation; waiting for the confirmatory event; time becomes finite and worrisome.
Mid-Life Transition (early 40's)	Create a better fit between life structure and self; resolve experience of disparity between inner sense of the benefits of living within a particular structure and what else one wants in life.	Change in activities from realization that life ambitions might not develop; change of career; remarriage, empty nest; a second career for women whose first career was in the home; loss of fertility; death of friend, sibling or child.	Awareness of bodily decline aging; own mortality; emergence of feminine aspects of self for men, masculine aspects for women.
Restabilization (a three-year period around 45)	Enjoy one's choices and life style.	Become a mentor; share knowledge and skills with younger friends and associates; contribute to the next generation; develop new interests or hobbies; occupational die is cast for men.	
Transition into the 50's (late 40's to mid-50's)	Another reexamination of the fit between life structure and self; need for re-direction, a whole new beginning for some.	Last chance for women to have a career, or vigorously pursue a deferred life goal or interests; family crises; home duties diminished; change in husband's job status.	An imperative to change so that deferred goals can be accomplished.— "It is perhaps late, but there are things I would like to do in the last half of my life."

Life Phase	Major Psychic Tasks	Marker Events	Characteristic Stance
Restabilization, Mellowing and Flowering (late 50's, early 60's)	Accomplishing important goals in the time left to live.	New opportunities related to career and valued interests; personally defined accomplishments.	A mellowing of feelings and relationships; spouse is increasingly important, greater comfort with self.
Life Review, Finishing Up (60's and beyond)	Accepting what has transpired in life as having worth and meaning; valuing one's self and one's choices.	Retirement of self and spouse; aging; death of friends, spouse and self.	Review of accomplishments; eagerness to share everyday human joys and sorrows; family is important; death is a new presence.

As can be observed in this composite chart of "age-linked" periods of stability and transition that Weathersby and others say is embedded in our experience of living, certain concerns are highlighted. If we refer to our discussion of **motivation** as an important factor in the learning process, we may be able to chart a needs history that can be used in instructional strategies.

Weathersby (1978) states that "people's learning interests are embedded in their personal histories, in their visions of who they are in the world and in what they can do and want to do." Understanding these cycles can facilitate a structured learning environment to maximize adult learning.

Another aspect of personality characteristic in adult learners is the process of decision-making. Many psychologists have told us that making choices entails goal setting, accommodation, assertiveness and directing oneself. Some even suggest that there is also a mix of initiative and reactive behavior.

Adult learners develop an understanding of personal change and thus are generally more decisive than traditional learners. Adults seem to take a more active and self-directed approach to life and learning.

Being one's own person, in adulthood, seems especially important. There is a reexamination of self and participation of self in various commitments. Adults take stock more frequently than traditional college students (who generally have mixed views of their self-esteem). With this reevaluation, adults have stronger views of self in relation to how they assume more responsibilities, interact, and adapt to various environments.

In attempting to summarize the various factors that effect adults in their formal learning process, Knox in his classic text, ***Adult Development and Learning*** (1977), does an outstanding job. He identifies the following seven modifiers to adult learning. They serve as a pointed summary for this chapter.

1. ***Condition:*** Physiological condition and physical health can effect learning and cognition in various ways. Sensory impairment, such as poor vision or hearing loss, can restrict sensory input. Inadequate cerebral circulation or stress can impair memory. Ill health can restrict attention given to external events.

2. ***Adjustment:*** The effective facilitation of learning is less likely when there is substantial personal or social maladjustment in the learning situation.

3. ***Relevance:*** The adult's motivation and cooperation in the learning activity is more likely when the tasks are meaningful and of interest to the learner.

4. ***Speed:*** Especially for older adults, time limits and pressures tend to reduce learning performance.

5. ***Status:*** Socioeconomic circumstances are associated with values, demands, constraints, and resources that can affect learning ability. Level of formal education tends to be a status index most highly associated with adult learning.

6. ***Change:*** Social change can create substantial differences between older and younger age cohorts (such as two generations) regarding the experience and values internalized during childhood and adolescence.

7. ***Outlook:*** Personal outlook and personality characteristics, such as open-mindedness or defensiveness, can affect the way in which an adult deals with specific types of learning situations (Knox, 1977).

Adult learners have these modifiers to learning, but they also have strategies, intelligences, and drive that are built on life experiences and resources that can only be attained by living.

Paul Kazmierski, Ph.D., is the founding Director of the Center for Leadership, Assessment and Development. He is a former Assistant Vice President for Student Academic Development and the Director and Professor of the Learning Development Center at Rochester Institute of Technology. He retired in 1990 to continue teaching courses in cognitive, industrial, and educational psychology. He is a nationally recognized consultant in adult learning, organizational development, stress management, team building, curriculum development and evaluation.

He has also been a faculty member at a community college and headmaster of a private secondary school. He received his Ph.D. from Syracuse University.

Dr. Kazmierski has written extensively in his fields of interest, as well as making conference presentations on adult learning, cognitive psychology and organizational development.

Dr. Kazmierski is a former president of the Rochester Mental Health Association and serves as Legislative Action Chairperson. Dr. Kazmierski is a recipient of Rotary Service Awards and the A. B. Herr Award for Outstanding Contributions to Reading Psychology.

References

Benson, Herbert, *The Relaxation Response*, Morrow, New York, 1975.

Birren, James E. and Schare, Karen W., eds., *Handbook of the Psychology of Aging*, Van Nostrand Reinhold, New York, 1977.

Bloom, Benjamin, et. al., *Taxonomy of Educational Objectives*, David McKay Co., New York, 1956.

Boyett, Joseph H. and Coon, Henry P. *Work Place 2000: The Revolution Shaping American Business*, Dutton, New York, 1991.

Candy, Philip,"How People Learn to Learn," in Robert Smith and Associate, ed. *Learning to Learn Across the Life Span*, Jossey-Bass, San Francisco, 1990.

Cook, Mary F., ed., *The Human Resource Yearbook: 1993/94*, Prentice Hall, Englewood Cliffs, New Jersey, 1993.

Cross, K. Patricia, "The Adult Learner," *Current Issues in Higher Education*, American Association for Higher Education, Washington, D.C., 1978.

Cross, K. Patricia, *Adults as Learners*, Jossey-Bass, San Francisco, 1981.

Eisdorfer, Carl and Lawton, Michael P., *The Psychology of Adult Development and Aging*, American Psychological Association, Washington, D.C., 1973.

Gardner, Howard, *Frames of Mind: The Theory of Multiple Intelligences*, Basic Books, New York, 1983.

Gardner, Howard, *Multiple Intelligences*, Basic Books, New York, 1993.

Golladay, Michael A., *The Conditions of Education*, National Center for Education Statistics, U.S. Government Printing Office, Washington, D.C., 1976.

Gould, Roger, "The Phases of Adult Life: A Study in Developmental Psychology," *The American Journal of Psychiatry*, *129:5*, November 1972.

Jensen, G.H., "Learning Styles," in Provist, J.A. and Anchors, S., *Applications of the Myers-Briggs Type Indicator in Higher Education*, Consulting Psychologists Press, Palo Alto, CA, 1987.

Joyce, Bruce, and Weil, Marsha, *Model of Teaching*, (3rd edition), Prentice Hall, Englewood Cliffs, New Jersey, 1986.

Jung, Carl G., *Psychological Types*, Princeton University Press, Princeton, NJ, 1921.

Kagan, Jerome, *Information Process in the Child*, Readings in *Child Development*, Paul H. Musen, John J. Cooper and Jerome Kagan, eds., Harper Row, New York, 1965.

Knowles, Malcolm, *The Modern Practice of Adult Education*, Association Press, New York, 1970.

Knowles, Malcolm, *The Adult Learner: A Neglected Species*, Gulf Publishing Company, Houston, 1973.

Knox, Alan B., *Adult Development and Learning: A Handbook on Individual Growth and Competence in the Adult Years for Education and the Helping Professions*, Jossey Bass, San Francisco, 1977.

Knox, Alan B., "Proficiency Theory of Adult Learning." In D. Charles, ed., Special issue of *Contemporary Educational Psychology*, 5(3), 1980.

Lazear, David, *Seven Ways of Knowing: Understanding Multiple Intelligences* (2nd edition, Skylight Publishing, Palatine, IL, 1991.

Levinson, Daniel J., *The Seasons of a Man's Life*, Random House, New York, 1978.

Meacham, James A., "A Transactional Model of Remembering," In H. Hokem and H.W. Reese, eds., *Life Span Developmental Psychology*, Academic Press, New York, 1977.

Messick, Samuel and Associates, _Individuality in Learning,_ Jossey Bass, San Francisco, 1976.

Myers, I.B., _Gifts Differing,_ Consulting Psychologists Press, Palo Alto, CA, 1980.

Neugarten, Bernice, _Middle Age and Aging,_ University of Chicago Press, Chicago, 1969.

Padus, Edward, Gottlieb, Bert, and Bricklin, Michael, eds., _Your Emotions and Health,_ Rodale, Emmaus, PA, 1986.

Sheehy, Gail, _Passages: Predictable Crises of Adult Life,_ Dutton, New York, 1976.

Trough, Allen, _The Adults Learning Project,_ Canada: Ontario Institute for Studies in Education, 1977.

U.S. Bureau of Census, _Current Population Reports,_ Series P-20, No. 335, "School Enrollment - October 1990," U.S. Printing Office, Washington, D.C., 1991.

Weathersby, Rita, "Life Stages and Learning Interests," _Current Issues in Higher Education,_ American Association for Higher Education, Washington, D.C., 1978.

Williams, Robert H. and Werths, Carl G., _Lives Through the Years,_ Atherton Press, New York, 1965.

Witkins, Herman and Goodenough, Donald, _Field Dependence and Interpersonal Behavior,_ Research Bulletin RB-76-12, Educational Testing Services, Princeton, N.J., April 1976.

Yabroff, William, _Images of Inner Wisdom: Four Guided Journeys to Discover Your Own Inner Power,_ Yabroff and Associates, Mt. View, California, 1990.

Thoughts on Teaching

Elizabeth M. Hawthorne

Introduction

Effective instructors provide stimulation for students to learn. Each instructor has his or her own way of accomplishing this through a blend of personality, character, knowledge and style. Instruction is dynamic and successful instruction is situational, not all things work well all the time—a persuasive argument for a skilled teacher to be able to view teaching from a variety of perspectives and be able to adapt.

A recent survey of students in an undergraduate educational psychology class resulted in suggestions for college teachers. The overall theme among these students was that the best teachers are those who are *involved* with their subject matter and their students. They emphasized that college instructors should actively involve students by creating interest in their subject area, by facilitating discussion and by varying the way class time is spent. Students asked that their faculty members evaluate students fairly without trying to trick them, connect with students by being available for extra help, and show interest in students as individuals and as people with complex lives. Most students frequently mentioned that they wanted their professors to be organized and prepared, to have a complete syllabus, to explain expectations, to be consistent, and to avoid surprises!

First and foremost the instructor is a perpetual learner— about important things such as students, content, and the teaching environment. Because a key to good teaching is the relationship between instructors and students, good teachers pay attention to this relationship and to their own role in the relationship.

One observes to obtain data to enrich one's understanding. How and what the instructor observes is critical. Observing is complex; for example, one can use one's eyes to see what is happening in the classroom—who is paying attention, who is taking notes, who is asking questions, who is "resting his eyes," who is in attendance and who is not. One can listen to what students say, directly and indirectly. Listening may reveal a pattern of questioning that tells the instructor that the material is not being adequately explained to the students. One can ask students systematically for information that will inform one's teaching. Angelo and Cross (1993) present excellent ideas about "classroom research" which allows the instructor to understand the extent to which students are mastering the material. Based on the feedback the instructor receives from students, instruction can then be crafted to clarify and elucidate.

A different assessment procedure is that of seeking students' judgment of the course and the instruction. Rather than doing so at the end of the course, an instructor is advised to do so throughout a course; mid-course adjustments can be made. It is essential, however, if one asks students for opinions about the course and one's teaching that every effort is made to be responsive to their concerns. Otherwise, students will be less than candid. The message that a thoughtful instructor sends to students with these inquiries and systematic responses is that the instructor is interested in the success of the students.

Observation also involves scrutinizing the results of student examinations. Student response patterns may reveal the strengths and weaknesses of the instruction more than the student's ability or interest in learning.

Teaching is what one does to help students learn. Teaching is the face-to-face instruction, while learning and observing inform the teaching. Teaching also enhances and focuses the learning and observing.

Teaching is a dynamic activity in which the instructor affects changes in students who affect change in the instructor. Furthermore, teachers need to be alert to changes in students and adjust their instruction accordingly.

Getting Ready to Teach

Mastery of the Material

Advocates of the lecture or direct tuition approach to instruction focus on the mastery of the content (Broadwell, 1980). An excellent lecture reflects deep and abiding knowledge and passion for the subject material. There is no substitute for knowing a great deal about one's teaching area—none. But the mastery is not beneficial if teachers bury their students in their own accumulated knowledge and insight. Mastery of content is being able to know the material so well that one can understand how to teach it to others, that is how one might explain complex ideas and information in multiple ways for different student needs. Cohen (1990) shares provocative insights into the translation of knowledge from teacher to learner. Great teachers help students think through ideas; they don't simply spill ideas onto students. Skillful instructors anticipate how students may view the subject material and are prepared to adjust their presentations accordingly. A superior lecture does not send students away to memorize the lecture, but to think about the material, to be excited about it, and to be eager for mastery. Such is the purpose of all instruction.

Institutional Issues

Where one teaches makes a difference. An instructor should become familiar with the institution and the individuals in the institution upon whom one may call for assistance. A faculty handbook may be available. Securing this kind of information in advance of beginning a semester/quarter can free an instructor to focus on instruction. Some things one needs to do right away include:

> Go to the library and meet the librarians. Learn about the resources in the library, access to materials, time needed, checkout policies, student services provided, and reserved reading policies.

> Find where and how to order films and other audio-visual materials and equipment, including costs, and policies and procedures.

> Visit the computer center and find out what is available (hardware, software instruction) for faculty and for students.

> Go to the bookstore to learn about book orders and returns, items pertinent to your courses that are available, and any special services that can be provided.

Finally, familiarize oneself with policies and services concerning academic assistance for students, clerical assistance, attendance, the selection of reading assignments, grading, examinations, academic honesty, faculty identification card(s), class cancellation policy, and finally, parking permits.

About Students

It seems that faculty members view their students along a continuum from passive receptacles to active constructors of knowledge. Those who view their students as passive receptacles see their role as filling up these receptacles with the benefits of the faculty member's own learning. Paulo Friere (1986) used a banking metaphor for this idea—putting money into a bank where it can earn interest. At the other end of the continuum, faculty create a framework and setting for students to construct their own understandings of knowledge building upon their own experiences and understandings (Freire, 1986; Njogu, 1992). These faculty members will prompt discussion, provide opportunities for student exploration of ideas with feedback and guidance from the faculty member; they will pose problems for students to solve. McKeachie (1986)and his colleagues refer to the "student-cognition model" when students' cognitive and motivational characteristics mediate instructional approaches.

The kind of relationships with students will be affected by the teacher's view of students. Cranton and Weston (1989)posited three basic configurations of relationships. One is instructor-centered (lecture, questioning, or demonstration). Here students are passive learners receiving information from others. The second relationship is interactive. Interaction takes places in two ways: first, between teacher and student (discussion) and, second, between and among students (group projects, peer teaching, collaborative approaches). The third kind of learning relationship is individualized, e.g., students move through the course at different speeds requiring immediate feedback (workbooks, computer-aided instruction). Here students are active constructors of knowledge. Similarly the relationship the instructor promotes between and among students is affected by his or her view of students. Students who are passive receptacles work alone and relate primarily to the instructor. When students are constructors of knowledge, they can work alone but their work with peers is not only encouraged but structured to foster collaborative learning (Bouton and Garth, 1983; Bruffee, 1987, 1993). Constructors of knowledge are excited about learning. Instructors can help students develop these qualities through their own excitement, respect for students' efforts, frequent and constructive feedback, and promotion of active processing of ideas.

How students learn is affected by their own dispositions, the subject matter, and the context. Understanding different learning styles and how they merge with instructional approaches facilitates a focus on individual students.

Benjamin Bloom's (1956, appendix 4.5) taxonomy discussed in chapter 7, "Applying the Cognitive Domain," provides an excellent foundation for guiding the planning and implementation of instruction. Each of the six stages, (knowledge, comprehension, application, analysis, synthesis, and evaluation) builds on earlier stages.

Entering the Classroom

How one feels about oneself, what one believes (Fuhrmann and Grasha, 1983), what one has prepared for a class session, how one has thought about the students, and what one wants to happen at the end of the class and beyond all contribute to the classroom environment. Consider each class a piece of art that needs to be designed with a canvas that requires careful and insightful painting, and a frame to highlight the beauty and the message on the canvas. Preparing for each class involves attention to the syllabus, to what happened in previous sessions, and to new ideas the instructor has gleaned from reading and from discussions with colleagues and students. The more an instructor feels comfortable with the subject matter, the better prepared he or she is to enter the class. Having a choice of approaches to the material ready to use as student responses and questions enables the instructor to be more responsive to different student needs. Being confident fortifies instructors for the vagaries of classroom exchange. So will being relaxed! Class time is not the time to put a topic to rest but to stimulate students to think more about it— and to excite them to want to learn more.

Students respond positively to an instructor who is in charge—not through fear and intimidation, but through confidence and skill. Teachers set the stage for their courses and for each class by their manner, by what they say, and by what they do to the room in which the class meets. The faculty member sets the tone from the very first class. When instructors engage in pre-class conversation, they should encourage students to get to know one another, and share something of themselves. The instructor's own enthusiasm does make a difference to students.

Many student complaints seem to focus on one area: the instructor does not make things clear—students don't know what is expected of them. Here are difficult choices for instructors to make. What does one want of the students? Some expectations to consider attendance, in-class behavior, promptness in coming to class, conversation or silence, preparation for class, and appropriate preparation for and behavior during examinations.

Class notes should be brief, highlighting the main points one wants covered and the different ways in which the teacher might approach the material. Speaking to and with students is preferable to reading a lecture (McKeachie, 1986). Try to arrange the room to promote discussion.

Enter the room before students arrive. Greet them, give them a chance to reach out. Show interest in students as learners and as people. Most college students, especially the traditional aged student, will be responsive to a teacher's personal interest in their progress as well as their enthusiasm for the subject. Don't enter empty-handed. Have all the materials, e.g., notes, hand-outs, overheads, films, equipment in sufficient number and working order. Know what the class meeting will include and how it will come about. Communicate expectations for the class to the students at the beginning of each class. Tell them how the class will be conducted during that period, but be able to depart from the plans in response to student needs. A useful framework is shown in Figure 1, Class Schedule.

Figure 1
Class Schedule

> **Agenda**
> **Clarification**
> **Coverage of material**
> **Feedback**
> **Review of Main Points**
> **Next Steps**

Agenda

The agenda includes the topic, what the instructor plans to accomplish during the class, and what is expected of the students. It can be written on the board, put on an overhead, or verbally given to students at the beginning of the class. An agenda helps students focus their attention on the pertinent issues, rather than have them passively listening and wondering what's coming next. An example of a class agenda is shown in Figure 2. The agenda reflects some important teaching principles. First, a common framework for discussion is provided. Second, information and ideas are conveyed (reviewed in this case), helping students to acquire the knowledge and fostering comprehension. Third, students are expected to apply the knowledge through small groups. Fourth, students have the opportunity to learn from the instructor and from peers. Misconceptions can be corrected. Fifth, students' level of understanding can be assessed. Sixth, students are guided to the next assignments, which can build their anticipation for the tasks.

Figure 2
Sample Class Agenda

Introduction
Clarification of Assignments
Topic: Cognitive Development
Activity: Brief review of Piagetian stages (theory)
Small Group Reports (application): each group
 will report on the Piagetian activities it designed
Class discussion of reports
Summary
Feedback from students
Next Steps

Clarification of Assignments

Presumably students had been assigned outside reading and/or other activities in preparation for the class. It is important to ascertain at the beginning of the class the extent to which students did the assignments and understood the material. While asking students for questions can be a way of starting this process, generally two circumstances preclude students' questions. One, they didn't do the assignment and wouldn't have a clue what to ask. Two, they did the assignment and it made no sense; they have no idea where to begin to ask questions. These two conditions are not rare events! Rather than simply asking for questions, ask some pertinent questions. Questions should build from a focus on the content to student application of the material and, finally, to student evaluation of their knowledge (Bloom, 1956). It is important to establish the level of students understanding. Another value of this activity is for students' to understand the expectations that they are to come to class prepared while knowing that the instructor will offer clarification to them when needed.

Coverage of Material

This should constitute the bulk of the class period. The options are virtually limitless, but instructors should consider the match between instructional approaches and the level of mastery according to Bloom's taxonomy. In professional courses, inform students of issues and problems they may face during their careers. Not only lecture, but use activities that include students in the learning process. Give examples of how the subject matter being taught applies to life. Use several examples and explain well. If needed, explain topics in more than one way so students can understand better. Know when alternative explanations are needed. Be attentive to what students are learning more than how far the class is progressing in the text. Go over material in the text.

Selecting Instructional Approaches

Thus far this discussion has addressed considering the level of understanding and the kind of relationship an instructor wants to have in the course. Additional variables to consider in the selection of methods include the amount of time available, the students' learning styles, class size, access to materials, budget, and the instructor's own comfort level. The choices of instructional approach are extensive and each has its own merits. Cross (1976), Lowman (1984), Newble and Cannon (1989), and Kozma, Belle, and Williams (1978) are excellent sources for examining advantages of various instructional approaches. Figure 3, In-Class Activities, and Figure 4, Out-of-Class Activities, offer several instructional approaches. The creative and exciting aspect of teaching is best exemplified in developing well-designed methods that fit with the material to be taught and with the audience seeking to learn. One's extra effort in selecting appropriate and varied instructional approaches is one way of fulfilling one's obligation to help students learn. One cannot stress too much how important it is for teachers to know the difference between having high standards and the failure to help students master the material.

Figure 3
Instructional Delivery Methods
In-Class Activities

1. Presentations—by instructor, guests, students
   a) Lecture
   b) Demonstration
   c) Audio-Visual Aids
      (1) cassettes
      (2) videos
      (3) movies
      (4) TV
      (5) radio
      (6) slides
      (7) transparencies
      (8) artwork
      (9) artifacts and other objects
   d) Teleconferencing
   e) Interactive Television
   f) Drama—live presentation
   g) Personal Experience/self-disclosure
2. Group Activities
   a) Discussions led by instructor, guests, students
      (1) Socratic method
      (2) trigger
      (3) open-ended questioning
   b) Role-Playing
      (1) small groups
      (2) entire group

    c) Simulation
    d) Debates
    e) Panels
    f) Games
       (1) paper/pencil
       (2) board/etc.
       (3) computer
    g) Interviews
    h) Questionnaires: leadership measures,
         basic interest tests
    i) Case Studies
    j) Other small group exercises; problem solving
3. Individual Activities
    a) writing
    b) critiquing/correcting other's work
    c) problem-solving

Figure 4
Instructional Delivery Methods
Out-of-Class Activities

1. Laboratory: archives, dig sites, chemistry lab
2. Field Trip
3. Practica: internships, student teaching
4. Guided research
    a) library
    b) data collection
    c) seeking materials (rocks for geologists)
5. Projects
6. Programmed Instruction
    a) computers
    b) paper/pencil
7. Workbooks
8. Other audio-visual
9. Tutorials: peer, instructor
10. Study Groups, dissertation groups

About the Lecture

By all means plan to lecture, but confine lectures to ten to fifteen minutes. If one must lecture to 100 or more students for fifty minutes, pause during the lecture and engage students in thinking about the material. For example, after about ten minutes, ask students to write in their notebooks three important points that were covered or a question they might have or how this material is related to a previously addressed topic; their career goals, past experiences, or the like. Interject thoughtful questions about the topic throughout the lecture and allow students time to respond and discuss. Stay on the topic. Lecture according to the class's ability—don't go ahead or have students wait for information. This implies that one is paying attention to one's audience while speaking. Vary how the material is presented, the tone of voice; walk around and talk to students. Be sure the lecture is central to what students need to understand and know. (Broadwell, 1980).

Handouts

There are three questions an instructor should ask about any handouts proposed for distribution to students. (1) What would students do without the handout? (2) What should the handout accomplish? and (3) What would the instructor do with the handout if she were a student?

Discussions

Have some pertinent and provocative questions ready to ask to begin discussions. Be patient waiting for responses. Listen to what students say and be tolerant in allowing dissent. Respectful treatment of students will create a climate in which students feel confident to speak. Christensen and Hansen (1987) and Christensen, Garvin and Sweet (1991) give excellent and thought-provoking ideas about using discussions for teaching.

Teaching Materials

When speaking, reinforce important points using the chalkboard. Write only important information. Visual cues reinforce verbal communications. Use the overhead projector, but make materials that are colorful and readable and that make sense. There was once a conference speaker whose overheads each had 45 lines of numerical data and another speaker who was addressing an American audience using overheads in German. Extreme examples, but view overheads from a student perspective before using them. If one plans to use cassettes (audio or video), films, or other electric and electronic approaches, have a backup plan since light bulbs burn out, films break, and equipment does not always arrive on time. When planning to use such aids, view them first, have a clear reason for using them, and introduce them to the students, highlighting what to look for and offering some open-ended questions that they should be ready to discuss following viewing/hearing the presentation. Films and the like can also be assigned to be viewed outside of class in the library or media center. Limit the frequency that such aids are used since they are intended to enhance the instruction. The faculty member is expected to provide the instruction.

Guest Lecturers

By all means, when special experts are in town or on campus, invite them to class to share their expertise, but, like other instructional aids, don't overdo the number of guest speakers. Prepare the students for their visits, so the students constitute an informed and inquiring audience. Also, tell guest speakers what material has been covered thus far, the size of the class, the backgrounds of the students, what the students were assigned for the class, and the arrangement of the classroom. Guests may have materials they wish the students to read in advance of the class. Provide or assign these materials with sufficient advanced notice.

Assessment

In this phase of the class, ask some questions that address the major points and the goals set to check for student understanding. Such assessment of learning in progress is the instructor's responsibility. Students share their understanding of material with their instructors (in writing or orally) and instructors correct misunderstandings, misconceptions, and miscommunications along the way. It is also good practice to routinely review student responses on examinations to correct errors and misunderstandings. It is helpful to check to see if there are any questions that everyone (or a majority) of students get correct or incorrect. One may choose not to penalize students when the entire class answers the same question(s) wrong. Often, this can be attributed to the instructor's failure to explain the material sufficiently. Chapter 7, "Item Analysis Interpretation," presents a detailed view of how problem items can be identified. Evaluating students should be frequent, positive, and constructive—a grade is not enough feedback!

Review of Main Points

Reviewing a lesson offers a quick summary that highlights the major issues covered in class. Revisiting material is important because learners need time to digest and interpret difficult ideas and concepts.

Next Steps

Even when a teacher has a complete syllabus specifying the assignments due each class, students need verbal reminders of the instructor's expectations for the next class in terms of required preparation. More importantly, instructors should explain what is important/difficult/interesting in the reading or other assignments and what students should be looking for. This can include the order in which certain assignments are best read, the value of comparing one author's point of view with another's, and the like. Communicating one's excitement for the assignments can help move students toward the goals in a positive manner. At this point, clarification of more complicated assignments is very important and allows for shared discussion with students about on-going projects.

Classroom Management

One should communicate clearly what is important for student success. If the instructor holds promptness to be important, students should be aware of this. Discussing with the class their ideas of appropriate classroom behavior will help avoid making the instructor the keeper of order; it involves students in the responsibility for the classroom. Be reasonable about considering student suggestions. If a student disagrees with a professor, there are three alternatives. One, provide evidence in a calm manner to refute the student's position; two, provide evidence for the correctness of your position; or, three, admit that the student may be correct. More importantly, communicate continuously to students that what they have to say (or ask) is important and worthy of your attention. Show understanding for the everyday stresses of college life, especially when students are commuters, work part-time or full-time, and have families for whom they are responsible.

Other management problems may involve students who are not attentive in class or who are the perennial sleepers and letter writers. It is helpful for instructors to understand their own feelings about the behavior so that they can address student inattention professionally. One can call attention to the undesired behavior or one can find ways to make class more engaging. Talking outside of class with the non-attentive student can provide the instructor with helpful guidelines. Including material covered in class on examinations may induce students to attend class and concentrate on the subject at hand.

A potential area for disruptive behavior is when sensitive issues such as race, religion and sex are discussed in class. One can avoid potential problems by setting ground rules for discussion with the students in advance.

Promote questions in large classes. A skilled instructor will let students know that clarification questions are welcome—then entertain them and respond to them. If students seem unwilling to ask questions, request that they write the question and pass them on to the teacher for response. Instructors do not have to have all the answers all the time. It is quite appropriate to admit not knowing the correct answer, then to provide an answer in the next class meeting. If questions that are asked seem peripheral or irrelevant, write them on the board for a response at the end of class.

Classroom Preparation

Being unprepared for class is a rarity for the best faculty members and a danger for repeat offenders. Begin class with a clarification of any departures from students' expectations (based on the syllabus and any announcements). Jot some open-ended questions on the board, divide the class into small groups to discuss them, and then have each small group report back to the full group. Students can be asked to volunteer to offer questions for discussion. It is always helpful to have a supplementary lecture, film, or other class program available in emergencies. Summarize the highlights of discussion at the conclusion of class.

Finally, two areas that bear on classroom success are outside assignments and evaluation of students. Simply put, outside assignments should not be excessively demanding. Instructions for their accomplishment should be explicit, and assignments should have some realistic purpose. Specifically, make clear to the students the purpose and exact outcome of each assignment. Out of class group assignments are beneficial, but fraught with logistical problems that the instructor should anticipate and work to prevent. Develop some understanding of the level of students' skills regarding outside assignments and give extra assistance to those who need help.

Ethical Considerations

A number of institutional and instructor ethical issues merit consideration.

1. Institutional Behavior Toward Students
   a. Accepting students into programs where there is clear evidence that the student is not prepared to succeed
   b. Closing courses after students have registered for them without sufficient advanced notice for them to get into a comparable course
   c. Counseling students into "less demanding" programs against student's will
   d. Using out-dated equipment
   e. Using unsafe equipment/unsafe facilities

2. Faculty Vis-a-Vis the Student
   a. Failing to give frequent feedback to students on their performance in a class
   b. Letting students reinforce their own errors

    c. Misleading students into thinking they are doing well and then "zapping" them at the end of the course

    d. Passing students who do not perform up to established standards

    e. Giving outdated information to students

    f. Cancelling classes arbitrarily

    g. Tolerating sexual harassment/discrimination

    h. Tolerating racial harassment/discrimination

    i. Failing to clarify expectations

    j. Giving better or worse grades for certain students

    k. Testing on material not covered in course

3. Faculty Vis-a-Vis the Institution

    a. Collecting a paycheck from an institution while spending more than forty hours a week on outside consulting

    b. Refusing to serve on college or university committees but accepting outside paid assignments

4. Research

    a. Falsifying data

    b. Taking grants for research which limit the scope of intellectual inquiry or which define the outcomes

Faculties may want to expand upon this list to develop a statement of ethical practices for their own institutions. Finally, faculties should review their own practices and discuss measures to prevent and punish unethical behaviors.

Multiple Roles

Faculty members have multiple roles. The way in which they choose to enact these roles can help enrich their teaching. An ongoing discussion among faculty within and across departmental lines can clarify institutional expectations. Understanding the multiplicity of faculty roles can help build a coherent career in college teaching. Typical faculty roles are shown in Figure 5.

Figure 5
Faculty Roles

Teacher
Learner
Mentor
Advisor
Committee member
Curriculum planner
Researcher
Scholar
Community member
Leader
Change agent
Role model
Colleague

Professional Development

Central to being a successful teacher is continuing professional development. As faculty seek to foster a thirst for knowledge in their students, they, too, must have and model this thirst through a variety of learning experiences of their own. Reading is central to continuing professional development. Similarly, as one seeks to understand and be responsive to students' diverse learning styles, professional educators owe it to themselves to reflect on their own learning styles and to find what is effective for their own professional needs.

Some teachers flourish amidst colleagues and thrive on informal intellectual debate; others are stimulated by their own disciplined research; still others seek instruction through seminars, workshops, and coursework. Observing experts is another way to learn. Listening to students is another source for professional growth. Many institutions provide extensive support, internally and externally, for these activities. Learn what is available and take advantage of what there is. Seek out an experienced colleague who can provide intellectual and moral sustenance. Teaching is hard work; one's egos and self-esteem are on the line with every encounter one has with students. Share ideas about teaching with others and avoid isolation.

Conclusions

Teaching is not limited to classroom experiences. "Teaching" includes planning, implementation, and evaluation. The responsibility of the faculty member is to create a framework for learning through the syllabus, the assigned out-of-class work, and the in-class presentation of course material. Faculty are responsible for providing current treatment of course materials, alternative explanations of ideas and concepts, and both group and individual instruction and assistance to students. Most especially, derive great pleasure and meaning from teaching. It will show.

Elizabeth M. Hawthorne, Ph.D., is Director of Academic Affairs at Penn State-Berks Campus. She is the former Associate Professor, Coordinator of the Program in Higher Education and Director of the John Russel Center for Educational Leadership.

References

Angelo, Thomas A., and Cross, K. Patricia, *Classroom Assessment Techniques; A Handbook for College Teachers*, Second Edition, Jossey-Bass, San Francisco, 1993.

Bloom, B. S. et al., *Taxonomy of Educational Objectives, Handbook I: Cognitive Domain*, McKay, New York, 1956.

Broadwell, Martin M, *The Lecture Method of Instruction*, Educational Technology Publications, Englewood Cliffs, 1980.

Bouton, Clark and Garth, Russell Y., eds., *Learning in Groups*, New Directions for Teaching and Learning, No. 14, Jossey-Bass, San Francisco, 1983.

Bruffee, Kenneth A, "The Art of Collaborative Learning." *Change. 19*, 42-47, April 1987.

Bruffee, Kenneth A, *Collaborative Learning, Higher Education, Interdependence, and the Authority of Knowledge*, Johns Hopkins Press, Baltimore, 1993.

Christensen, C. Roland, Garvin, David A., and Sweet, Ann, eds., *Education for Judgment*, Harvard Business School Press, Boston, 1991.

Christensen, C. Roland with Hansen, Abby J., *Teaching and the Case Method*, Harvard Business School Press, Boston, 1987.

Cohen, David K, "A Revolution in One Classroom: The Case of Mrs. Oublier," *Educational Evaluation and Policy Analysis, 12(3)*, 327-345, Fall 1990.

Cranton, Patricia and Weston, Cynthia B., "Considering the Audience," In Patricia Cranton, *Planning Instruction for Adult Learners*, Wall and Thompson, 14-35, Toronto, 1989.

Cross, K. Patricia, *Accent on Learning*, Jossey-Bass, San Francisco, 1976.

Freire, Paulo, *Pedagogy of the Oppressed*, Continuum, New York, 1986.

Fuhrmann, Barbara Schneider and Grasha, Anthony F., *A Practical Handbook for College Teachers*, Little, Brown, and Company, Boston, 1983.

Kozma, Robert B., Belle, Lawrence W., and Williams, George W., *Instructional Techniques in Higher Education*, Educational Technology Publications, Englewood Cliffs, NJ, 1978.

Lowman, Joseph, *Mastering the Techniques of Teaching*, Jossey-Bass, San Francisco, 1984.

McKeachie, Wilbert J, *Teaching Tips*, 8th Edition, D.C. Heath and Company, Lexington, MA, 1986.

McKeachie, Wilbert J., Pintrich, Paul R., Lin, Yi-Guang, and Smith, David A.F., *Teaching and Learning in the College Classroom*, National Center for Research to Improve Postsecondary Teaching and Learning, Ann Arbor, 1986.

Newble, David and Cannon, Robert, *A Handbook for Teaching in Universities and Colleges: A Guide to Improving Teaching Methods*, St. Martin's Press, New York, 1989.

Njogu, Kimani wa, "Decolonizing the Child," *Paintbrush*, XX, 39&40, 129-140, 1992.

Planning Student Evaluation, Constructing Tests and Grading

Bill J. Frye, Ph.D.

Forward

Having suffered the emotional damage of a divorce, then the esteem-destroying effects of two years of un/underemployment, Pat, a returning adult student, faces yet another hurdle—an advisor demanding an explanation for a 1.5 GPA. It matters not that twelve years ago, when Pat last attended college, all thoughts were of love and a forthcoming marriage—one that would last forever. That 1.5 now is a serious matter. It was influential in the jobs Pat applied for and did not get. And now, Pat is withered by the suspicious stare of the advisor still waiting for an explanation, "What about that GPA?"

Although Pat is a fictitious composite of many returning students, the indelible and far-reaching effects of grades are real. Using GPAs as a measure of the person is not restricted to the academic community. The popular literature abounds with stories of too many college graduates vying for too few jobs.

Facing a flood of applications, it is easy for a prospective employer to pick a number, let's say 3.5, and discard all others that fall short. Thus, a 3.5 may get an interview; a 3.4, a "don't call us, we'll call you" letter.

Considering the importance and permanence of college grades, it is remarkable that many institutions give responsibility for their assignment to instructors who have had not a moment's study in testing and grading. The same presumption that anyone who knows a subject can teach it seems to apply to testing and grading. While failings in either teaching or testing are injurious to both the instructor and the student, the student is the one far more likely to receive a permanent scar—visible for all to see on the transcript.

Although most experienced instructors are happy to forget about their early struggles with testing and grading, some are quite candid in recounting their first teaching experiences. Liotta (1990) describes his first year as an English instructor by noting that although he had "served as an aircraft commander . . . responsible for a $10 million airplane . . . and the lives of [his] crew," his greatest difficulty was the struggle of grading student work (p.97).

Difficulties with creating student tests were also addressed by Murray (1990) who, speaking from his community college teaching perspective, noted that "most teachers will go to any extreme to avoid . . . the time and energy [of] writing and grading exams . . . . They will adopt only textbooks that have an accompanying test bank . . ." (p.148). Grading that relies solely on publisher provided textbook exams is a tacit admission that only text material will be covered in class. One can almost envision the extension of this practice, with students calling the publisher, seeking video tapes of the lectures.

Peter Seldin, known for his work on faculty development, states that "College and university professors are hired with the expectation that they eventually will be effective teachers" (Seldin in Lucas, 1989, p.89). Similarly, viewing each new offering of a course as a reason to reexamine the evaluation plan and every administration of a test as an opportunity for its improvement, can eventually lead to effective grading.

Introduction

This chapter is organized, to the extent possible, in the same order as the steps an instructional planner might go through during the development of a new course. In so doing, more measures are presented than are likely to occur in any one particular course. Consequently, some readers may benefit from using parts of the chapter as a reference.

Topics covered include how to develop a college course evaluation plan, methods for quantifying various forms of student work, spreadsheet grade management, computer item analysis, and course syllabus contents. Suggestions for developing test items are also offered. The latter portion of the chapter addresses assignment of letter grades. Beginning instructors are urged to check their faculty manual for possible grading, testing and evaluation policies before reading this chapter.

Course Evaluation Plan

A course evaluation plan is a listing of the measures, e.g., tests, projects, papers, etc. that contribute to a student's grade. Percentage weightings determine the relative influence each measure has in determining the grade.

In all likelihood, the faculty manual requires that an evaluation plan be included in the course syllabus and given to students at the beginning of the quarter or semester. For beginning instructors, developing a detailed plan with so many unknowns is particularly difficult: how many tests to have; what projects to require; attendance; etc. Whether new to teaching or simply facing a new course, one can only apply reasoned judgement with the expectation that the plan will need to be changed the next time the course is taught. Given the realities of students' perceptions of grades, it is perhaps wise for the beginning instructor to ask the department chair to review the completed plan before distributing it to students.

As the term progresses the instructor may find that students cannot complete all of the requirements. In such a case, it is perhaps safe to withdraw a requirement. However, to realize at midterm that something important was forgotten, then to **add** to the workload would no doubt upset some students.

Steps for Developing an Evaluation Plan

1. List all the activities and measures that will contribute to a course grade. Table 1 lists several typical measures. Other completed course evaluation plans are contained in Appendix 7.1 and Appendix 7.2.

WORKSHEET FOR EVALUATION PLAN

Evaluation Measures	Grade Weight (100%)	Points ( )
1. Tests		
2. Class Participation		
3. Attendance		
4. Written Papers		
5. Laboratory Projects		
6. Technical Reports		
7. Other: Subjective		
	100%	

Table 1

2. Distribute the percentage weightings across the measures. Students usually understand evaluation plans and will target their efforts toward the heavily weighted measures. Weighting considerations vary according to the course:

—A course in "Sales Presentation Skills" might weight class participation and presentations highly.

—An engineering technology course in "Laboratory Instrumentation" might highly weight laboratory projects and technical reports.

—An introductory course such as "Medical Terminology" might weight objective tests most heavily.

—An introductory composition course might assign low weight to objective tests and high weight to written papers.

—An advanced composition class might weight essays heavily and not use objective tests at all.

Table 2 illustrates a possible weighting scheme:

WORKSHEET FOR EVALUATION PLAN

Evaluation Measures	Grade Weight (100%)	Points ( )
1. Tests (3)	(40%)	
2. Class Participation	(3%)	
3. Attendance	(2%)	
4. Written Papers	(10%)	
5. Laboratory Projects (3)	(30%)	
6. Technical Reports	(10%)	
7. Other: Subjective	(5%)	
	100%	

Table 2

The evaluation plan in Table 2 assigns 70% of the grade to test scores and laboratory projects and 5% to class participation and attendance. The proportion of weighting should reflect the instructor's thoughtful priorities about what is important for this particular course.

3. Select a total number of points for the course. While any total point value can be used, starting with a sizable even number will keep the plan simple and easily understood by students. Table 3 illustrates a choice of 1000 points. Thus, students achieving 100% on all measures, would earn 1000 points.

WORKSHEET FOR EVALUATION PLAN

Evaluation Measures	Grade Weight (100%)	Points (1000)
1. Tests (3)	(40%)	
2. Class Participation	(3%)	
3. Attendance	(2%)	
4. Written Papers	(10%)	
5. Laboratory Projects (3)	(30%)	
6. Technical Reports	(10%)	
7. Other: Subjective	(5%)	
	100%	(1000)

Table 3

4. Compute the number of points each measure is worth by multiplying total points by the measure percentage:

$$
\begin{array}{rcccr}
40\% & = & .40 \times 1000 & = & 400 \text{ points} \\
3\% & = & .03 \times 1000 & = & 30 \text{ points} \\
2\% & = & .02 \times 1000 & = & 20 \text{ points} \\
10\% & = & .10 \times 1000 & = & 100 \text{ points} \\
30\% & = & .30 \times 1000 & = & 300 \text{ points} \\
10\% & = & .10 \times 1000 & = & 100 \text{ points} \\
5\% & = & .05 \times 1000 & = & 50 \text{ points} \\
\hline
\end{array}
$$

Totals: 100%   1000 points

Table 4

Table 5 illustrates the evaluation plan's percentages and points:

WORKSHEET FOR EVALUATION PLAN

Evaluation Measures	Grade Weight (100%)	Points (1000)
1. Tests (3)	(40%)	(400)
2. Class Participation	(3%)	(30)
3. Attendance	(2%)	(20)
4. Written Papers	(10%)	(100)
5. Laboratory Projects (3 X 100)	(30%)	(300)
6. Technical Reports	(10%)	(100)
7. Other: Subjective	(5%)	(50)
	100%	1000

Table 5

Each measure on an evaluation plan is supported by other measures. For example, Table 5 identifies tests as being worth 400 points. As will be shown later, the 400 points will be divided into three different tests, each with its own point assignment. Similarly the three 100-point laboratory projects involve three different point assessments.

Test Weighting and Item Weighting

The sample evaluation plan allocates 400 points for the three tests. How each test will contribute to the 400 point total can be decided in several ways: Three equally weighted unit tests? Two unit tests and a comprehensive final? Three unequally weighted unit tests? The institution or department may have a policy of requiring a comprehensive final. Or, a department may have a non-written practice of requiring comprehensive finals. A beginning faculty member may wish to inquire about the department's policy on final exams when meeting with the department head to review the evaluation plan.

A course that has fairly discrete units and is not a prerequisite for an advanced class is often a candidate for equally weighted unit testing. Conversely, some courses such as math, physics, accounting, and programming often involve units that build upon one another. These type of courses are also often part of a series, with advanced courses building upon prerequisite courses. For this type of course, a weighted comprehensive final is perhaps appropriate.

The following are three different ways of looking at test weighting:

—Three equally weighted unit tests with a total of 400 points would be:

400 points divided by 3 tests = 133 points per test

—With a comprehensive final, the 400 points might be distributed:

Two unit tests = 100 points each; final = 200 points

—Three unequally weighted unit tests might have a point assignment similar to the following:

Test 1 = 100 points; Test 2 = 125; Test 3 = 175

Table 6 shows how "Three unequally weighted unit tests" might appear in a final evaluation plan:

WORKSHEET FOR EVALUATION PLAN

Evaluation Measures	Grade Weight (100%)	Points (1000)
1. Tests: 1 = 100 pts @ 10.0%	(40%)	(400)
2 = 125 pts @ 12.5%		
3 = 175 pts @ 17.5%		
400 pts = 40.0%		
2. Class Participation	(3%)	(30)
3. Attendance	(2%)	(20)
4. Written Papers	(10%)	(100)
5. Laboratory Projects (3 X 100)	(30%)	(300)
6. Technical Reports	(10%)	(100)
7. Other: Subjective	(5%)	(50)
	100%	1000

Table 6

The final step in test point assignment is item weighting. Item weighting means determining the number of points each test item is worth. The example that follows assumes that all test items are of equal importance. Presume that after writing the tests in accordance with the recommendations in this chapter, the following number of items were created:

TEST#	# OF ITEMS WRITTEN
1	53
2	48
3	86

The item weights for each test would be determined as follows:

Test 1: 100 points divided by 53 items = 1.89 points per item
Test 2: 125 points divided by 48 items = 2.60 points per item
Test 3: 175 points divided by 86 items = 2.03 points per item

When applying the above item weights, multiply the number of correct items by the item weight value:

53 correct items multiplied by 1.89 points = 100.17 points
40 correct items multiplied by 1.89 points = 75.60 points

Uneven numbers, such as the above, can be easily handled by spreadsheet software. College students should not have to contend with test questions that were "thrown in" to reach some even item count.

> **The following information is presented in the same order as in the sample evaluation plan shown in Table 6**

1. Writing Achievement Tests

Classroom tests are normally **Achievement** tests. **Achievement** is growth resulting from instruction. Such growth may be either knowledge (cognitive domain), skills (psychomotor domain), attitudes (affective domain), or combinations of the three.

Properly stated objectives specify the domain and level of desired student performance. Achievement tests measure the attainment of the performance. Consistent with the prescriptions in Chapter 2, all achievement measures must be linked to stated student objectives.

Good tests are not just written; they evolve. Even skilled professional test writers must rely on respondent feedback and statistical analyses to create an acceptable test. For beginning college teachers, whose only knowledge of testing may be their own experience as students, writing good achievement tests is a formidable challenge.

When designing instructor-prepared achievement tests, consideration should be given to objectivity, validity, efficiency, and comprehensiveness.

Objectivity provides freedom from instructor subjective judgments when grading student work. Objectivity also affords a level of scoring consistency that is difficult to achieve with more subjective measures such as essay or short answer questions.College students are usually familiar with objective measures. Objective tests also offer the advantage of computer scoring capability.

Validity has several different forms. However, **Content** and **Construct** validity are the primary concerns for the college test maker. A test has **Content Validity** if it properly measures the stated objectives. For example, a unit may have many Level III performance objectives. An essay test, with its characteristic in-depth treatment of limited content, can cover only one or two of the objectives. Conversely, an objective test can easily cover many or all objectives. Content validity can be assured through the use of a table of specifications that helps in monitoring linkages between performance objectives and test items.

Construct validity refers to consistency between the level of behaviors specified in the objectives and level of behaviors measured by the tests. If the performance objectives specify the *analysis* level and the test used to measure the performance is written at the *knowledge* level, then construct validity has not been attained. Similarly, if *knowledge* level objectives are tested with *synthesis* level test items, then the criterion for construct validity has not been met. Test items should require the level of performance specified by the performance objectives.

A table of specifications, covered later in this chapter, is the best means to assure content and construct validity. Although at first glance a table of specifications looks like the work of a mad behaviorist, experienced instructors find it to be a valuable and practical planning tool.

Efficiency of measurement is important for all college instructors. With the incredible time demands on beginning instructors, employing efficient testing and evaluation methods is an absolute necessity. The need for efficient measures is illustrated by comparing the efficiency of an essay test and a multiple-choice test for a class of thirty students. The essay test requires approximately ½-hour for development, and at 30 minutes each, 15 hours for grading for a total of 15-½ hours. Writing 50 multiple choice items at 20 minutes each would take about 17 hours plus 1 hour for grading for a total of 18 hours. Not much difference. However, what about the next term? Figuring two hours for revisions and one hour for scoring, the multiple choice test requires only three hours; but the essay test remains at 15-½ hours. Objective tests, or at least tests that are primarily objective, with perhaps some short answer items, are time efficient measures of student achievement.

Comprehensiveness is important for having confidence that a test score is representative of what a student actually knows. Calling for a large number of items on a test will raise the ire of many professional psychometricians. The relative merits of short versus long tests hinge on the intended purpose of the measure and the level of writer expertise. If the goal is a professionally-created commercial test for making reliable statistical inferences, then the shorter the better. If the goal is an instructor-created reliable assessment and diagnostic measure, then the longer the better. Virtually all time-constrained tests are no more than estimates of a student's full knowledge and understanding of a given subject. Having a large number of items increases the probability that a student's test score is an accurate measure of objective attainment and what was actually learned.

Just as a table of specifications can help confirm content and construct validity, so too can it assure that in achieving comprehensiveness the test developer does not stray from the stated performance objectives.

Evaluating Objective Test Items

No one style of objective test item is best for all forms of measurement. Examining item strengths and weaknesses before attempting to develop a test may prove beneficial.

True-False

Strengths:
1. simple to construct
2. numerous aspects of a topic can be examined
3. particularly good as a pre-test to stimulate interest in a topic
4. ease of answering allows coverage of a large body of content
5. good where only two plausible answers exist
6. familiar to students
7. readily scored

Weaknesses:
1. even with correction factors applied can encourage guessing—student has 50-50 chance of guessing right answer
2. low in reliability due to guessing
3. often difficult to construct completely true or false **brief** statements
4. true statements are usually longer than false statements

5. gives equal attention to both minor details and significant points
6. not appropriate for argumentative material
7. suited only to lowest levels of cognitive domain— knowledge and comprehension
8. although higher level statements could be written, guessing factor eliminates effectiveness

Matching Items

Strengths:

1. valuable in measuring student's ability to recognize relationships, associations, etc.
2. can readily treat numerous aspects of a single concept
3. fairly easy to construct

Weaknesses:

1. typically requires only rote memorization
2. the type of content suited to short matched phrases is limited
3. difficult to measure higher level behaviors with a question format requiring only short phrases
4. promotes process-of-elimination guessing
5. risk of wasting student time if not properly structured
6. if using sequential material, can be difficult to score

Recall/Supply/Fill-in-the-Blank

Strengths:

1. relatively simple to construct
2. can readily treat many forms of content
3. requires student to recall the term—unlike matching in which one must simply identify the term
4. greatly reduces guessing factor

Weaknesses:

1. unless it is essential that the student recall the exact word from memory, this form may waste time
2. students often cannot recall the requested word, but can recall a similar word—forcing subjectivity in grading

3. difficult to measure higher level behaviors
4. tends to measure rote memory only
5. can lead to "lifting" sentences from text with a one word blank—danger of trivializing content
6. sloppy student writing can waste grading time

Multiple-Choice

Strengths:
1. can be used effectively to measure higher cognitive levels (application, analysis, synthesis)
2. students normally familiar with this question format
3. guessing factor greatly reduced
4. computer scoring can provide valuable item analysis information

Weaknesses:
1. requires skill and thorough understanding of cognitive domain to write higher level items
2. difficult to devise items so that the three distractors are both plausible and incorrect
3. sometimes difficult to construct items that have only one correct answer
4. too often the item is constructed to measure recall only
5. requires considerable time to construct good items
6. danger of making correct answer noticeably longer than other three
7. higher level items can lead to student differences in interpretation

Once the decision has been made on the type of item to be used to measure a particular objective, the following test item construction suggestions may prove useful. In addition to the technical structuring, the test appearance is also important. Students place so much importance on tests, presenting them with a professional looking error free exam is a way of showing that the instructor also takes testing seriously.

Constructing Standards for Objective Tests

True-False

1. avoid using "not" in statement; can become confusing for false answers
2. make the point of the item clear, avoiding "trick" questions
3. attempt to develop questions that require responses beyond the knowledge level, perhaps comprehension
4. have provision for a clear marking of a true or false response
5. do not "overload" with either true or false items
6. make both true and false items similar in length
7. avoid ambiguous words and statements
8. avoid direct textbook quotes
9. avoid specific determiners (specific determiners are words such as always, never, cannot, etc.; they are usually found in incorrect or false answers)
10. monitor sequence of true and false answers; students will look for a pattern

Matching

1. group the longer statements on the left side of the page and the shorter statements on the right side
2. include at least 3 or 4 extra choices in the right side column to avoid a simple process of elimination
3. when using numbers or dates in the right-hand column, arrange in sequential or alphabetical order so student does not waste time looking for the location of a known answer
4. put all items in matching set on same page; do not make the student turn from one page to another to complete the items
5. have at least 5 to 12 responses in each matching exercise
6. group only related content in each matching exercise
7. if certain responses in the right side column are used more than once, mention this in the directions

Recall/Supply/Fill-in-the-Blank

1. if the question requires that answers be listed in a given order, include information in the directions explaining how the responses are to be scored
2. avoid beginning a sentence with a blank; give the information portion before the blank
3. write sentence-completion items with sufficient information to clearly qualify the required response
4. attempt to develop items requiring responses beyond the knowledge level
5. give sufficient information to allow only one correct response
6. allow sufficient space for a handwritten answer
7. do not copy statements directly from textbooks
8. avoid ambiguous statements

Multiple-Choice

Of the various types of objective test items, college students are perhaps most familiar with multiple-choice. Although it is difficult to construct good multiple-choice items, the advantages offered by this form of question normally offset the considerable investment in development time.

A charge often leveled against multiple-choice items is that they can only measure the lowest level of recall. "However, with some effort, instructors can write multiple-choice and short-answer questions to examine and require higher order thinking skills, especially application and analysis" (Cameron, 1991, p.154). The key to writing higher level items is a thorough understanding of the cognitive domain. The quality of any multiple-choice test item depends upon the skill of the item writer.

> **As a further aid in constructing multiple-choice items, an example for each level of the domain is offered**

The cognitive domain is a taxonomy or hierarchy. This means that achieving a higher level performance requires successful achievement of all subordinate levels. Stated differently, application level can be achieved only if 1.) pertinent knowledge can be recalled and 2.) the knowledge is sufficiently understood to explain its meaning in one's own words (comprehension). In practice, achievement of an application level objective may be measured by test items written to the knowledge, comprehension and applications levels. This notion is also developed in the Table of Specifications section in a later part of the chapter.

Applying the Cognitive Domain

Knowledge: The recall of specific and possibly isolated bits of information characterizes the knowledge level. The performance objective should state specifically what is to be recalled, such as specific facts, ideas, titles, processes, dates, formulas, etc. The student does not need to have an understanding of the information.

performance objective: From the text and discussion, cite the name and year of enactment of civil rights laws and executive orders.

test item: In what year was The Civil Rights Act passed?
*A. 1964   B. 1968   C. 1972   D. 1978

rationale: Student need only recall the name of the act and the year passed—not required to know major provisions, social conditions leading up to passage, etc.

Comprehension: A comprehension level objective requires not only knowledge of specific facts, ideas, etc., but also a level of understanding. The simplest example of comprehension is if a student can explain in his or her own words what a fact, formula, event, etc. means. Translation from symbols to meaning and modest levels of predicting given trends are also forms of comprehension.

performance objective: Given an example from the Federal Appendix of Forms book, decide whether the form would be classified as an interrogatory, a request for production of documents or a request for admissions, 100% accuracy.

test item: The form located on page 6 of this test is commonly
used for a(n) . . .
A. statement of proof for an expert witness
B. interrogatory
*C. request for production of documents
D. request for admission

rationale: The objective called for memorizing characteristics
and categories from the Forms book. The test has
an example of a form that has the same characteristics as a Request for Production of Documents
form from the text. Requires a modest level of
translation.

Application: This level is similar to comprehension in that
the student is again confronted with an objective requiring
understanding. However, the use or application of the fact,
formula or theory is also required. Problem solving questions are
typical measures of this level of performance.

performance objective: Given specific problems and without
conversion charts, be able to correctly convert
temperatures between the Fahrenheit, Celsius,
Rankine and Kelvin scales.

test item: Sixty-six (66) degrees Fahrenheit equals _____
degrees Celsius.
A. 36   *B. 18.9   C. 34   D. 47.4

rationale: The objective is written is such a way that many,
many different conversion combinations could
be tested. This characteristic is termed "content
generality" and is usually the mark of a good
application level objective.

Analysis: This level requires the student to break down or
take apart a problem. Correct performance at this level means
that the student can correctly identify the root cause of a given
problem or symptom. Analysis—one level above application—is
often a matter of applying all the theories, rules, etc. that bear
upon the presented problem, then figuring out what combination
of applications could account for the problem.

performance objective: Diagnose given adult learning problems and support using research findings from the text and class discussions.

test item: An instructor noticed that the adult students in the evening two-credit hour class do substantially better on the tests than the day adult students. The day class meets 10-10:50 two days a week, the evening class meets 7-8:40 one night a week. What would you recommend that the instructor investigate to determine a possible cause for the difference in test scores?

A. Compare the IQ scores for each group
B. Ask evening students why they are doing so well
*C. Determine if day students have enough time to complete tests
D. Compare the GPAs for each group

rationale: This question is based on a student's thorough knowledge of research on adult learners. From the conditions given in the question and for the four possible responses, inadequate time for test completion should be the first thing to investigate. A correct answer requires the student to mentally sort through the various empirical findings on adults, then to prioritize the conclusions to find the most likely answer.

Synthesis: This level of performance requires that the student be able to put together elements and parts to form a whole. Synthesis performance requires a combining of elements in such a way as to constitute a pattern or structure not present before. Stated in a simpler fashion, synthesis is achieved if the student can take apart a complex problem, identify the root cause of the problem, then cite a specific and correct solution.

performance objective: Correctly diagnose and repair given malfunctioning microcomputers. Repair must be within repair manual flat rate time and with no unnecessarily replaced parts.

test item: Two identical 640K microcomputers vary in the time it takes to execute the same program. Which action to the slower computer will make it run the program faster?

    A. Replace the power cord
  *B. Deactivate RAM-resident programs and buffers
    C. Change printer
    D. Unhook printer and modem

rationale: For the cited performance problem, the student must logically go through each of the possible repairs (answers) and determine how, or if, each might cause the slowdown. Also requires knowledge of how a computer uses RAM in the execution of a program. In this example, the student does not actually make the physical repair, but when the correct solution is cognitively determined, synthesis is achieved. Full achievement of the objective would require the student to fulfill a psychomotor product objective calling for the actual "fixing."

Evaluation: The evaluation level of performance involves making judgments about the perceived value of ideas, solutions, methods, etc. An example is a student making a qualitative judgment about the value or merits of a solution to a problem. Evaluation is troublesome because "The criteria may be those determined by the student or those which are given to him" (Bloom, 1956, p.207). Letting students determine their own criteria for evaluating something would be impossible to objectify. Further, by allowing students to use their own list of evaluation standards how could they ever be wrong?

Evaluation is one level above synthesis. Thus, within the taxonomy, one evaluates the solution that was reached at the synthesis level. This is completely rational. One cognitively works through a problem then embarks upon a solution. When finished, one reflects upon whether or not the solution was a good one. While fully agreeing that the highest level of cognitive processing is largely a matter of reflective assessment of the merits of cognitive decisions, such judgements do not readily lend themselves to objective measurement. Although an evaluation example is offered, instructors wishing to make this level a significant part of their planning are urged to examine the explanations and examples in the Taxonomy (Bloom, 1956).

performance objective: Given a technical computer problem, select a solution that is technically correct and least disruptive to the equipment users.

test item: Assume that in the above question the computer that ran the software slower is used by many people, with only one person using that particular software. For this circumstance, which is the best solution?

    A. Should satisfy the person who asked for the speed up; the other people can take care of themselves

    B. Each person should learn to setup the computer each time they use it

   *C. Leave the computer setup alone, and advise the person complaining about the slowness to wait until you contact other users

    D. As long as the software actually works, the person has no right to complain about the slowness

rationale: This question asks the student look beyond the immediate problem and consider that the RAM resident programs and special buffers were set-up by one of the other users. To remove the set-up will then disrupt that person's work—thus fixing one problem will create another. The student who appreciates the importance of keeping the computer working for everyone will get the correct answer.

Formatting Multiple-Choice Items

Multiple-choice items are typically composed of a question (stem), with one correct response (reinforcer) and three incorrect responses (distractors). Uniform adherence to the following format recommendations will add to the professional appearance of the questions:

1. The following format is recommended for items in which the stem is a complete sentence.

   a. punctuation (period or question mark) at the end of the stem
   b. each response should begin with a capital letter
   c. periods are **Not** normally used at the end of the responses

2. The following format is recommended for test items in which the stems are of the completion type.
   Example: High quality roller bearings are made from steel . . .

   A. castings
   *B. forgings
   C. centrifugal castings
   D. machine turned stock

Classroom achievement tests have a measurement purpose and a diagnostic purpose. The three examples below will suffice for measurement, but not for diagnosing deficiencies. All the instructor knows about a student who misses one of these types of questions is that the student may know none, one, some, or all but one of the possible answers. To take corrective action for missed material, the instructor needs feedback on what a student does know and what he or she does not know. If a question has three important parts, then three questions should be asked. Then the instructor will have clear evidence of what students have mastered and where they have fallen short.

3. The following responses are **Not** recommended:

   A. "all of the above"
   B. "none of the above"
   C. "A and B only," etc.

4. Avoid the use of specific determiners such as "never" and "always." A test-wise student will know that these words are usually found in incorrect responses.

5. State the stem in a positive form as opposed to negative. It is important to always reinforce a correct answer. If a negative stem must be used, underline or highlight **Not**.

Example: positive- "Which of the following is . . ."
            negative- "Which of the following is **Not** . . ."

6. Attempt to keep all the responses the same length. Correct answers are often longer that incorrect answers.

7. Avoid using a "give-away" or obviously wrong response just to save time in writing the last distractor; doing so can give a mistaken impression that the instructor is not serious about the test.

Constructing Essay Tests

Essay or short answer type questions are best suited to higher level behaviors. Written responses afford the student a level of individuality of interpretation that cannot be readily achieved by objective measures. In the section of this chapter dealing with efficiency of measure, it was noted that short answer essay type questions are not normally considered high in efficiency. Consequently, before preparing an essay question one should make certain that the situation being tested merits the time invested by the student in writing a response and by the instructor in reading, evaluating and reacting to the response. With this in mind, the following points should be considered in identifying suitable content for short answer or written response questions.

1. The objectives from which the question is developed should be written to one of the higher levels.

2. The answers sought should be significant in terms of content.

3. The questions posed should be realistic in terms of the student's understanding of the content. The question(s) should require the student to do something such as drawing inferences and developing relationships, not simply repeating textbook arguments.

4. The question should be a challenge for the student, i.e. if asked to articulate a particular **problem**, has the student a realistic expectation of understanding the problem from the class readings and lectures? If the

student is asked to discuss an **issue**, has the content required for understanding the variety of factors affecting the issue been presented? Lastly, is the issue significant enough to merit in-depth treatment?

5. Can the question be stated in such a way that (1) the task of the student is clearly communicated and (2) the question is not reduced to a knowledge level response.

With the above criteria met, the essay or short answer item(s) may be written. A primary consideration in structuring the question is the length of the answer. If the question can be properly treated in one or two paragraphs (short answer), then this should be clearly communicated to the student. If the answer will require several pages to develop, then time and directions to this effect must be provided.

Questions should be specific in identifying what the student is to do. For example, the question, *"Discuss the positions of Alan Greenspan and Paul Volcker"* is not stated correctly. The student is being asked to "discuss positions" that allow too many different interpretations. A better statement of this question might be, *"Compare and contrast the positions of Alan Greenspan and Paul Volcker on (1) domestic economic issues affecting international balance of trade and (2) interest rate policies as they influence inflation and recession. In the treatment of each of these two issues, identify similarities and differences in position for each of the two men."* In this statement of the question, the student is told more clearly what is expected.

Grading Essay Questions

With the time/length factor established and the question suitably phrased, the method for determining how the responses will be graded must still be decided. This is an important consideration and should be addressed before administering the question. The test developer should write his or her response to the questions. This answer then serves as the criterion against which student answers will be compared (it is not surprising for a student to develop a better answer than the instructor's). If, while developing the criterion answer, a specific number of key points or positions are identified, then the task is somewhat simplified. One can assign a given number of points to each point or position, and mark the papers accordingly. However, if the answer to the question requires a free response, one in which the problem relates more to a student's individual perspective and opinion, then the grading problem is much different, and indeed more difficult. If a question asks for a student's opinion, then it would be difficult to judge an opinion as being either right or wrong. In this case, evaluation would be limited to the student's development, rationale, and presentation, regardless of the opinion held.

It is recommended that essay test answers be evaluated in terms of average, above average, and below average. Some measurement experts recommend rereading the tests and reclassifying each answer. It has been the writer's experience that sorting answers into three stacks corresponding to average, plus or minus, is a realistic and workable treatment. In using this grading method, two cautions are offered:

1. Since the difference between an average and an above average answer is one of **degree,** the point spread awarded for each level of response should not be extremely high.

2. An exceptionally good essay and an exceptionally bad one may be anticipated. A below average writing should be awarded some points to differentiate it from a blank paper or a nonsense answer. The exceptionally good answer should not be used to downgrade otherwise acceptable responses.

Another caution in the use of short answer or essay questions pertains to the instructor's treatment of the answer. In reading the answer, the evaluator should give as much attention to the writing as did the student. By providing a testing situation that allows student individuality to emerge, the evaluator should take the opportunity to provide thoughtful, individual feedback to the student. Evaluator notes on a returned paper can be a valuable means for influencing a student. This is not to say that the evaluator needs to rebuild a student's answer, but one should certainly point out weak and strong areas of the response. To omit this facet of the essay test, the feedback component, is a serious misuse of the question format.

Essay answers should be evaluated on the basis of how well the text and lecture material is articulated by the student. Consider the case of a student who may have had other related classes or perhaps firsthand experience relating to the question. This student should develop a response superior to other class members. However, it is unfair to give lesser grades to responses that dealt only with the class material. An inherent problem in grading essay tests occurs when a student's superior answer draws upon information external to the class being taken and results in a downward evaluation of other students' essays.

2. Evaluating Class Participation

Including class participation as a part of a student's grade is difficult. As humans, instructors are more likely to remember those students making good comments near the end of the grading period. The reason for including class participation in the evaluation plan is to reward

1. active participation, i.e. numerous comments throughout the quarter or semester, and
2. quality comments that are well targeted to the discussion and thoughtfully presented.

Both of the above categories are important. However, disregarding all comments except those that are well developed and articulately presented is perhaps unfair to the student who is struggling to overcome a lack of self-confidence.
A plan must be found that will

1. give adequate recognition to the bright, verbal student.
2. give some credit to the person who is trying to be actively involved in class discussion but occasionally misunderstands.
3. give only incidental points to the student who talks a lot but says little.

The following specific points are recommended:

1. assign columns in the grade book or spreadsheet for entries after each class meeting
2. award points in a fashion similar to the following:
   2.1. spoke in class = 1 or 0 points: regardless of the quality of the comment, if the student spoke in class 1 point is earned; if not, 0 points

2.2. contributed quality comments = 1 to 5 points: disregarding how many times the student spoke and looking only at the quality of the comments, award from 1 (low) to 5 (high) points for the class period

3. Including class participation in a course evaluation plan requires instructor discipline. If marks are routinely entered after each class session, then participation assessment can work. However, time demands and back-to-back classes can add to the difficulty of maintaining up-to-date class participation assessment records.

3. Considering Attendance

Before establishing evaluation plan weighting for attendance, it may be wise to check the faculty manual and student handbook for any institutional policy statements. Frequently, institutions have policies requiring "regular class attendance" and stated instructor responsibility for "maintaining student attendance records."

How much influence attendance should have on a course grade should be considered judiciously. With more and more adult students attending college classes, one may expect to find:

1. legitimate business or family obligations that may force the adult student to occasionally miss a class;
2. and the adult student showing the courtesy of advising the instructor of forthcoming absences well in advance.

It is suggested that such absences be allowed on an individual basis. The most important consideration in required attendance is to keep careful and accurate records. In the sample evaluation plan in Table 6, 20 points were assigned for attendance. A policy of one allowed absence and a five-point penalty for each additional absence might be reasonable.

4. Evaluating Written Papers

Written papers, whether detailed and documented research papers or laboratory technical reports, require written evaluation criteria. These criteria should be given to the student along with the assignment. It is wrong to give a written requirement and then leave it to the student to guess how the paper is to be graded.

The following are two college instructors' evaluation criteria for written papers:

TECHNICAL WRITING
Written Paper Evaluation Form

CRITERION	POSSIBLE POINTS	POINTS RECEIVED
- STRUCTURE -		
Typed	6	
8 to 10 pages	6	
Spelling and grammar	10	
Organization (table of contents, headings, etc.)	8	
- CONTENT -		
Accuracy of report	20	
Validity and strength of conclusions	30	
Proper documentation	10	
All supporting data included	10	
TOTAL	100	

Table 7

The heavy weighting on content in the above form is perhaps typical for an engineering technology report. If this were a typing class or a "History of Man and Technology" paper, the relative weighting might be different.

The following plan is from an Introduction to Legal Assisting class and reflects a heavy weighting on the arguments, evidence, and conclusion sections of the paper.

INTRODUCTION TO LEGAL ASSISTING
Written Paper (case analysis) Evaluation Form

CRITERION	POSSIBLE POINTS	POINTS RECEIVED
Length (3-4 pages)	5	
Typed	5	
Spelling and grammar	10	
Strength of Arguments	20	
Strength of Supporting Evidence	10	
Strength of Conclusion	10	
TOTAL	60	

Table 8

Having a paper returned with the only instructor mark being a grade is frustrating. No doubt many instructors recall such an experience from their own student days. If the intent is to develop student written communications skills, then providing written evaluation criteria with the assignment and giving clear feedback on the returned work are mandatory. To do otherwise is to reduce assigned papers to no more than a process of certifying by grade the skills already possessed by students.

5. Evaluating Laboratory Projects

Similar to the preceding categories, a laboratory project evaluation form details the criteria that will be used when grading a completed student project. Including the form with the assignment allows students to evaluate their own project during its completion.

INTRODUCTION TO MACHINE TOOLS
and CNC EQUIPMENT
Laboratory Project Evaluation Form

CRITERION	POSSIBLE POINTS	POINTS RECEIVED
- overall dimensions +/- .005	25	
- hole placement +/- .010	20	
- finish (random mill marks)	10	
- threads (Go/No-Go gauge)	15	
- channel depth +/- .002	10	
- channel width +/- .005	10	
- channel location +/- .015	10	
TOTAL	100	

Table 9

6. Evaluating Technical Reports

Similar to **"4. Written Paper,"** the following form provides the student with the written criteria that will be used to evaluate this advanced report.

TECHNICAL WRITING
Technical Presentation Evaluation Form

CRITERION	POSSIBLE POINTS	POINTS RECEIVED
Succinct, no excessive verbiage	25	
Narrative targeted to audience	20	
Media selection for presentation of data	15	
Proper headings	5	
Glossary included	5	
Accuracy of graphs	10	
Conclusions supported by data	10	
Spelling and grammar	5	
Overall neatness and organization	5	
TOTAL	100	

Table 10

7. Including Subjective Evaluation

Including subjective evaluation as a part of a course grade is clearly not for everyone. Large classes where instructors have little opportunity to know their students beyond a seat assignment chart and a test score prohibit consideration of this measure.

Career courses, seminars, and other small classes may offer a level of student interaction that would warrant subjective evaluation. Some suggest that college career program instructors are professionally compelled to include subjective evaluation as an integral part of their course grade.

Including subjective evaluation means that there are certain non-testable student characteristics that may impact their success or failure in related employment. Faculty choosing to include subjective evaluation are urged to attach small percentage weight to the category—perhaps no more than 5%.

SAMPLE
Subjective Evaluation Form

CRITERION	POSSIBLE POINTS	EARNED POINTS
Cleanliness and Grooming	5	
Communication Skills	5	
Observed Social Skills	5	
Personality Suited for Profession	15	
Likely Success in Profession	20	
TOTAL	50	

Table 11

Table of Specifications

A table of specifications is a tool for systematically document-ing the linkage between performance objectives and test items. It was mentioned earlier in this chapter as a means for assuring content and construct validity and as an aid to achieving test comprehensiveness. Appendix 7.3 and Appendix 7.4 contain examples of completed tables. Since tables of specifications con-vey so much important information, instructors are encouraged to choose their own design. However, the following information may prove useful in guiding the design.

Typically, a table would be developed for each instructional unit and would illustrate the unit content and cognitive domain level for each performance objective and for each test item. Tables usually have **Behavior** as column headings and **Content** as rows. The *content* would normally be the headings from the unit content outline. Table 12 represents a portion of a blank table of specifications. Note that each of the cells has a broken horizontal dividing line. Objective numbers will be entered in the top half of the cell and test item numbers in the bottom half.

Table of Specifications

	knowledge	compre-hension	application	analysis	syn/eval

Table 12

The following three knowledge level performance objectives were written from the content "internal/external memos, letters and instruments":

1. From the text, identify the three primary differences between an internal research memorandum and an external memorandum of law, no errors (knowledge).

2. From class lecture and class notes, given the terms internal memoranda, external memoranda, letters and instruments, match each term with the appropriate definition, one error permitted (knowledge).

3. Without the use of notes, list the five documents that are classified as legal agreements, 100% accuracy (knowledge).

Using the above numbers, all three objectives are listed in the table adjacent to the appropriate content; "Int/Ext memos and instruments," and under the "knowledge" column as shown in Table 13.

Table of Specifications

	knowledge	compre-hension	application	analysis	syn/eval
Int/Ext memos letters and instruments	Obj 1-3				

Table 13

Achievement of the three objectives was measured with eleven matching questions as shown below:

Match each of the following descriptions (Questions 1-11) with one of the Key categories.

Key: A. Letters
      B. Instruments
      C. Legal Agreements
      D. Internal Research Memoranda
      E. External Memoranda

1. Identifies, summarizes, analyzes and evaluates
2. Classifies a promise that is enforceable in court
3. Focuses on arguments in support of a legal issue
4. Persuasive advocacy document
5. Comparable to an appellate brief
6. May seek an action or create a record for a case
7. Attempts to preserve in writing agreement terms
8. Shows the results of legal research to the legal team
9. An agreement where the property owner gives someone else the right to use the property for a certain period of time
10. Wills, deeds and bank notes are classified as this
11. Informs other members of the law firm's team

The above eleven questions are classified as "knowledge level" and would be entered as shown in Table 14:

Table of Specifications

	knowledge	compre-hension	application	analysis	syn/eval
Int/Ext memos letters and instruments	1, 2, 3 Que 1-11				

Table 14

Table 14 illustrates the content and level for the three objectives and eleven test items. The large number of test items assures the instructor of adequate feedback to determine if any of the forms are misunderstood by students.

For illustration purposes, Table 15 shows two objectives (5 and 6) and three test items (12,13,14) all at the analysis level.

Table of Specifications

	knowledge	compre-hension	application	analysis	syn/eval
Unit				5, 6	
Content				12,13,14	

Table 15

Presume that two students missed all three questions in Table 15. The instructor would have convincing evidence that neither of the students had mastered the objectives. At this point, the two students appear equal, and both would receive a minus three points toward their test score. If additional questions had been asked, more could be revealed about these two hypothetical students. The hierarchical nature of the cognitive domain allows questions at the analysis level as well as all subordinate levels. Table 16 illustrates the inclusion of additional questions:

Table of Specifications

	knowledge	compre-hension	application	analysis	syn/eval
Unit				5, 6	
Content	5, 6	7, 8	9,10,11	12,13,14	

Table 16

A comparison of the two students with feedback from the additional seven questions proves to be revealing:

Student A: Correct = 5,6,7,8,9,10
            Wrong = 11,12,13,14

Student B: Correct = 5,6
            Wrong = 7,8,9,10,11,12,13,14

The two students no longer appear equal. Clearly, student A was much better prepared than student B. All student A needs is help getting from the application level to the analysis level. Student B on the other hand has memorized some things but has no understanding beyond rote recall. With the added questions the scores are more reflective of the level of learning, and, more importantly, the instructor can make informed diagnoses for helping both students.

An additional benefit of using tables of specifications can be seen by examining the "totals" row and column in the examples in Appendix 7.3 and Appendix 7.4. The bottom row totals are a simple count of the number of objectives and the number of test items for each level of the cognitive domain. These totals offer a clear profile of the required level of student cognitive processing. Many introductory courses may be expected to have knowledge as the dominant level; advanced courses should have a greater emphasis on application and higher level behaviors.

The totals along the rightmost column are also a simple count of how many objectives and how many test items are written for each unit content heading. These totals reveal the influence each topic has on the unit test. Both the objectives and the test item totals in this column are useful for assuring testing balance.

It is important to note that a table of specifications has particular merit during the development of a course. By entering each objective in the table as it is written, the instructor can see the overall behavioral and content patterns emerge. Similarly, as each test item is written and entered, diagnostic strategies can be implemented.

Assigning Grades Has Never Been Easy

> College and university instructors continually refer to grades and grading as "onerous," "odious," "challenging," and the most disliked part of teaching. Perhaps such disdain swells from the paradoxical union of instructors striving to bring enlightenment and students striving for good grades.

College grades are an interesting part of the history of higher education. Hammons and Barnsley(1992) cite the event that led to the first use of letter grades in American higher education: A University of Missouri professor, in the early 1900s, failed an entire class. The resulting system was based on percentages: "top 3% — A; next 22% — B; middle 50% — C; next lowest 22% — D; and the bottom 3% — F" (p.52). This system was, no doubt, the precursor to the normal distribution grade assignment system. Later, some colleges experimented with **Pass/Fail** systems but encountered problems with employers and graduate schools more accustomed to hiring and admitting on the basis of letter grades and GPAs.

The mid-1960s, throughout the 1970s and into the 1980s, marked a period of grade inflation in American higher education. Summerville et al. (1990), credit Bejar and Blew with coining the definition of grade inflation as "an increase in grade point average without a concomitant increase in achievement" (p.33). One of the many studies that investigated the inflation phenomenon was conducted by Frank Thomas (1983) who concluded that "Such inflation began in the 1960s when many American professors gave higher grades to help keep students from being drafted" (p.2). Once started, the inflation spread quickly as college after college quietly adjusted grades upward to keep their graduates competitive in the job market.

Currently, many public schools and some higher education institutions are exploring multiple-assessment and alternative-assessment methods of student evaluation to offset possible culturally different learning patterns. It remains to be seen how these methods may reshape the nature of student evaluation and grading.

Whatever form grades may take in the future, it will still be the task of the instructor to make their assignment. The intent of this chapter is to offer guidelines to assist the college instructor in assigning grades under current systems.

> Instructors must accept that no matter how fair the system for evaluating achievement some students will be displeased and blame the instructor for their low grade.

What is a Grading Curve and Where Did it Go?

Many of today's higher education instructors attended college during the 1950s and 1960s, a time when grades were likely given on the basis of a normal curve. At that time, grading was often done by mathematically computing a standard deviation then assigning grades based on how far each score varied from the mean of the group. This norm-based method used test results as the basis for grade assignments. Grades were simply a measure of how each score **related** to all the other scores. This method also established in advance the following approximate percentages of each grade:

PERCENTAGE OF STUDENTS		LIKELY GRADE
2%	=	A
13%	=	B
68%	=	C
13%	=	D
2%	=	F

Table 17

Under this system, no matter how well a total class may have done, only +/-2% of the students were destined to receive A's. Similarly, approximately 2% of the class was going to fail. This method clearly had several flaws, but it did serve to keep grades low. Also, it was based on a normal curve, standard deviation units, and other things mysterious to students.

The advent of computerized scoring meant that computers could do the computations and assign letter grades accordingly. This added much to the "scientific" aura of norm-based grading. It also created a competitive classroom environment that pitted every student against the rest of the class. Cooperative learning was unheard of except for the fabled fraternity and sorority files.

More recently, some in higher education have shifted toward a criterion-based orientation. This method is based on objectives, with grade assignment dependent upon **each** student's level of success in attaining the objectives—**Independent of All Other Students.** Herein is the major difference between these two methods of grading:

NORM-BASED = grade earned is dependent upon other students' scores

CRITERION-BASED = grade earned is independent of other students' scores

Although criterion-based methods are certainly a superior means for awarding and earning grades, they have been a contributor to grade inflation. With the advent of objectives, tables of specifications, and tests based on known objectives, student achievement levels rose.

Without benefit of empirical data from which contemporary higher education grading practices can be determined, generalizing is at best speculative. Nonetheless, drawing from anecdotal accounts and direct observation of institutional practices, it appears that vestiges of the norm-based systems are alive and well in many, if not most, universities. If university professors are not schooled in alternative practices, then they are likely to grade as they were graded—usually leading to a norm-based system.

Two-year colleges and colleges of education, where pedagogy is recognized and practiced, are far more likely to assign grades on a criterion-based system. The work of Boyer (1990) and several universities working toward redefining scholarship suggest that some universities may be moving toward alternate methods of teaching and testing. If those methods include criterion-based testing in more university classes, then students will be better served.

Drawing the Line: A or B?   D or F?

Norm-based advocates had formulas, curves and computers to aid their labors in grade assignment. Their methods were bolstered by the very look and title of a "Normal Curve"—see Figure 1.

Figure 1
Normal Curve of Percentages and Grades Based on Standard Deviations

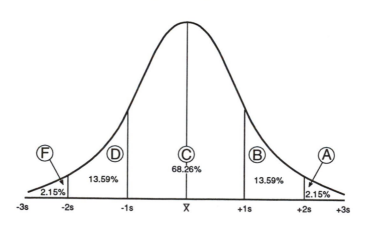

Effective criterion-based methods will probably result in a curve similar to Figure 2. Although instructors could take pride in an achievement curve like Figure 2, they are left without benefit of mysterious formulas to determine the difference between an A and a B.

A beginning instructor, looking at a curve drawn from the first and only students to have taken his or her class, may agonize over having to draw lines to differentiate the letter grades. The best an instructor can do is to give thoughtful deliberation about the following questions:

1. How rigorous are the objectives?
2. What is the caliber of student capable of maximum achievement of the objectives?
3. What does an A or an F mean for this class and for my instruction?
4. How much student time and effort is required to achieve the objectives?
5. How much confidence do I have in my tests?
6. Could I defend the number of students receiving As?
7. Have I plotted the test results and other measures for each of my classes graphically to see the student performance profile?
8. What do "excellent," "good," "average," "below average," and "failure" mean in terms of my course?

Figure 2
Typical Curve for Criterion-Based Achievement Levels

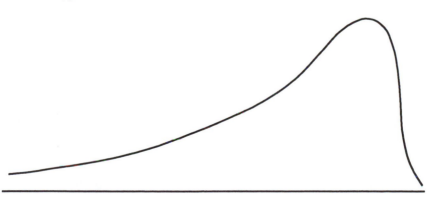

Beginning instructors are urged to consider the above questions, graph the student final scores, draw grade lines on the curve, and take it to their department head. The safest way to avoid conflict over grades is to be open about them **before** they reach the transcript. Continuing with the 1,000 point example, the grade cut-offs may look something like Figure 3.

Figure 3
Sample Criterion-Based Curve with Points and Grades

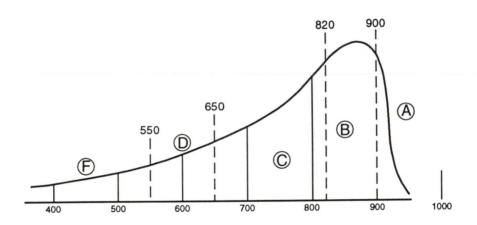

Equal point increments between grades are not required, as is the case in the above example. A, B, C, D and F are symbols of what "excellent," "above average," average," "below average" and "failure" mean to the institution, the program, and most importantly, the instructor. As the class is taught again, the teaching and the tests will improve. The graphs will grow to represent many classes. The placement of lines to separate grades may also change. Grading is both an imprecise and painful science. The last time grading was done with precision and without pain is when computers did it with standard deviations—precisely but wrong.

Although this chapter advocates criterion-based grading, it is clear that a norm-based flavor is added when urging graphing and examination of student performance profiles. The way in which the graphs are used is important. A norm-based proponent would seek to achieve a curve that approaches a normal distribution. A criterion-based advocate who achieves a normally distributed student profile is probably doing something wrong. Criterion-referenced teaching and testing seek a profile that moves as many students as possible to the high side of the curve. Effective criterion-referenced teaching and testing will never result in a normally distributed curve.

Grade Management With a Spreadsheet

Grading based on points and percentages is easily managed with a microcomputer and appropriate spreadsheet software. Even if one must learn how to use a spreadsheet, grade management efficiencies will offset the learning time many fold.

With the constant upgrading of software versions, it is difficult to identify with certainty which spreadsheets are suited to grade management. Spreadsheet software must be capable of

1) having a "LOOKUP" feature that can lookup a value (percentage) and return an alphabetical character (letter grade), and
2) adding a combination of values and alphabetic characters without producing an error message.

To be useful for instructors, spreadsheets need the capability of looking up a percentage value and returning a letter grade or alpha note. Some spreadsheets can only lookup a value and return a value. Of the spreadsheets tested at the time of this writing, the following performed the grade assignment lookup without error:

— Macintosh[1], MS-DOS[2] and Windows[3] versions of Excel[4]
— Lotus 1-2-3[5], version 3.+

Other popular spreadsheets that proved incapable of performing the grade assignment lookup follow:

— Appleworks[6]
— Lotus 1-2-3[7,] version 2.01 and earlier
— Microsoft Works[8]

---

[1] *Copyright 1986, Apple Computer, Inc. and McIntosh Laboratories, Inc.*
[2,3,4,8] *Copyright 1985-1992, Microsoft Corporation*
[5,7] *Copyright 1986, Lotus Development Corporation*
[6] *Copyright 1987, Apple Computer, Inc.*

Other advantages of using a spreadsheet for grade management include:

1) One or many years of classes can be stored one disk.
2) Grade information, weightings, and changes peculiar to each class can be retained—a particular advantage when doing make-up grades long after the class has been taught.
3) Any instructor error in student grading can be reentered in spreadsheet with resultant effect on student grade shown immediately.
4) Throwing out a test item, or adding bonus questions to a test, is easily accommodated by a spreadsheet.
5) Periodically printing grade-to-date reports and distributing to students throughout the quarter or semester gives accurate feedback to students on their class achievement.

Table 18 represents a simple two measure spreadsheet (Test-1 + Paper) to illustrate the steps for setting-up a grade management template.

1. Enter "Name" as first column; ID# as second column. This will allow instructor printouts listing the student name first and student distribution printouts listing the ID# first. **Important Note:** The Test-1 points (25) and Paper points (100) must be initially entered as alpha characters (alphabetic or numeric character entered as text) and **Not** values (numeric characters that will be used in formulas). The less-than($<$)/greater-than($>$) characters are used so one can visually see that the numbers are entered as ALPHAs.

Grade Management Spreadsheet

	A	B	C	D	E	F	G
1	Name	ID#	Test-1	Paper	Pts.to	% to	Grade
2			<25>	<100>	Date	Date	to Date
3							
4							
5							
6							

Table 18

2. Enter student names, ID#s, and scores for Test-1 as shown in Table 19:

Grade Management Spreadsheet

	A	B	C	D	E	F	G
1	Name	ID#	Test-1	Paper	Pts.to	% to	Grade
2			<25>	<100>	Date	Date	to Date
3							
4	Able. H.	1255	25				
5	Burn, L.	6289	20				
6	Chen, C.	5071	15				

Table 19

3. Enter formula for summing points to date in cell E4 as shown in Table 20. Note that formulas are stated in the syntax of two popular spreadsheets:

Grade Management Spreadsheet

	A	B	C	D	E	F	G
1	Name	ID#	Test-1	Paper	Pts.to	% to	Grade
2			<25>	<100>	Date	Date	to Date
3							
4	Able. H.	1255	25		=SUM(C4:D4)		
5	Burn, L.	6289	20		or		
6	Chen, C.	5071	15		@SUM(C4..D4)		

Table 20

4. Copy the summation formula down to include the number of students in a typical class as shown in Table 21:

Grade Management Spreadsheet

	A	B	C	D	E	F	G
1	Name	ID#	Test-1	Paper	Pts.to	% to	Grade
2			<25>	<100>	Date	Date	to Date
3							
4	Able. H.	1255	25		25		
5	Burn, L.	6289	20		20		
6	Chen, C.	5071	15		15		

Table 21

5. Enter the formula for computing percentage to date in cell F4. Use SUM for the points possible for each measure on row 2(C2 to D2). Although Table 22 has only two values (25 points and 100 points), a real grade template must accommodate all measures listed in the evaluation plan. Note the use of $ to indicate absolute cell locations in the percent formula. Copy the formula down when completed.

Grade Management Spreadsheet

	A	B	C	D	E	F	G
1	Name	ID#	Test-1	Paper	Pts.to	% to	Grade
2			<25>	<100>	Date	Date	to Date
3							
4	Able. H.	1255	25		=E4/SUM($C$2:$D$2)		
5	Burn, L.	6289	20		@E4/SUM($C$2..$D$2)		
6	Chen, C.	5071	15		15		

Table 22

6. Change the ALPHA <25> to a VALUE 25 and the resultant percentage should appear for each student as shown in Table 23:

Grade Management Spreadsheet

	A	B	C	D	E	F	G
1	Name	ID#	Test-1	Paper	Pts.to	% to	Grade
2			<25>	<100>	Date	Date	to Date
3							
4	Able. H.	1255	25		25	100	
5	Burn, L.	6289	20		20	80	
6	Chen, C.	5071	15		15	60	

Table 23

7. Pick a location under the student list that will show on a student printout (not column 1) and enter the grade LOOKUP table as shown in Table 24. Note that the LOOKUP table has the percent to be looked-up in one column and the letter grade to be returned in the adjacent column. The percentage-to-grade table is one actually used in a college class that employs criterion-referenced teaching and testing:

Grade Lookup Table

0.00%	no data
1.00%	F see me
70.00%	D-
72.50%	D
75.00%	D+
77.50%	C-
80.00%	C
82.50%	C+
85.00%	B-
87.50%	B
90.00%	B+
92.50%	A-
95.00%	A

Table 24

8. NAME the area of the LOOKUP table. GRADE is the name used in Table 25:

Grade Lookup Table

0.00%	no data
1.00%	F see me
70.00%	D-
72.50%	D
75.00%	D+
77.50%	C-
80.00%	C
82.50%	C+
85.00%	B-
87.50%	B
90.00%	B+
92.50%	A-
95.00%	A

Table 25

9. Enter the grade LOOKUP formula in cell G4 as shown in Table 26 and copy down:

Grade Management Spreadsheet

	A	B	C	D	E	F	G
1	Name	ID#	Test-1	Paper	Pts.to	% to	Grade
2			<25>	<100>	Date	Date	to Date
3							
4	Able. H.	1255	25		25		=VLOOKUP(F4,GRADE,1)
5	Burn, L.	6289	20		20		@VLOOKUP(F4,GRADE,1)
6	Chen, C.	5071	15		15		

Table 26

10. Table 27 depicts the completed spreadsheet. Many of the newer spreadsheets have the capability of sharing grade data with integrated graphing programs. This adds yet another benefit to grade management with a spreadsheet.

Grade Management Spreadsheet

	A	B	C	D	E	F	G
1	Name	ID#	Test-1	Paper	Pts.to	% to	Grade
2			<25>	<100>	Date	Date	to Date
3							
4	Able. H.	1255	25		25	100	A
5	Burn, L.	6289	20		20	80	C
6	Chen, C.	5071	15		15	60	F see me

Table 27

Item Analysis Interpretation

Developing good tests requires continual analysis and revision. Computerized test scoring and item analysis services are mandatory tools for enabling faculty to develop quality achievement tests. Even professionally prepared publisher tests merit local item analysis inquiry to assure that specific instructor methods and/or related coursework do not alter the way students interpret and answer test questions.

What follows is not a technical treatment of the statistical characteristics of item analysis. Rather, it is a simple anecdotal accounting of how technical information can be used to improve classroom achievement tests.

Appendix 7.5 contains an item analysis report for a college test that has undergone continuing revision. Table 28 shows the left half of the report and information on test questions 1 and 2.

ITEM ANALYSIS

QUES NO	A NO/%	B NO/%	C NO/%	D NO/%	E NO/%	OMIT NO/%	MULT.RESP. NO/%
1	5/16	17/54*	4/12	5/16	0/0	0/0	0/0
2	1/3	1/3	28/90*	1/3	0/0	0/0	0/0

Table 28

The asterisk in Table 28 indicates the correct keyed answer. For question 1, B is the correct answer; 17 students selected B; 17 is 54% of the 31 students who answered the question. The percent of students selecting each answer is not in itself persuasive. For example, 50% of a class answering a question correctly reveals nothing about whether the question should be retained, revised, or thrown-out. Determining the merit of an item rests upon an examination of the pooled scores of the 50% who got the item right, as well as the scores of the 50% who missed the question. Table 29 shows the right half of the report wherein key information is contained:

AVERAGE SCORE BY RESPONSE

QUES NO	A	B	C	D	E	OMIT
1	67.60	68.53	62.50	69.40	0.00	0.00

BIS: 0.097
PBIS: 0.078
T-VALUE: 0.419

Table 29

Table 29 reveals that the five students (see Table 28) who selected answer A had an average score on the total test of 67.60; the 17 students who selected B, the correct answer, averaged 68.53; the 4 students selecting C averaged 62.50; and the 5 students selecting D averaged 69.40. The low T-value suggests that something may be wrong with the item.

The 17 students selecting the correct answer averaged 68.53; the 5 selecting D averaged 69.40—the five wrong answers had a higher average score. All good test items should result in the correct answer having the highest average score, regardless of how many people select it. This characteristic of the correct answer having the highest average, and all incorrect answers having lower averages, is termed "positive discrimination" and is indicative of good items.

What if question one could be amiss? It had always been a good question, and an argument could be made that the students selecting A and D, both wrong answers, had lower average scores than the 17 correct answers. Also, although the T-value is low, it is not a negative number. What to do? Ignore the five higher scoring students?

For this particular item, during the class meeting following the test, each student was given a copy of his/her test along with a computer generated list of answers, and the class was asked why they selected each answer. What followed was a simple explanation: during the teaching of the unit, the instructor used an example that related to a student's comment. In developing the example, the instructor unwittingly made answer D equally correct as answer B. The remedy was to give the five students who selected D credit for a correct answer.

Item 23 from the report is interesting. The negative T-value flags the question as a negatively discriminating item. However, as shown in Table 30, the negative T was actually caused by just one person's score being substantially higher than the 30 correct answers.

ITEM ANALYSIS

QUES NO	A NO/%	B NO/%	C NO/%	D NO/%	E NO/%	OMIT NO/%	MULT.RESP. NO/%
23	30/96*	1/3	0/0	0/0	0/0	0/0	0/0

AVERAGE SCORE BY RESPONSE

QUES NO	A	B	C	D	E	OMIT
23	67.60	72.00	0.00	0.00	0.00	0.00

BIS: -0.175
PBIS: -0.077
T-VALUE: -0.416

Table 30

While it may sound harsh, one score does discredit an item, even when the one score is high enough to produce a negative T-value. Even the highest scoring student in a class can make mistakes—both clerical and logical mistakes. It is suggested that a problem, such as item 23 presents, be ignored during post-test analysis.

Finally, item 44 distinguishes itself with a prodigious negative T-value as shown in Table 31:

ITEM ANALYSIS

QUES NO	A NO/%	B NO/%	C NO/%	D NO/%	E NO/%	OMIT NO/%	MULT.RESP. NO/%
44	6/19	22/70	1/3	1/3	1/3*	0/0	0/0

AVERAGE SCORE BY RESPONSE

QUES NO	A	B	C	D	E	OMIT
44	71.83	69.27	56.00	38.00	51.00	0.00

BIS: -0.661
PBIS: -0.264
T-VALUE: -1.472

Table 31

The reason for this problem serves to modify the forgoing recommendation to ignore the mistake of any one person. If the one person making the mistake is the instructor, do not ignore it! During the revision of item 44 from the prior administration and revision, the item was botched by the instructor. The remedy was to give all students credit for the item. Perhaps the most meaningful lesson from this event was that without an item analysis an instructor error such as this could go unnoticed.

The class that contributed the above item analysis report was a real college class. The same class also used the Grade Lookup Table in Table 25 for assigning grades. If a student in that class earned 84.50% then a C+ resulted; if an 85.00% was earned, a B- resulted. The ½ percentage point separating these two grades equates to a five point difference on a 1000-point evaluation plan. Instructor made tests that have never undergone computer scoring and item analysis are likely to contain far more than five points of mistakes and misunderstandings.

Nothing will make the discomfort of assigning student grades go away. However, the uneasiness can be lessened if the instructor has taken all reasonable steps to assure that the mistakes that led to a poor grade were made by students, not by the instructor.

The Syllabus: Putting it All Together

Some departments and institutions have a preferred style of syllabus format. Others may maintain "official" syllabi that are periodically revised in response to pending accreditation reviews. Some offer guidelines for what should be included but allow instructors to develop their own syllabus format. The nature of the course, whether lab or lecture, also affects what should be included in a syllabus.

With the many variables surrounding what may be contained in a syllabus, it is difficult to suggest any one format. However, examples are offered in Appendix 7.6 and Appendix 7.7.

Dr. Bill J. Frye is an Associate Professor at the University of Akron, where he teaches technical education curriculum and instructional design and development. He has been an active consultant to many higher educations institutions.

Dr. Frye received his B.S. and M.S. degrees from Indiana State University, and his Ph.D. from Ohio State University. He is noted for his work in the areas of competency-based instructional development and the non-traditional learner.

References

Bloom, Benjamin S., ed., et al., *Taxonomy of Educational Objectives, Handbook I: Cognitive Domain*, David McKay, New York, 1956.

Cameron, Beverly J., "Using Tests to Teach," *College Teaching, 39*, 154-155, Fall 1991.

Hammons, James O., and Barnsley, Janice R., "Everything You Need to Know About Developing a Grading Plan for Your Course (Well, Almost)," *Journal on Excellence in College Teaching*, Miami University, Oxford, Ohio, 1992.

Liotta, P.H., "All My Best Students Are Flunking," *College Teaching, 38*, 96-100, Summer 1990.

Lucas, Ann F., ed., *The Department Chairperson's Role in Enhancing College Teaching*, New Directions for Teaching and Learning, *27*, 89, Jossey-Bass, San Francisco, 1989.

Murray, John P., "Better Testing for Better Teaching," *College Teaching 38*, 148-152, Fall 1990.

Seldin, Peter, in A. Lucas, ed., *The Department Chairperson's Role in Enhancing College Teaching*, New Directions for Teaching and Learning, *27*, 89, Jossey-Bass, San Francisco, 1989.

Summerville, Richard M., Ridley, Dennis, R., and Maris, Terry L., "Grade Inflation: The Case of Urban Colleges and Universities," *College Teaching*, 33-38, Winter 1990.

Thomas, Frank B., "Grade Inflation as Determined by Comparison of Education and Noneducation Majors," Ph.D. Diss., University of Akron, Ohio, 1983.

Appendix

Appendix 2.1

Chapter 2

Colleges in America

Historical Developments

Significant Historical Developments Affecting Higher Education

1636 Harvard College Founded

1647 Massachusetts School Law—Towns of fifty households required to provide a teacher.

1785 & 1787 The Northwest Ordinance—Sale of public lands set aside the 16th lot for schools—First federal aid to education.

1819 The Dartmouth College Case—Supreme Court provided legal support for private higher education.

1828 Yale Report of 1828—First formal statement of educational philosophy.

1862 Morrill Act—Established "land grant" colleges to promote agriculture, sciences, and teachers.

1874 The Kalamazoo Case—Public high schools to be free and supported by "taxation levied on the people at large."

1887 Hatch Act—Provided extension teaching for farmers.

1896 Plessy vs Ferguson—Equal and separate educational facilities are legal.

1914 Smith-Lever Act—Established cooperative extension service.

1917 Smith-Hughes Act—Federal vocational education grants for agriculture, higher education, and trades and industrial.

1925 The Oregon Case—Allowed for mandatory attendance at public or private schools.

1944 G. I. Bill of Rights—Direct financial assistance to military veterans.

1945 Harvard Report on General Education—In A Free Society defined courses to meet general education goals.

1947 Truman Commission on Higher Education—Placed emphasis on community and two-year colleges.

1950 National Science Foundation established—Promotion of science and research.

1954 Brown vs Board of Education—Revised Plessy vs Ferguson—Segregation at any level is illegal.

1958 The National Defense Education Act—Provide support for educational services, mathematics, and sciences.

1963 Vocational Education Act—Broadened scope of vocational education and included disadvantaged students.

1965 National Endowment for the Humanities established.

1965 Higher Education Act of 1965—Provided financial aid to private and public colleges, loans to students, grants for books and materials.

1970 The Regents External Degree created by New York state.

1972 Establishment of the Fund For Improvement of Post-Secondary Education.

1973 CETA—Manpower Retraining approved.

1983 A Nation at Risk: The Imperative for Excellence in Educational Reform—A report by the national commission on excellence in education outlining that educational institutions have lost sight of basic purposes of schooling.

Appendix 4.1

Chapter 4

Instructional Planning for College Courses

Basic Programming Course Level I Goals

The following is an example from a BASIC programming course:

MATH 100 INTRODUCTION TO BASIC

The application of BASIC language to typical business problems. Includes creating and executing programs using all conventional commands and current micro computer equipment.

Breakdown of course description:

1. application of BASIC to typical business problems
2. creating programs
3. executing programs
4. all commands
5. micro computer equipment

Content: application of BASIC to typical business problems

Level I Goal: Develop simple BASIC programs employing combinations of the four mathematical operators.

Content: creating programs

Level I Goal: Write and test programs common to business financial management.

Content: executing programs

Level I Goal: Be familiar with commonly used micro-computer business software.

Content: all commands

Level I Goal: Use all conventional commands of the Beginners All-purpose Symbolic Instruction Code language.

Content: micro-computer equipment

Level I Goal: Be familiar with IBM compatible and APPLE MacIntosh micro-computers.

Appendix 4.2

Chapter 4

Instructional Planning for College Courses

Respiratory Care Physics Course Level I Goals

RESP-119 APPLIED PHYSICS FOR RESPIRATORY CARE

An overview of matter and energy as it pertains to human physiology, diagnostics, and therapeutic modalities employed in the field of respiratory therapy. Emphasis is on motion; states of matter; energy as it applies to work; fluid pressures; humidity and electricity. 4 credits

Content: motion; states of matter; energy as it applies to work; fluid pressures; humidity and electricity

Level I Goal: Know the various properties, principles, characteristics and laws associated with matter and energy; specifically, motion; states of matter; work; fluid pressures; humidity and electricity.

Content: overview of matter and energy as it pertains to human physiology

Level I Goal: Become familiar with matter and energy as it pertains to human physiology.

Content: diagnostics, and therapeutic modalities employed in the field of respiratory therapy

Level I Goal: Understand the importance of matter and energy in relation to diagnostic laboratories, tests and equipment.

Level I Goal: Be able to apply principles and laws of matter and energy to therapeutic modalities used in the field of respiratory care.

Appendix 4.3

Chapter 4

Instructional Planning for College Courses

Legal Assisting Course Outline

INTRODUCTION TO LEGAL ASSISTING
Course Content Outline*
Patricia E. Ruth

UNIT 1

1.0.0 Legal Assisting - What Is It?
    1.1.0 Historical Development
        1.1.1 early forms of practice
        1.1.2 developing a need for legal assistants
        1.1.3 ABA's recognition and support
        1.1.4 growth in use of legal assistants
        1.1.5 forming legal assistant organizations
        1.1.6 associate membership in bar organizations
    1.2.0 Access to the Profession
        1.2.1 basic qualifications
        1.2.2 education and training
        1.2.3 licensing certification
    1.3.0 The Nature of the Work
        1.3.1 litigation
        1.3.2 corporate law
        1.3.3 estate planning and probate
        1.3.4 real estate
        1.3.5 family law
        1.3.6 government positions
        1.3.7 other specialty areas
    1.4.0 Career Considerations
        1.4.1 independence, creativity, responsibility
        1.4.2 compensation
        1.4.3 opportunities for advancement
        1.4.4 working environment

2.0.0 Organization and Management of Law Offices
    2.1.0 Organizational Structures
        2.1.1 private practice arrangements
        2.1.2 other forms of practice
    2.2.0 Support Personnel
        2.2.1 legal assistants
        2.2.2 law clerks, investigators and librarians
        2.2.3 clerical personnel

---

*Adapted with permission of Little, Brown and Company, Boston, **Fundamentals of Paralegalism**, by Thomas E. Emermann, Second Ed., 1987.*

2.2.4 administrators
2.2.5 outside contractors
2.3.0 Fee Structure
   2.3.1 fixed fees
   2.3.2 contingency and percentage fees
   2.3.3 time charges
   2.3.4 retainers and advances
   2.3.5 prepaid legal services
2.4.0 Standard Operating Procedures
   2.4.1 office procedures manual
   2.4.2 client files
   2.4.3 work product files
   2.4.4 tickler systems
   2.4.5 timekeeping and billing
2.5.0 Office Automation and Computerization
   2.5.1 computer equipment and terminology
   2.5.2 word processing
   2.5.3 file indexing and retrieval
   2.5.4 number crunching
   2.5.5 communications
   2.5.6 future developments

3.0.0 Legal/Ethical Requirements for Legal Assistants
3.1.0 The Structure of Professional Responsibility
   3.1.1 legal requirements
   3.1.2 code of ehtics
   3.1.3 bar guidelines on the use of legal assistants
   3.1.4 enforcement
3.2.0 Unauthorized Practice of Law
   3.2.1 justifications for restrictions
   3.2.2 defining the practice of law
   3.2.3 applications to laypersons
   3.2.4 laypersons supervised by attorneys
3.3.0 Ethical Responsibilities of Legal Assistants
   3.3.1 avoiding unauthorized practice of law
   3.3.2 maintaining confidentiality
   3.3.3 avoiding conflict of interest
   3.3.4 avoiding deception
   3.3.5 avoiding solicitation

UNIT 2

4.0.0 Organization and Structure of U.S. Legal System
    4.1.0 Functions of Law
    4.2.0 Sources of Law
    4.3.0 Criminal Law and Civil Law
    4.4.0 Types of Courts
    4.5.0 Federal Courts
    4.6.0 State Courts
    4.7.0 Court Personnel

5.0.0 Finding and Interpreting the Law
    5.1.0 Publication of Primary Source Material
        5.1.1 statutes
            5.1.1.1 literalism
            5.1.1.2 intrinsic factors
            5.1.1.3 extrinsic factors
            5.1.1.4 conclusion
        5.1.2 administrative regulations
        5.1.3 constitutions
        5.1.4 court cases
    5.2.0 Publication of Secondary Sources
    5.3.0 Interpreting the Law
        5.3.1 statutes
        5.3.2 administrative regulations
        5.3.3 constitutions
        5.3.4 court cases
            5.3.4.1 the sample case
            5.3.4.2 the facts
            5.3.4.3 the judicial history
            5.3.4.4 the issues
            5.3.4.5 the decision
            5.3.4.6 the reasoning
            5.3.4.7 the disposition
    5.4.0 The Role of Precedent
        5.4.1 mandatory and persuasive authority
        5.4.2 overturning precedent
        5.4.3 sidestepping precedent

UNIT 3

6.0.0 Basic Legal Concepts
   6.1.0 Criminal Law
      6.1.1 classification of crimes
      6.1.2 elements of a crime
      6.1.3 parties to the crime
      6.1.4 defenses
      6.1.5 application of the exclusionary rule
   6.2.0 Torts
      6.2.1 negligence
         6.2.1.1 elements
         6.2.1.2 defenses
      6.2.2 intentional torts
         6.2.2.1 types
         6.2.2.2 defenses
      6.2.3 sovereign immunity
      6.2.4 strict liability
      6.2.5 damages
   6.3.0 Contracts
      6.3.1 elements of a contract
      6.3.2 remedies for breach
      6.3.3 defenses
      6.3.4 rights of third parties
      6.3.5 parole evidence rule
   6.4.0 Property
      6.4.1 real estate
         6.4.1.1 ownership
         6.4.1.2 sales
         6.4.1.3 rental
      6.4.2 chattel
         6.4.2.1 the Uniform Commercial Code
         6.4.2.2 formation of a contract
         6.4.2.3 warranties
         6.4.2.4 unconscionability
         6.4.2.5 remedies for breach of contract
         6.4.2.6 commercial paper
      6.4.3 estates and trusts

6.5.0 Corporate Law
   6.5.1 business organizations
      6.5.1.1 sole proprietorships
      6.5.1.2 partnerships
      6.5.1.3 corporations
   6.5.2 agency law
      6.5.2.1 principal and agent
      6.5.2.2 employer and employee
      6.5.2.3 employer and independent contractor
6.6.0 Constitutional Law
   6.6.1 federalism
   6.6.2 separation of powers
   6.6.3 due process
   6.6.4 equal protection
6.7.0 Administrative Law
   6.7.1 delegation of authority
   6.7.2 rulemaking
   6.7.3 adjudication
   6.7.4 judicial review

7.0.0 Litigation and Adjudication
7.1.0 Civil Procedure
   7.1.1 filing the suit
      7.1.1.1 parties to the suit
      7.1.1.2 selection of the court
      7.1.1.3 notice
   7.1.2 the pleadings
      7.1.2.1 the complaint
      7.1.2.2 the defendant's responses
      7.1.2.3 additional responses
   7.1.3 discovery
      7.1.3.1 interrogatories
      7.1.3.2 depositions
      7.1.3.3 requests for admissions
      7.1.3.4 motions on documents & physical exams
      7.1.3.5 enforcing discovery rights
   7.1.4 pretrial motions
   7.1.5 negotiation and pretrial conferences

UNIT 4

8.0.0 Interviewing and Investigation
  8.1.0 The Client Interview
    8.1.1 principles of good communication
    8.1.2 putting the subject at ease
    8.1.3 starting the interview
    8.1.4 keeping the interview going
    8.1.5 ending the interview
  8.2.0 The Investigation
    8.2.1 getting started
    8.2.2 physical and photographic evidence
    8.2.3 locating witnesses
    8.2.4 interviewing witnesses
    8.2.5 taking formal statements
    8.2.6 obtaining documentary evidence
    8.2.7 using computer data bases
    8.2.8 the investigative report

9.0.0 Legal Research
  9.1.0 Analyzing the Problem
  9.2.0 Library Research
    9.2.1 discovering basic principles
      9.2.1.1 American Jurisprudence 2d
      9.2.1.2 Corpus Juris Secundum
      9.2.1.3 local reference encyclopedias
      9.2.1.4 special subject encyclopedias, treatises
      9.2.1.5 legal periodicals
      9.2.1.6 American Law Reports, annotated
      9.2.1.7 citations for secondary sources
    9.2.2 finding statutes and regulations
      9.2.2.1 subject index technique
      9.2.2.2 using popular-name tables
      9.2.2.3 checking subsequent legislative or
        judicial action
      9.2.2.4 locating the legislative history
      9.2.2.5 administrative actions
    9.2.3 finding court decisions
      9.2.3.1 digests
      9.2.3.2 Shepard's citations

9.3.0 Computer Assisted Research
    9.3.1 contents of the data bases
        9.3.1.1 LEXIS
        9.3.1.2 WESTLAW
        9.3.1.3 other data bases
    9.3.2 operation of the systems

UNIT 5

10.0.0 Legal Writing
    10.1.0 Internal Research Memoranda
        10.1.1 purpose
        10.1.2 format and content
        10.1.3 application of format
    10.2.0 Letters
        10.2.1 purpose
        10.2.2 format and content
    10.3.0 Instruments
        10.3.1 purpose
        10.3.2 format and content
    10.4.0 Pleadings and Motions
        10.4.1 purpose
        10.4.2 format and content
    10.5.0 Interrogatories and Other Discovery Requests
        10.5.1 purpose
        10.5.2 format and content
        10.5.3 responding to interrogatories
    10.6.0 External Memoranda of Law
        10.6.1 purpose
        10.6.2 format and content
    10.7.0 Appellate Briefs
        10.7.1 purpose
        10.7.2 format and content of appellant's brief
            10.7.2.1 digesting or abstracting the record
            10.7.2.2 identifying the issues
            10.7.2.3 presenting the facts
            10.7.2.4 developing the argument
            10.7.2.5 summing it up
            10.7.2.6 table of authorities

Appendix 4.4

Chapter 4

Instructional Planning for College Courses

Physics for Respiratory Care Course Outline

PHYSICS FOR RESPIRATORY CARE
Course Content Outline
Bonita L. Lusardo

UNIT 1

1. Introduction to Physics
1.1 Definition of Physics
   1.1.1 definition of matter
   1.1.2 definition of energy
1.2 Review of Scientific Method
   1.2.1 hypothesis
   1.2.2 experiment
      1.2.2.1 testing
      1.2.2.2 recording
      1.2.2.3 controls
   1.2.3 theory
   1.2.4 law
      1.2.4.1 inductive reasoning
      1.2.4.2 deductive reasoning

2. Measurement
2.1 Definition of Measurement
2.2 System Internationale (SI units)
   2.2.1 metric system
      2.2.1.1 quantities and units used
      2.2.1.2 conversion of units
   2.2.2 centimeter-gram-second (CGS)
      2.2.2.1 quantities and unit used
      2.2.2.2 conversion of units
   2.2.3 British system
      2.2.3.1 quantities and units used
      2.2.3.2 conversion of units
2.3 Scientific Notation
   2.3.1 definition
   2.3.2 use
2.4 Temperature Scales
   2.4.1 Fahrenheit and Celsius
      2.4.1.1 boiling and freezing points
      2.4.1.2 conversion factors

      2.4.2 Kelvin and Rankine
           2.4.2.1 absolute zero
           2.4.2.2 conversion factors
      2.4.3 relationship between temperature scales
           2.4.3.1 Fahrenheit to Rankine conversion
           2.4.3.2 Celsius to Kelvin conversion
           2.4.3.3 use with gas laws
   2.5 Lung Flow Rates and Volumes
      2.5.1 spirometer and respirometer
           2.5.1.1 volume collecting device
           2.5.1.2 flow measuring device
      2.5.2 pulmonary function tests (PFT)
           2.5.2.1 measure
                  2.5.2.1.1 integrity of the airways
                  2.5.2.1.2 function of the diaphragm
                  2.5.2.1.3 function of the thoracic muscles
                  2.5.2.1.4 cardiovascular status
                  2.5.2.1.5 condition of lung tissue
           2.5.2.2 indications of PFT
                  2.5.2.2.1 screen for pulmonary disease
                  2.5.2.2.2 preoperative evaluation
                  2.5.2.2.3 assess disease progression
                  2.5.2.2.4 assist in determining disability
                  2.5.2.2.5 modify therapeutic approach
           2.5.2.3 lung parameters
                  2.5.2.3.1 tidal volume (Vt)
                  2.5.2.3.2 vital capacity (VC)
                  2.5.2.3.3 residual volume (RV)
                  2.5.2.3.4 total lung capacity

3. Motion and Forces
   3.1 Kinematics (study of motion)
      3.1.1 speed (velocity=v)
      3.1.2 distance (s)
      3.1.3 time (t)
      3.1.4 acceleration (a)
   3.2 Newton's Laws of Motion
      3.2.1 #1 objects remain at rest unless external forces act
      upon them

3.2.2 #2 acceleration of an object is directly proportional to the net external force, and inversely related to the objects mass
    3.2.2.1 cardiovascular system
    3.2.2.2 sputum expectoration
3.2.3 #3 for every action there is an equal and opposite reaction
    3.2.3.1 breathing
    3.2.3.2 closed head injuries
3.3 Forces
  3.3.1 vectors
    3.3.1.1 magnitude, direction and sense
    3.3.1.2 represented by a straight line
  3.3.2 torque
    3.3.2.1 equilibrium
    3.3.2.2 static equilibrium
  3.3.3 gravity
    3.3.3.1 center
      3.3.3.1.1 determinant of net torque
      3.3.3.1.2 determines stability of equilibrium
    3.3.3.2 lung fluids and secretions
    3.3.3.3 Archimedies' Principle
      3.3.3.3.1 buoyancy
      3.3.3.3.2 specific gravity
  3.3.4 centrifugal
    3.3.4.1 "center fleeing"
    3.3.4.2 laboratory centrifuge
  3.3.5 frictional
    3.3.5.1 static
    3.3.5.2 kinetic
    3.3.5.3 mucous membranes
  3.3.6 surface tension
    3.3.6.1 forces at the surface of a liquid
    3.3.6.2 cohesion
    3.3.6.3 adhesion
    3.3.6.4 meniscus
      3.3.6.4.1 concave
      3.3.6.4.2 convex

3.3.7 low surface tension
3.3.8 high surface tension
    3.3.8.1 inward attraction force
    3.3.8.2 atelectasis
    3.3.8.3 alveolar patency
    3.3.8.4 surfactant
    3.3.8.5 premature infant
    3.3.8.6 ideopathic respiratory distress syndrome (IRDS)

UNIT 2

4. Matter

4.1 Three States
    4.1.1 determinants of each state
        4.1.1.1 molecular arrangement
        4.1.1.2 molecular activity
4.2 Mass
    4.2.1 quantity of matter
    4.2.2 units of measurement
    4.2.3 forumla
4.3 Weight
    4.3.1 earth's gravitational pull
    4.3.2 units of measurement
    4.3.3 formula
4.4 Density
    4.4.1 mass per unit of volume
    4.4.2 characteristics of density
        4.4.2.1 kinetic activity
        4.4.2.2 Brownian movement
    4.4.3 relationship to gravity
    4.4.4 formula
4.5 The Mole Concept
    4.5.1 gram molecular weight
    4.5.2 Avogadro's number
4.6 Density of Gases Used in Respiritory Therapy and Diagnosis

5. Work, Energy and Simple Machines

5.1 Work
    5.1.1 characteristics of work
    5.1.2 relationship to power

5.2 Types of Energy
    5.2.1 kinetic
    5.2.2 potential
5.3 Work-Energy Principle
5.4 Conservation of Energy
    5.4.1 forms of energy
    5.4.2 mechanical energy
5.5 Principles of Simple Machines
    5.5.1 a first class lever, a fulcrum
        5.5.1.1 fulcrum is between effort and resistance
        5.5.1.2 diaphragm
    5.5.2 inclined plane, a second class
        5.5.2.1 resistance is between fulcrum and effort
        5.5.2.2 intercostals
    5.5.3 a third class lever
        5.5.3.1 effort is between fulcrum and resistance
        5.5.3.2 pectoralis major
5.6 Muscles as Simple Machines used in Respiration
    5.6.1 respiratory muscles
        5.6.1.1 diaphragm
    5.6.2 accessory muscles
        5.6.2.1 inspiraton
            5.6.2.1.1 scalene
            5.6.2.1.2 sternocleidomastoid
            5.6.2.1.3 pectoralis major
        5.6.2.2 expiration
            5.6.2.2.1 external oblique
            5.6.2.2.2 internal oblique
            5.6.2.2.3 transverse rectus

6. Fluid Pressures
    6.1 Definition of Pressure
    6.2 Fluids
    6.3 Properties of Gases
        6.3.1 kinetic activity
        6.3.2 Brownian movement
        6.3.3 in relation to temperature, volume and pressure
            6.3.3.1 Charles' law
            6.3.3.2 Boyle's law
            6.3.3.3 Universal Gas law

6.4 Relationship of Pressure to Force and Area
    6.4.1 larger area = decrease in pressure (inverse relationship)
    6.4.2 higher force = increase in pressure (direct relationship)
6.5 Atmospheric Pressure
    6.5.1 14.7 lbs. per square inch
    6.5.2 evenly distributed
    6.5.3 pressure dependent on height of container
    6.5.4 measurement of manometer (weight density x height)
    6.5.5 relationship of gauge pressure to atmospheric pressure
6.6 Pascal's Principle
    6.6.1 pressure in an enclosed fluid
    6.6.2 application to pericardial fluid
    6.6.3 application to pleural fluids
    6.6.4 mechanical ventilation
6.7 Pressure in Flowing Fluids
    6.7.1 pressure gradient
    6.7.2 formula
    6.7.3 flow rate
        6.7.3.1 characteristics of flow rate
        6.7.3.2 relationship between flow rate, volume and resistance
        6.7.3.3 normal resistance
        6.7.3.4 increased resistance
        6.7.3.5 decreased resistance
        6.7.3.6 Poiseuille's law
    6.7.4 types of flow
        6.7.4.1 laminar
        6.7.4.2 turbulent
        6.7.4.3 discriminating types of Renold's number
    6.7.5 transport gas laws
        6.7.5.1 Dalton's law
        6.7.5.2 Henry's law
        6.7.5.3 Grahm's law
        6.7.5.4 Fick's law
    6.7.6 airways and air flow
        6.7.6.1 airway generations

6.7.7.5 blood pressure
   6.7.7.5.1 variations
   6.7.7.5.2 measurement
6.7.8 law of La Place
   6.7.8.1 behavior of spheres
   6.7.8.2 pressure in a drop
      6.7.8.2.1 2 gas/liquid interface
      6.7.8.2.2 4 x surface tension/radius
      6.7.8.2.3 expressed in dynes/cm squared

UNIT 3

7. Heat Transfer and Humidification
7.1 First Law of Thermodynamics
   7.1.1 applying work on matter
   7.1.2 applying heat on matter
7.2 A Body's Internal Energy
   7.2.1 metabolism = internal energy
   7.2.2 increased metabolism = digestion + increased core temperature
      7.2.2.1 digestion = work
      7.2.2.2 core temperature = heat
   7.2.3 increased metabolism produces increased levels of CO_2
   7.2.4 heat is directly proportional to calorie intake
   7.2.5 calorie
   7.2.6 dietary calorie
7.3 Heat Transfer
   7.3.1 conduction
   7.3.2 convection
   7.3.3 evaporation
   7.3.4 radiation
7.4 Preventing Heat Transfer with Liquid Oxygen
   7.4.1 store in Dewar vessel
      7.4.1.1 prevents conduction and convection
      7.4.1.2 silver coating prevents radiation
7.5 Liquid Oxygen Production
   7.5.1 true gas
   7.5.2 critical temperature
   7.5.3 critical pressure

8.7.1 galvanic fuel cell
   8.7.1.1 semipermeable membrane
   8.7.1.2 gold and lead electrodes
   8.7.1.3 $O^2 + H^2O = OH-$
   8.7.1.4 oxidation
   8.7.1.5 reduction
   8.7.1.6 current is measured as % of O^2
   8.7.1.7 advantages and disadvantages
      8.7.1.7.1 electrode life
      8.7.1.7.2 response time
   8.7.1.8 concerns
      8.7.1.8.1 pressure
      8.7.1.8.2 H^2O
8.7.2 polarographic
   8.7.2.1 similar to galvanic
   8.7.2.2 has a battery
   8.7.2.3 advantages and disadvantages
      8.7.2.3.1 electrode life
      8.7.2.3.2 response time
   8.7.2.4 concerns
      8.7.2.4.1 pressure
      8.7.2.4.2 H^2O
8.7.3 physical analyzer
   8.7.3.1 Pauling principle
   8.7.3.2 magnetic fields
   8.7.3.3 measures partial pressures
   8.7.3.4 disadvantage
8.7.4 electrical analyzers
   8.7.4.1 thermal conductivity
      8.7.4.1.1 Wheatstone bridge
      8.7.4.1.2 heated wires
      8.7.4.1.3 accuracy
      8.7.4.1.4 measurement by percentage
8.7.5 chemical analyzers
   8.7.5.1 mercury displacement
   8.7.5.2 CO^2
   8.7.5.3 measures % of O^2
   8.7.5.4 accuracy

Appendix 4.5

Chapter 4

Instructional Planning for College Courses

Cognitive Domain

COGNITIVE DOMAIN
Benjamin S. Bloom

1.0 KNOWLEDGE
    1.1 Knowledge of Specifics
        1.1.1 knowledge of terminology
        1.1.2 knowledge of specific facts
    1.2 Knowledge of Ways & Means of Dealing with Specifics
        1.2.1 knowledge of conventions
        1.2.2 knowledge of trends & sequences
        1.2.3 knowledge of classifications & categories
        1.2.4 knowledge of criteria
        1.2.5 knowledge of methodology
    1.3 Knowledge of Universals & Abstractions in a Field
        1.3.1 knowledge of principles & generalizations
        1.3.2 knowledge of theories & structures

2.0 COMPREHENSION
    2.1 Translation
    2.2 Interpretation
    2.3 Extrapolation
3.0 APPLICATION

4.0 ANALYSIS

    4.1 Analysis of Elements
    4.2 Analysis of Relationships
    4.3 Analysis of Organizational Principles

5.0 SYNTHESIS
    5.1 Production of a Unique Communication
    5.2 Production of a Plan or Proposed Set of Operations
    5.3 Derivation of a set of Abstract Relations

6.0 EVALUATION
    6.1 Judgements in Terms of Internal Evidence
    6.2 Judgements in Terms of External Criteria

Appendix 4.6

Chapter 4

Instructional Planning for College Courses

Affective Domain

AFFECTIVE DOMAIN
David R. Krathwohl
Benjamin S. Bloom
Bertram B. Masia

1.0 RECEIVING (ATTENDING)
1.1 Awareness
1.2 Willingness to Receive
1.3 Controlled or Selected Attention

2.0 RESPONDING
2.1 Acquiescence in Responding
2.2 Willingness to Respond
2.3 Satisfaction in Response

3.0 VALUING
3.1 Acceptance of a Value
3.2 Preference for a Value
3.3 Commitment

4.0 ORGANIZATION
4.1 Conceptualization of a Value
4.2 Organization of a Value System

5.0 CHARACTERIZATION BY A VALUE OR VALUE COMPLEX
5.1 Generalized Set

Appendix 4.7

Chapter 4

Instructional Planning for College Courses

Unit Content and Level I and II Goals

UNIT 5 CONTENT OUTLINE

10.0.0 LEGAL WRITING
    10.1.0 Internal Research Memoranda
        10.1.1 purpose
        10.1.2 format and content
        10.1.3 application of format
    10.2.0 Letters
        10.2.1 purpose
        10.2.2 format and content
    10.3.0 Instruments
        10.3.1 purpose
        10.3.2 format and content
    10.4.0 Pleadings and Motions
        10.4.1 purpose
        10.4.2 format and content
    10.5.0 Interrogatories and Other Discovery Requests
        10.5.1 purpose
        10.5.2 format and content
        10.5.3 responding to interrogatories
    10.6.0 External Memoranda of Law
        10.6.1 purpose
        10.6.2 format and content
    10.7.0 Appellate Briefs
        10.7.1 purpose
        10.7.2 format and content of appellant's brief
            10.7.2.1 digesting or abstracting the record
            10.7.2.2 identifying the issues
            10.7.2.3 presenting the facts
            10.7.2.4 developing the argument
            10.7.2.5 summing it up
            10.7.2.6 table of authorities
            10.7.2.7 assembling appendixes, table of contents
            10.7.2.8 preparation of the cover sheet

11.0.0 TRIALS AND HEARINGS
    11.1.0 Preparations for Trial
        11.1.1 assembling a trial notebook
            11.1.1.1 outline of the case

11.1.1.2 identification lists

11.1.1.3 witness section

11.1.1.4 exhibits file

11.1.1.5 pleadings file

11.1.1.6 motions file

11.1.1.7 jury trial

11.1.1.8 computerized litigation support

11.1.2 coordinating and preparing witnesses

11.2.0 Assistance during the Trial

11.3.0 Adjudicatory Hearings

11.3.1 preparation for the hearing

11.3.2 conduct of the hearing

Unit 5 Goals

Level I Goal: Become familiar with the common skills and duties needed by the legal assistant for trial and administrative hearings, including legal writing skills.

Supporting Level II Goals*:

5.1 Know the various types of non-trial documents the legal assistant is expected to prepare (cognitive).

5.2 Know the various types of trial documents the legal assistant is expected to prepare (cognitive).

5.3 Identify the elements of an appellate and an appellee brief (cognitive).

5.4 Appreciate the uses of a legal assistant during trial (affective).

5.5 Identify the elements of a trial notebook (cognitive).

5.6 Understand the procedures for preparing a witness (cognitive).

5.7 Understand the basic skills utilized by a legal assistant during advocacy of an administrative hearing (cognitive).

---

* *First digit (5) identifies the: Unit 5.*

Appendix 4.8

Chapter 4

Instructional Planning for College Courses

Sample Level III Objectives

SAMPLE LEVEL III OBJECTIVE
Relationship to Unit Topic and Level II Goals

Unit: Family Planning

Cognitive Goal: Understand the need for proper prenatal nutrition.

Performance Objective: Cite at least two of the text examples of adverse effects upon newborns from illegal drug abuse during pregnancy.

Performance: cite
Conditions: none
Criterion: two of the text examples

Performance Objective: Prepare a sample diet plan for the first term of pregnancy. Must meet the calorie and food group requirements in the text.

Performance: prepare
Conditions: none
Criterion: calorie and food group requirements in the text

Performance Objective: Using the text weight gain data, graph your current weight from pregnancy to first month after; accurate +/- 1 lb.

Unit: Allied Health

Psychomotor Goal: Take and record patient vital signs.

Performance Objective: Under instructor supervision, take the pulse of another student; within thirty seconds and +/-two beats of instructor's reading.

Performance: take the pulse
Conditions: under instructor supervision
Criterion: within thirty seconds and +/- two beats

Performance Objective: Given patient descriptions, pulse rates, and norms chart, categorize each as NORMAL or ABNORMAL; 100% accuracy

Performance: categorize

Conditions: patient descriptions, pulse rates and norms chart

Criterion: categorized as normal or abnormal, 100% accuracy

Performance Objective: Read the blood pressure of a student within forty-five seconds and accurate within +/- 5% of instructor determined reading.

Performance: read

Conditions: none

Criterion: within forty-five seconds, accurate +/- 5% of instructor reading

Performance Objective: From the hand-out on age, weight and conditioning norms, compute your projected blood pressure; 5% accuracy.

Performance: compute

Conditions: age, weight and conditioning norms

Criterion: 5% accuracy

Unit: Programming Fundamentals

Psychomotor Goal: Use conventional keyboarding techniques for alpha and numeric data entry.

Performance Objective: Label all characters and symbols for the standard "QWERTY" keyboard; from memory, with 100% accuracy.

Performance: label

Conditions: from memory

Criterion: 100% accuracy

Performance Objective: On a timed three-minute speed test, and with no more than four errors, type at least twenty-five words per minute.

Performance: type

Conditions: three-minute speed test

Criterion: no more than four errors, at least twenty-five words per minute

Appendix 4.9

Chapter 4

Instructional Planning for College Courses

Legal Assisting Objective Hierarchy

INTRODUCTION TO LEGAL ASSISTING
OBJECTIVE HIERARCHY
Patricia E. Ruth-Instructor

I. Become familiar with the role of the legal assistant, including ethical considerations and the organization of the modern law office.

  II. Identify the various requirements needed to access the legal assisting profession (cog)*.

  II. Identify the different areas of practice of law and the scope of activities performed by the legal assistant in each area of practice (cog).

  II. Value the desirable characteristics a legal assistant should possess (aff).

  II. Know the different types of organizational structures and the different types of support personnel used in these structures (cog).

  II. Identify the various types of standard operating procedures used in law offices (cog).

  II. Know the ABA's Code of Professional Responsibility (cog).

  II. Understand the restrictions (avoidances) placed on the activities that legal assistants undertake (cog).

I. Understand the organization of the legal system and case and statutory laws.

  II. Know the different elements of criminal and civil law (cog).

  II. Know the different types of state and federal courts (cog).

  II. Identify the various types of publications of primary source materials, which aid the legal assistant in legal research process (cog).

  II. Identify the procedures taken to interpret statutes (cog).

  II. Identify the methods used to interpret a court case (cog).

  II. Understand the role of precedence for the American legal system (cog).

Identifies domain for Level II goal.

II. Appreciate the importance of "stare decisis" in founding the American legal system (aff).

I. Understand basic legal concepts, including the litigation and adjudication process of the courts.

II. Identify the defenses used in criminal, tort and contract law (cog).

II. Know the types of remedies for breach of contract in property law (cog).

II. Understand the legal structures in corporate law and administrative law (cog).

II. Understand the most frequent applications of constitutional law (cog).

II. Value the need to litigate and adjudicate an unsettled dispute in civil and criminal law (aff).

II. Know the basic stages involved in a civil litigation action (cog).

II. Know the major stages involved in a criminal law actions (cog).

II. Know the various procedures involved in an administrative hearing (cog).

I. Become familiar with the common skills and duties needed by the legal assistant during the investigative, and legal research phases of cases.

II. Know the common abilities needed when conducting a client interview (cog).

II. Understand the various skills exercised when conducting an investigation (cog).

II. Know the alternative methods followed when conducting library research to seek the same piece of information (cog).

II. Identify the steps taken in analyzing a legal research problem (cog).

II. Identify the various techniques commonly used to find statutes and court decisions (cog).

II. Identify the major computer-assisted data bases used in research and the basic legal information contained in each (cog).

II. Value the proper procedures for checking for subsequent judicial or legislative actions (aff).

II. Understand the proper formats for the citation of cases and statutory materials (cog).

I. Become familiar with the common skills and duties needed by the legal assistant for trial and administrative hearings, including legal writing skills.

II. Know the various types of non-trial documents the legal assist is expected to prepare (cog).

III. From the text, identify the three primary differences between an internal research memorandum and an external memorandum of law, no errors (know)**.

III. From class lecture and class notes, given the terms internal memoranda, external memoranda, letters and instruments, match each term with the appropriate definition, one error permitted (know).

III. Without the use of notes, list the 5 documents that are classified as legal agreements, 100% accuracy (know).

II. Know the various types of trial documents the legal assistant is expected to prepare (cog).

III. From text and class discussion, identify the 4 pleadings that are filed with the court at the beginning of a lawsuit, no errors (know).

III. Without the use of notes or text, identify, in order, the format requirements for pleadings and motions as defined in Rule 10 of the Federal Rules of Civil Procedure, all requirements must be included (comp).

III. Given an example from the Federal Appendix of Forms book, decide whether the form would be classified as an interrogatory, a request for production of docu-

---

**Identifies category of the cognitive domain for Level III objectives.

ments or a request for admissions, 100% accuracy (comp).

II. Identify the elements of an appellate and an appellee brief (cog).

III. From text and class lecture, list the eight items that should be present in a completed appellant's brief, no errors (know).

III. Given a set of facts surrounding a case and using class notes, determine what method of statutory or constitutional analysis should be used to best support the position being advocated, 100% accuracy (analy).

III. From class lecture and notes, list the two duties a legal assistant will perform before drafting the appellate brief, no omissions allowed (know).

III. From class lecture and notes, identify the 7 duties a legal assistant will perform when preparing a brief, no errors (know).

III. From text and class lecture, describe in writing, 100 words or less, the process that takes place when a legal assistant prepares a reply brief, all factors must be included (comp).

II. Appreciate the uses of a legal assistant during trial (aff).

III. From class discussion and handout, list the 5 primary responsibilities of the legal assistant when acting as "second chair" during trial, no errors (comp).

III. From text and class lecture, describe the advantages of using a legal assistant as a "second chair" rather than using a secretary, no errors (comp).

II. Identify the elements of a trial notebook (cog).

III. Identify each section of the trial notebook, in order, from text and lecture, include all sections (know).

III. From text and lecture, identify the documents that are found in the pleadings files, one error permitted (know).

III. Given a document, determine in which section of the trial notebook it belongs, without the use of notes or handouts, no errors (appl).

II. Understand the procedures for preparing a witness (cog).

III. Without the use of notes, list the types of general advice a legal assistant should give to prospective witnesses, at least five of the seven types must be included (know).

III. From class text and videotape, identify the types of substantive duties a legal assistant may perform when preparing a witness for testimony, one omission out of the five types is permitted (know).

III. From handout, describe the advantage of taking the witness through the exhibit system just prior to trial, no error (comp).

III. Given a section from a court transcript, determine whether the section is an example of a direct examination or a cross-examination, no errors (analy).

II. Understand the basic skills utilized by a legal assistant during advocacy of an administrative hearing (cog).

III. Without the use of notes, list the three main functions a legal assistant may perform in an administrative hearing, all functions must be included (know).

III. In 100 words or less, describe in writing the process of preparing for an administrative hearing, all factors must be presented (comp).

III. From speaker and class discussion identify the two primary reasons for successful advocacy of an administrative hearing, no errors (know).

III. From text, describe why you should never ask a question of an adverse witness for which you do not know the answer, no errors (know).

III. From handout and class lecture, identify the only way to effectively combat impeachment when opposing counsel is cross-examining a witness, no errors (comp).

Appendix 4.10

Chapter 4

Instructional Planning for College Courses

Physics for Respiratory Care Lesson Plans

PHYSICS FOR RESPIRATORY CARE
LESSON PLANS
Bonita L. Lusardo-Instructor

Tuesday—1:00-2:15 PM

Pick up overheads and handouts

Introduce self and course
Welcome perspective respiratory care professionals
Hand out syllabus (for lec. and lab.)
Go over syllabus and materials needed for course: Questions?
Inform:

1st: Responsibility of assignments are the student's alone.

2nd: Participation in lab activities will be permitted only after the Program Medical/Safety packet has been properly filled, signed and handed to me at the beginning of the first lab session.

LECTURE: Introduction to Physics

Level II: 1. Know what the study of physics is and how the scientific method is applied to the study of physics (cog).

Level III: 1. Be able to define physics as it was stated in class (know).

Q—What is physics?
Does anybody have an idea?
We know from other courses that it is a study—
Q—but a study of what? (Matter & Energy)

Matter = anything that has mass & occupies space
Energy = capacity for doing work

With all sciences we must use a universal method of study which brings us to the scientific method.

Level III: 2. Be able to list, as it was stated in class and in order, the phases of scientific method (know).

Hypothesis, Experimentation, Theory and Law

Level III: 3. Given four written statements; be able to identify, without error, the phase of scientific method used (comp).

Material: Deals with thought and action—A way to seek out the truth.

1st there is an observation (controlled or uncontrolled)—and then there is a Hypothesis—an idea or educated guess regarding the observation.

Q—Anybody see *Medicine Man* played by Sean Connery?

Experimentation—test the hypothesis & collect data.
   Included are:

Q—What happened to Sean's experimentation?

   Did he———> establish questions?
   ———> perform the experiment?
   ———> record the data?

Q—Do you think—maybe—there was a problem with the controls?

Q—What do controls do?
Controls add validity to the experiment
   1. time
   2. amount
   3. unknown

Q—Do you think Sean Connery had Controls????

Theory—is a statement forming results of experimentation
   other researchers must conclude with the same results

Law—Formal summary taken from repeated observations and experimentations.

Inductive reasoning—going from specific information to a general conclusion.
   ◆ Joe is a communist
   ◆ Joe is from U.S.A.
   ◆ U.S.A. is a communist country

Deductive reasoning—going from a general statement to a specific conclusion.

- U.S.A. is a democratic country
- Joe is from U.S.A.
- Joe is a democrat

Q—Is Joe a democrat or a communist??

Qs—Inductive:

- Are there enough instances to prove your point??
- Are the instances typical??
- Are the instances recent??

Qs—Deductive:

- Is the major premise true??
- Have I chosen the best possible conclusion from the major premise??

When we study physics we not only need to use the scientific method but we also need to use some form of universal measurement. (Explain the System Internationale)

Level II: 2. Know the quantities, units and formulas used when converting to and from the System Internationale (cog).

Level III: 4. Given specific problems or scenarios and without conversion charts be able to correctly convert and calculate areas of length, weight and volume by employing the English and Metric systems (app).

* *Give information sheet handouts* *
* *Use overheads to explain the handout* *

Overhead #1 For length, weight and volume we will use the metric system.

Mega—largest that we are dealing with.

going down in size:
Kilo, Hecto, Deca——and now we have reached base which are Meter——Gram——Liter

going below base or the quantity of 1

deci, centi, milli and micro—smallest that we are dealing with.

Overhead #2 Conversion from English to Metric

Step by step examples on board: lead the students into answering

$5in = ?cm$ $5in \times \dfrac{2.54cm}{1in} =$ $8lbs = ?kg$ $8lbs \times \dfrac{454gms}{1lb} =$

$4qts = ?L$ $4qt \times \dfrac{.95L}{1qt} =$ $6.4in = ?cm$ $6.4in \times \dfrac{2.54}{1in} =$

$6cm = ?in$ $6cm \times \dfrac{.39in}{1cm} =$ $4kg = ?lb$ $4kg \times \dfrac{2.2lb}{1kg} =$

$8L = ?qts$ $8L \times \dfrac{1.06}{1L} =$ $6.5cm = ?in$ $6.5cm \times \dfrac{.39in}{1cm} =$

Level III: 5. Given numerical values, be able to select the correct scientific notation for each one (comp).

Overhead #1 repeated:

** Notice to the right where it says "power" you will see each value stated in scientific notation. Explanation of zeros.

Q—What did I say?
Give me some examples....
**HOT CHALK—from seat

Q—What did I say?

Explain-CGS will be used later on in the course

In order to avoid confusion we will cover CGS at the point in the course where it well be used. For now, just know that it is used when small masses and lengths are measured and it is expressed in terms of mass, length and time.

Summarize today's info
—HOT CHALK—
Define physics
Scientific method
SI, including Scientific Notation

Ed. Note: *Hot Chalk is a technique in which the student holding the chalk must respond to the instructor's questions. See "Improving Timeliness of Student Reading with Hot Chalk,"* **Adjunct Info,** *2, 2, Info-Tec, Inc., Cleveland, 1994.*

We will be going over temperature scales in Wednesday's lab—
so be sure and do your reading assignment in "Nave" and go
over the information in your handout. Be prepared to hand in
a work sheet at the end of Wednesday's lab—so be sure and
know your Metric/English conversions and scientific notation.

Wednesday— 10:45-12:45

Don't forget overheads & assignment sheets
write problems on board

LAB: Temperature scales and feedback on SI and Scientific
notation.

Collect Medical/Safety packets.

Overhead #2 reviewed
*review conversion from English to Metric with HOT CHALK
** avoid calling on the "real adult student" today
*** Go over board problems:
1. 2' = ?cm
2. 6cm = ?in
3. 80lbs = ?kg
4. 4kg = ?lbs
5. 2.5qts = ?L
6. 7L = ?qts

Level II: 3. Understand the relationships between various
temperature scales and their conversion factors
(cog).

Level III: 6. Given specific problems and without conversion
charts, be able to correctly convert temperatures
between the Fahrenheit, Celsius, Rankine and
Kelvin scales (app).

Overhead #3

Celsius scale   ——> 0 degrees = Freezing point of H_2O

                 ——> 100 degrees = Boiling point of H_2O

Fahrenheit scale ——> 32 degrees = Freezing point of H_2O

                 ——> 212 degrees = Boiling point of H_2O

Temperature scale used most often in US is Fahrenheit, while in science, the Celsius scale is used. One medical institution may use Fahrenheit while another will use Celsius; therefore, it is necessary to know how to convert one to the other.

Overhead #4

Q—Where do the #'s 100 & 180 come from?

For Celsius the difference between its boiling and freezing point = 100

For Fahrenheit the difference between its boiling and freezing point = 180

Remember how we got these #'s

Q—What fact would determine the first (top)# of the fraction? If no answer ask:

Q—Why would it be 9/5 instead of 5/9 or vice/versa? Answer: What you are solving for?

Remember:
  1) What determines the top # of the fraction
  2) You add 32 degrees to the larger scale (F) & you subtract 32 degrees from the smaller scale (C).

Level III: 7. Be able to define, as stated in class, absolute temperature (know).

Overhead #5

Kelvin & Rankine scales: —> are used to depict large variations in temperatures.
—> represent Absolute Temperature

Absolute temperature is one in which all molecular activity has ceased.

The Kelvin scale is same as Celsius scale but the "0" point is down to -273 degrees.

The Rankine scale is same as Fahrenheit scale with "0" point down to -460 degrees.

Q—How would you convert from C to K?
    Think about how you converted C to F
    To convert C to K add 273
    And F to R?
    To convert F to R add 460

Hand out work sheets, students to finish in 1-hr. Monitor/Aid

Thursday: 1:00 - 2:15

> *Remember Overheads*

LECTURE:

Review: In Tuesday's lecture we addressed physics as a valid study using the scientific method. We discussed the 4 main characteristics of the scientific method, including what constitutes a valid experiment. We went over the SI measuring standards and conversion of units to that standard.

In Wednesday's lab we reviewed Tuesday's lecture. We learned how to convert US standard temperatures into universally accepted values. We discussed absolute temperatures and the conversion factors for those 2 scales.

Today: We will learn the normal values of lung volumes, the techniques by which we evaluate them and the alterations involved in obstructive and restrictive disease.

Level II: 4. Associate lung volumes to the integrity and function of the cardiopulmonary system (cog).

Level III: 8. Given a diagram based on a typical spirogram, be able to correctly label all lung compartments with their titles and normal values, as stated in class (know).

Overhead #6

A spirometer is a volume-displacement device, used to determine lung volumes and flow rates. The Collins spirometer is a water sealed collecting device, suspended by a chain and pulley system. It has a pen connected to record movement of the bell on a graph. The patient breathes in and the bell moves downward. The amount of displacement of the bell, will correspond to the pen movement which in turn corresponds to the volume.

Demonstrate with colored pen on overhead

A respirometer is a flow-sensing device used to determine lung volumes and flow rates.

The (Wrights) respirometer consists of a vane connected to a series of gears. Gas flows through the instrument, rotating the vanes to register a volume. At flows greater than 300L/min, the vane-gear system may cause erroneous measurements because the vane is subject to distortion.

Demonstrate with colored pen on overhead

Overhead #7

Pulmonary Function Test can measure values below:

Volumes: IRV = 3.1L   Capacities: IC = IRV + Vt
$\quad$ Vt = .5L $\qquad\qquad\qquad$ FRC = ERV + RV
$\quad$ ERV = 1.2L $\qquad\qquad\quad$ VC = IRV + Vt + ERV
$\quad$ RV = 1.2L $\qquad\qquad\qquad\quad$ IC + ERV

$\qquad\qquad\qquad\qquad\qquad$ TLC = IRV + Vt + ERV + RV
$\qquad\qquad\qquad\qquad\qquad\qquad$ VC + RV
$\qquad\qquad\qquad\qquad\qquad\qquad$ IC + FRC

** *Demonstrate with colored pen on overhead***

Qs—*Hot Chalk* give Normal values for the following:
$\quad$ 1) IC
$\quad$ 2) FRC
$\quad$ 3) VC
$\quad$ 4) TLC

Qs—*Hot Chalk* what volumes are found in the following capacities?
$\quad$ 1) IC
$\quad$ 2) FRC
$\quad$ 3) VC
$\quad$ 4) TLC

Level III: 9. Without error, recognize the lung volume or capacity by the technique used to measure it (comp).

Qs— Identify the following maneuvers:

Vt   1) Normal resting breathing

IRV 2) Largest volume of gas that can be inspired above a normal tidal volume

IC   3) Largest volume that can be inspired from resting end-expiration.

ERV 4) Largest volume of gas that can be expired from a resting end-expiratory level

RV   5) Volume of gas in the lung at the end of maximum expiration.

FRC 6) Volume of gas remaining in the lung at the end- expiratory level.

VC   7) Maximum inspiration followed by maximum expiration.

TLC 8) Total amount of gas in the lungs following a maximum inspiration.

VE   9) Vt x RR

Qs—*Hot Chalk* for above.

Level III: 10. Correctly identify all lung volume alterations in obstructive and restrictive patterns (comp).

Overhead #8

Distensibility can be judged by establishing the change in length or size that results when force is applied. The distensibility of the springs can be generalized by the force necessary to stretch and hold them at a certain point. It is not possible to measure the force applied to the lungs and thoracic cage; therefore, the pressure that is applied is measured, and instead of measuring the changes in length we measure the change in volume.

In a restrictive disorder the lungs are stiff and they require a lot of pressure to ventilate.

Qs—What effect would this have on TLC?
Would this affect lung volumes?
Would this influence respiratory rate?

TLC, FRC, RV and forced VC (FVC) are reduced. Diseases and Conditions = Pulmonary fibrosis, Obesity, Kyphoscoliosis and Pregnancy.

In an obstructive disorder the lungs have increased compliance. It takes very little pressure to ventilate this patient—but because—the lung parenchyma may be irritated by an allergen or may have lost its elastic properties the air-way may collapse, resulting in air trapping or hyperinflation.

Qs—What do you think would happen to certain lung
compartments if you had air trapping?
What would happen to the FRC?
Would this effect the TLC? Why?

Increased TLC, FRC and RV. Diseases and Conditions = Emphysema, Chronic Bronchitis and Asthma.

*Summarize: We discussed the spirometer and respirometer and how they measure lung volumes. We know the normal values for lung volumes and capacities—also the maneuvers required for PFTs. We have had an introduction to abnormal lung physiology, thus, making it possible to identify specific lung disorders and diseases.

*Reminder: During today's lab we will be learning the indications of PFT's.

Thursday 3:00 - 5:00

Don't forget overheads & graded assignment sheets

LAB:

Review: In Wednesday's lab we reviewed the metric system and SI. We learned how to convert US standard temperatures into universally accepted values. We became acquainted with

absolute temperature and the conversion factors for those
2 scales.

Earlier today in lecture two measuring devices were discussed.

Q—What were the names of these devices?
   ans: Spirometer and Respirometer

Q—What do they measure and how?
   ans: A spirometer is a volume-displacement device, used
   to determine lung volumes and flow rates. A respirometer
   is a flow-sensing device used to determine lung volumes
   and flow rates.

** *Ask for volunteer ** for a ***
** *Demonstration of a Collins Water-seal Spirometer ***

** Point out the bell, Kymograph, gas analyzer and CO^2
absorber and how the bell rises during expiration and the
pens on the kymograph move downward. Watch how one pen
records respiratory excursions during inspiration and expiration while the other records only during inspiration (tracing
accumulated volumes).

*Demonstration of a Wrights respirometer and a "Slow Vital Capacity"
maneuver*

Pass out 1 respirometer per 2 students. Each student will be
equipped with bed-side PFT equipment that has one-way
valves. Explain how to assemble it and attach this equipment
to the respirometer.

Note
Liters are the whole number and "cc" have a decimal.

Level II: 5. Appreciate the value of pulmonary function testing
          (PFT) in relation to diagnostics (aff).

Level III: 11. Given a scenario, be able to correctly distinguish
          between indicated PFTs and those PFTs that are
          not indicated (analy).

Lung volumes are collected and measured to establish the
lung's ability to remove CO^2 and maintain a set level of O^2.
After volumes are collected, calculations are performed accord-

ing to the patient's height, weight, age and sex. These results are then compared with predicted normal values and the end result will aid the therapist in assessing and evaluating the patient's condition.

Indications for PFTs:
      1) Screen for pulmonary disease
      2) Preoperative evaluation
      3) Assess disease progression
      4) Assist in determining disability
      5) Modify therapeutic approach

Appendix 7.1

Chapter 7

Testing and Evaluation

Evaluation Plan

RESPIRATORY CARE
EVALUATION PLAN

Lecture:

Unit Exams (3) 40 points/exam .... 120 ...... 40%

Comprehensive Final .... 102 ...... 34%

Subjective .... 21 .... 7%

Lab:

Weekly Assignments (9) .... 27 .... 9%

Comprehensive Lab Final .... 30 ...... 10%

                       Total Points .... 300 .... 100%

Subjective evaluation (21 points):

Class participation 7pts

Attendance 7pts

Professionalism 7pts

            Total 21pts

A = 100 - 93%

B = 92 - 84%

C = 83 - 75%

D = 74 - 68%

Appendix 7.2

Chapter 7

Testing and Evaluation

Evaluation Plan

LEGAL ASSISTING
EVALUATION PLAN

Measure	Percentage	Points
Five Unit Tests	50%	200
Final Examination	6%	24
Class Participation	10%	40
Attendance (2-unexcused absences allowed)	11%	44
Subjective	8%	32
Group project 5%		
Client interview 3%		
Written Paper	15%	60
Total	100%	400

A = 93% - 100%

B = 85% - 92%

C = 77% - 84%

D = 69% - 76%

F = below 69%

EVALUATION PLAN FOR WRITTEN PAPER, GROUP PROJECT AND CLIENT INTERVIEW

Measure	Points
Written Paper (case analysis)	
Criterion:	
Length (3-4 pages)	5
Typed	5
Spelling and Grammar	10
Strength of Arguments	20
Strength of Supporting Evidence	10
Strength of Conclusion	10
	60
Group Project	
Criterion:	
Active Participation	4
Proper Sources and Citations	4
Proper Conclusions in Interpretation	5
Presentation	7
	20
Client Interview	
Criterion:	
Preparation	2
Open Ended Questioning	3
Closed Ended Questioning	3
Withdrew Relevant Information	4
	12

Appendix 7.3

Chapter 7

Testing and Evaluation

Table of Specifications

Table of Specifications

Key =
Objec-tive	
	Test Item

Behaviors

Each cell is divided diagonally: the lower-left value is the **Objective** number(s); the upper-right value is the **Test Item** number(s).

Unit Content	**Cognitive** knowledge (obj / test)	comprehension (obj / test)	application (obj / test)	analysis (obj / test)	syn./eval.	**Affective**	**Psychomotor**	**Totals** (obj / test)
Introduction To Physics	1, 2 / 3	3						3 / 3
Measurement	4, 7 9, 12, 13 / △ 7, 8	5, 8,10 14-17 / 5, △10	6, 11 / 4, 6	18, 19 / 11				8 / 16
Motion & Force	20, 26-34 / 12, 14-17	21-25 / 13						6 / 15
Totals	9 / 17	5 / 13	2 / 2	1 / 2			17 /	17 / 34

△ = Supports Affective Goal

Appendix 7.4

Chapter 7

Testing and Evaluation

Table of Specifications

Table of Specifications

Unit 5

Key = Objective / Test Item (diagonal cell split: upper-left = Objective, lower-right = Test Item)

Behaviors

Content	Cognitive: knowledge	Cognitive: comprehension	Cognitive: application	Cognitive: analysis	Cognitive: syn./eval.	Affective	Psychomotor	Totals
Internal/External Memos, Letters, Instruments	1, 2, 3 / 1-11							3 / 11
Pleadings, Motions, Interrogatories, Other Discovery	4-7 / 12, 15	5, 6 / 13, 14						6 / 4
Appelate/EE Briefs	9-10 / 18-26	11 / 48	/ 16	8 / 17				4 / 12
Trial/Trial Notebook	14, 15 / 29, 36	[12, 13] / [27, 28]	16 / 37			[12, 13] / [27, 28]		5 / 11
Preparing a Witness	17, 18 / 38, 39	19 / 40	/ 41	20 / 42				4 / 5
Administrative Hearings	21, 23 / 43, 44, 45	22, 24, 25 / 46, 47, 49						5 / 6
Totals	13 / 33	9 / 9	1 / 3	2 / 2		2 / 2		27 / 49

[box] = Affective listed twice - once for comprehension level, once for affective level

Appendix 7.5

Chapter 7

Testing and Evaluation

Test Item Analysis Report

THE UNIVERSITY OF AKRON
COMPUTER CENTER
TEST SCORING SERVICES
INSTRUCTOR'S STATISTIC REPORT FOR
5400-421-080

INSTRUCTOR : B. FRYE
TEST FORM: A
NO. OF STUDENTS: 31
MEAN: 67.742   ST. DEV.: 11.196
ITEM ANALYSIS

QUES. NO.	A NO/%	B NO/%	C NO/%	D NO/%	E NO/%	Omit NO/%	Mult.Resp. NO/%	A	B	C	D	E	Omit	
										AVERAGE SCORE BY RESPONSE				
								A	B	C	D	E	Omit	
1	5/16	17/54*	4/12	5/16	0/0	0/0	0/0	67.60	68.53	62.50	69.40	0.00	0.00	BIS: 0.097 / PBIS: 0.078 / T-VALUE: 0.419
2	1/3	1/3	28/90*	1/3	0/0	0/0	0/0	52.00	56.00	69.32	51.00	0.00	0.00	BIS: 0.746 / PBIS: 0.437 / T-VALUE: 2.619
3	2/6	27/87*	1/3	1/3	0/0	0/0	0/0	59.00	69.56	53.00	51.00	0.00	0.00	BIS: 0.670 / PBIS: 0.422 / T-VALUE: 2.508
4	11/35*	18/58	1/3	0/0	1/3	0/0	0/0	73.64	66.44	56.00	0.00	38.00	0.00	BIS: 0.501 / PBIS: .389 / T-VALUE: 2.275
5	13/41	8/25	1/3	9/29*	0/0	0/0	0/0	71.31	61.50	73.00	67.56	0.00	0.00	BIS: -0.014 / PBIS: -0.011 / T-VALUE: -0.057
6	0/0	0/0	2/6	29/93*	0/0	0/0	0/0	0.00	0.00	58.50	68.38	0.00	0.00	BIS: 0.427 / PBIS: 0.225 / T-VALUE: 1.244
7	1/3	1/3	3/9	0/0	26/83*	0/0	0/0	51.00	38.00	53.67	0.00	71.15	0.00	BIS: 0.999 / PBIS: 0.674 / T-VALUE: 4.920
8	2/6	1/3	0/0	27/87*	1/3	0/0	0/0	44.50	56.00	0.00	69.96	66.00	0.00	BIS: 0.820 / PBIS: 0.517 / T-VALUE: 3.253
9	0/0	0/0	4/12	27/87*	0/0	0/0	0/0	0.00	0.00	60.00	68.89	0.00	0.00	BIS: 0.424 / PBIS: 0.267 / T-VALUE: 1.492
10	1/3	30/96*	0/0	0/0	0/0	0/0	0/0	52.00	68.27	0.00	0.00	0.00	0.00	BIS: 0.647 / PBIS: 0.285 / T-VALUE: 1.599

PAGE: 2

THE UNIVERSITY OF AKRON
COMPUTER CENTER
TEST SCORING SERVICES
INSTRUCTOR'S STATISTIC REPORT FOR
5400-421:080

INSTRUCTOR: B. FRYE
TEST FORM: A
NO. OF STUDENTS: 31
MEAN: 67.742   ST. DEV.: 11.196

ITEM ANALYSIS

QUES. NO.	A NO/%	B NO/%	C NO/%	D NO/%	E NO/%	Omit NO/%	Mult.Resp. NO/%	AVERAGE SCORE BY RESPONSE A	B	C	D	E	Omit	
11	0/0	29/93*	2/6	0/0	0/0	0/0	0/0	0.00	68.14	62.00	0.00	0.00	0.00	BIS: 0.265 PBIS: 0.140 T-VALUE: 0.761
12	2/6	25/80*	2/6	0/0	2/6	0/0	0/0	63.50	69.28	54.00	0.00	66.50	0.00	BIS: 0.405 PBIS: 0.284 T-VALUE: 1.595
13	5/16	22/70*	4/12	0/0	0/0	0/0	0/0	60.20	70.36	62.75	0.00	0.00	0.00	BIS: 0.486 PBIS: 0.370 T-VALUE: 2.142
14	1/3	1/3	13/41*	16/51	0/0	0/0	0/0	52.00	53.00	70.31	67.56	0.00	0.00	BIS: 0.245 PBIS: 0.194 T-VALUE: 1.066
15	7/22	5/16	0/0	1/3	18/58*	0/0	0/0	64.57	53.00	0.00	70.00	72.94	0.00	BIS: 0.690 PBIS: 0.547 T-VALUE: 3.518
16	0/0	1/3	1/3	2/6	27/87*	0/0	0/0	0.00	52.00	38.00	59.50	70.04	0.00	BIS: 0.848 PBIS: 0.534 T-VALUE: 3.404
17	11/35	18/58*	1/3	1/3	0/0	0/0	0/0	67.64	69.50	52.00	53.00	0.00	0.00	BIS: 0.233 PBIS: 0.185 T-VALUE: 1.013
18	0/0	2/6	0/0	28/90*	1/3	0/0	0/0	0.00	58.50	0.00	68.43	67.00	0.00	BIS: 0.324 PBIS: 0.190 T-VALUE: 1.043
19	1/3	0/0	4/12	3/9	23/74*	0/0	0/0	73.00	0.00	57.75	64.33	69.70	0.00	BIS: 0.400 PBIS: 0.297 T-VALUE: 1.672
20	23/74*	2/6	0/0	1/3	5/16	0/0	0/0	71.30	62.00	0.00	38.00	59.60	0.00	BIS: 0.730 PBIS: 0.541 T-VALUE: 3.462

THE UNIVERSITY OF AKRON
COMPUTER CENTER
TEST SCORING SERVICES
INSTRUCTOR'S STATISTIC REPORT FOR
5400-421:080

INSTRUCTOR: B. FRYE
TEST FORM: A
NO. OF STUDENTS: 31
MEAN: 67.742   ST. DEV.: 11.196

ITEM ANALYSIS

QUES. NO.	A NO/%	B NO/%	C NO/%	D NO/%	E NO/%	Omit NO/%	Mult.Resp. NO/%	Avg A	Avg B	Avg C	Avg D	Avg E	Avg Omit	BIS / PBIS / T-VALUE
21	1/3	0/0	4/12	0/0	26/83*	0/0	0/0	53.00	0.00	60.75	0.00	69.38	0.00	BIS: 0.506 / PBIS: 0.342 / T-VALUE: 1.958
22	27/87*	0/0	0/0	0/0	4/12	0/0	0/0	70.41	0.00	0.00	0.00	49.75	0.00	BIS: 0.984 / PBIS: 0.620 / T-VALUE: 4.261
23	30/96*	1/3	0/0	0/0	0/0	0/0	0/0	67.60	72.00	0.00	0.00	0.00	0.00	BIS: -0.175 / PBIS: -0.077 / T-VALUE: -0.416
24	30/96*	0/0	0/0	0/0	0/0	1/3	0/0	68.30	0.00	0.00	0.00	0.00	51.00	BIS: 0.688 / PBIS: 0.303 / T-VALUE: 1.711
25	2/6	21/67*	0/0	0/0	8/25	0/0	0/0	45.00	71.00	0.00	0.00	64.88	0.00	BIS: 0.550 / PBIS: 0.424 / T-VALUE: 2.522
26	1/3	12/38	14/45*	4/12	0/0	0/0	0/0	52.00	64.58	69.71	74.25	0.00	0.00	BIS: 0.201 / PBIS: 0.160 / T-VALUE: 0.872
27	0/0	0/0	31/100*	0/0	0/0	0/0	0/0	0.00	0.00	67.74	0.00	0.00	0.00	BIS: 0.436 / PBIS: 0.000 / T-VALUE: 0.000
28	1/3	0/0	29/93*	0/0	1/3	0/0	0/0	53.00	0.00	68.66	0.00	56.00	0.00	BIS: 0.612 / PBIS: 0.323 / T-VALUE: 1.835
29	6/19	0/0	15/48*	0/0	10/32	0/0	0/0	67.50	0.00	70.07	0.00	64.40	0.00	BIS: 0.252 / PBIS: 0.201 / T-VALUE: 1.105
30	3/9	1/3	12/38*	15/48	0/0	0/0	0/0	64.00	52.00	71.92	66.20	0.00	0.00	BIS: 0.376 / PBIS: 0.295 / T-VALUE: 1.664

AVERAGE SCORE BY RESPONSE

PAGE: 4

THE UNIVERSITY OF AKRON
COMPUTER CENTER
TEST SCORING SERVICES
INSTRUCTOR'S STATISTIC REPORT FOR
5400-421:080

INSTRUCTOR: B. FRYE
TEST FORM: A
NO. OF STUDENTS: 31
MEAN: 67.742   ST. DEV.: 11.196

ITEM ANALYSIS

QUES. NO.	A NO/%	B NO/%	C NO/%	D NO/%	E NO/%	Omit NO/%	Mult.Resp. NO/%	Avg A	Avg B	Avg C	Avg D	Avg E	Omit	BIS	PBIS	T-VALUE
31	1/3	5/16	18/58*	7/22	0/0	0/0	0/0	72.00	63.60	68.22	68.86	0.00	0.00	0.064	0.050	0.272
32	3/9	0/0	1/3	27/87*	0/0	0/0	0/0	58.00	0.00	57.00	69.22	0.00	0.00	0.547	0.345	1.977
33	5/16	14/45*	7/22	5/16	0/0	0/0	0/0	71.00	68.86	63.86	66.80	0.00	0.00	0.114	0.090	0.489
34	0/0	4/12	6/19	21/67*	0/0	0/0	0/0	0.00	60.50	56.17	72.43	0.00	0.00	0.791	0.610	4.147
35	5/16	15/48*	0/0	9/29	2/6	0/0	0/0	74.80	68.40	0.00	67.67	45.50	0.00	0.071	0.057	0.307
36	4/12	22/70*	0/0	1/3	3/9	1/3	0/0	65.75	72.23	0.00	51.00	48.67	51.00	0.852	0.632	4.396
37	3/9	26/83*	0/0	2/6	0/0	0/0	0/0	47.33	71.19	0.00	53.50	0.00	0.00	0.999	0.674	4.920
38	29/93*	1/3	0/0	1/3	0/0	0/0	0/0	68.66	52.00	0.00	57.00	0.00	0.00	0.612	0.323	1.835
39	0/0	30/96*	0/0	0/0	1/3	0/0	0/0	0.00	68.27	0.00	0.00	52.00	0.00	0.647	0.285	1.599
40	2/6	1/3	28/90*	0/0	0/0	0/0	0/0	58.50	70.00	68.32	0.00	0.00	0.00	0.160	0.274	0.875

THE UNIVERSITY OF AKRON
COMPUTER CENTER
TEST SCORING SERVICES
INSTRUCTOR'S STATISTIC REPORT FOR
5400-421:080

INSTRUCTOR : B. FRYE
TEST FORM: A
NO. OF STUDENTS: 31
MEAN: 67.742   ST. DEV.: 11.196

ITEM ANALYSIS

QUES. NO.	A NO/%	B NO/%	C NO/%	D NO/%	E NO/%	Omit NO/%	Mult.Resp. NO/%	A	B	AVERAGE SCORE BY RESPONSE C	D	E	Omit	
41	5/16	6/19	18/58*	2/6	0/0	0/0	0/0	56.60	64.67	73.28	55.00	0.00	0.00	BIS: 0.735 PBIS: 0.582 T-VALUE: 3.854
42	1/3	0/0	0/0	30/96*	0/0	0/0	0/0	52.00	0.00	0.00	68.27	0.00	0.00	BIS: 0.647 PBIS: 0.285 T-VALUE: 1.599
43	0/0	0/0	2/6	0/0	29/93*	0/0	0/0	0.00	0.00	44.50	0.00	69.34	0.00	BIS: 0.999 PBIS: 0.526 T-VALUE: 3.334
44	6/19	22/70 /	1/3	1/3	1/3*	0/0	0/0	71.83	69.27	56.00	38.00	51.00	0.00	BIS: -0.661 PBIS: -0.264 T-VALUE: -1.472
45	25/80*	1/3	4/12	1/3	0/0	0/0	0/0	71.80	38.00	53.75	52.00	0.00	0.00	BIS: 0.999 PBIS: 0.701 T-VALUE: 5.289
46	11/35	7/22	10/32*	3/9	0/0	0/0	0/0	71.18	64.00	69.90	56.67	0.00	0.00	BIS: 0.173 PBIS: 0.133 T-VALUE: 0.721
47	20/64*	4/12	0/0	1/3	6/19	0/0	0/0	71.85	61.25	0.00	73.00	57.50	0.00	BIS: 0.636 PBIS: 0.496 T-VALUE: 3.079
48	3/9	1/3	25/80*	2/6	0/0	0/0	0/0	57.00	56.00	69.96	62.00	0.00	0.00	BIS: 0.584 PBIS: 0.409 T-VALUE: 2.417
49	1/3	23/74*	6/19	1/3	0/0	0/0	0/0	80.00	66.83	69.50	66.00	0.00	0.00	BIS: -0.188 PBIS: -0.139 T-VALUE: -0.756
50	1/3	1/3	0/0	26/83*	2/6	0/0	1/3	56.00	52.00	0.00	70.08	59.50	51.00	BIS: 0.719 PBIS: 0.486 T-VALUE: 2.992

THE UNIVERSITY OF AKRON
COMPUTER CENTER
TEST SCORING SERVICES
INSTRUCTOR'S STATISTIC REPORT FOR
5400-421:080

INSTRUCTOR: B. FRYE
TEST FORM: A
NO. OF STUDENTS: 31
MEAN: 67.742   ST. DEV.: 11.196

ITEM ANALYSIS

QUES. NO.	A NO/%	B NO/%	C NO/%	D NO/%	E NO/%	Omit NO/%	Mult.Resp. NO/%	Avg A	Avg B	Avg C	Avg D	Avg E	Avg Omit	BIS	PBIS	T-VALUE
51	2/6	0/0	25/80*	1/3	3/9	0/0	0/0	73.50	0.00	69.12	70.00	51.67	0.00	0.363	0.254	1.416
52	0/0	1/3	2/6	28/90*	0/0	0/0	0/0	0.00	66.00	66.00	67.93	0.00	0.00	0.088	0.052	0.279
53	1/3	1/3	2/6	27/87*	0/0	0/0	0/0	38.00	52.00	52.00	70.59	0.00	0.00	0.999	0.630	4.365
54	1/3	30/96*	0/0	0/0	0/0	0/0	0/0	72.00	67.60	0.00	0.00	0.00	0.00	-0.175	-0.077	-0.416
55	0/0	0/0	30/96*	1/3	0/0	0/0	0/0	0.00	0.00	68.27	52.00	0.00	0.00	0.647	0.285	1.599
56	0/0	0/0	28/90*	0/0	3/9	0/0	0/0	0.00	0.00	69.00	0.00	56.00	0.00	0.594	0.348	2.001
57	3/9	1/3	25/80*	1/3	0/0	1/3	0/0	58.00	38.00	71.36	53.00	0.00	51.00	0.952	0.668	4.832
58	28/90*	1/3	1/3	1/3	0/0	0/0	0/0	68.82	70.00	38.00	65.00	0.00	0/00	0.510	0.299	1.687
59	1/3	1/3	3/9	26/83*	0/0	0/0	0/0	52.00	51.00	48.33	71.23	0.00	0.00	0.999	0.674	4.920
60	0/0	11/35	10/32*	10/32	0/0	0/0	0/0	0.00	65.82	71.00	66.60	0.00	0.00	0.200	0.261	1.101

INSTRUCTOR: B. FRYE
TEST FORM: A
NO. OF STUDENTS: 31
MEAN: 67.742   ST. DEV.: 11.196

THE UNIVERSITY OF AKRON
COMPUTER CENTER
TEST SCORING SERVICES
INSTRUCTOR'S STATISTIC REPORT FOR
5400-421:080

QUES. NO.	ITEM ANALYSIS							AVERAGE SCORE BY RESPONSE								
	A NO/%	B NO/%	C NO/%	D NO/%	E NO/%	Omit NO/%	Mult.Resp. NO/%	A	B	C	D	E	Omit	BIS	PBIS	T-VALUE
61	0/0	3/9	28/90*	0/0	0/0	0/0	0/0	0.00	61.33	68.43	0.00	0.00	0.00	0.324	0.190	1.043
62	24/77*	2/6	5/16	0/0	0/0	0/0	0/0	69.50	54.00	64.80	0.00	0.00	0.00	0.405	0.293	1.648
63	1/3	2/6	24/77*	3/9	0/0	1/3	0/0	72.00	54.50	70.08	62.00	0.00	51.00	0.539	0.390	2.279
64	30/96*	0/0	1/3	0/0	0/0	0/0	0/0	68.27	0.00	52.00	0.00	0.00	0.00	0.647	0.285	1.599
65	0/0	1/3	29/93*	1/3	0/0	0/0	0/0	0.00	66.00	68.34	52.00	0.00	0.00	0.404	0.213	1.174
66	0/0	1/3	0/0	1/3	29/93*	0/0	0/0	0.00	38.00	0.00	52.00	69.31	0.00	0.999	0.526	3.334
67	2/6	0/0	7/22	15/48*	7/22	0/0	0/0	54.50	0.00	67.57	70.67	65.43	0.00	0.317	0.253	1.407
68	1/3	22/70*	7/22	0/0	0/0	1/3	0/0	53.00	71.64	60.00	0.00	0.00	51.00	0.723	0.549	3.538
69	24/77*	4/12	0/0	3/9	0/0	0/0	0/0	67.50	66.75	0.00	71.00	0.00	0.00	0.056	0.040	0.217
70	0/0	0/0	8/25	17/54*	6/19	0/0	0/0	0.00	0.00	56.50	72.59	69.00	0.00	0.600	0.478	2.928

THE UNIVERSITY OF AKRON
COMPUTER CENTER
TEST SCORING SERVICES
INSTRUCTOR'S STATISTIC REPORT FOR
5400-421:080

INSTRUCTOR: B. FRYE
TEST FORM: A
NO. OF STUDENTS: 31
MEAN: 67.742   ST. DEV.: 11.196
ITEM ANALYSIS

QUES. NO.	A NO/%	B NO/%	C NO/%	D NO/%	E NO/%	Omit NO/%	Mult.Resp. NO/%	AVG A	AVG B	AVG C	AVG D	AVG E	AVG Omit	BIS / PBIS / T-VALUE
71	2/6	0/0	29/93*	0/0	0/0	0/0	0/0	45.00	0.00	69.31	0.00	0.00	0.00	BIS: 0.999 / PBIS: 0.526 / T-VALUE: 3.334
72	4/12	24/77*	0/0	0/0	3/9	0/0	0/0	55.25	70.96	0.00	0.00	58.67	0.00	BIS: 0.741 / PBIS: 0.535 / T-VALUE: 3.414
73	3/9	22/70*	6/19	0/0	0/0	0/0	0/0	61.00	68.14	69.67	0.00	0.00	0.00	BIS: 0.073 / PBIS: 0.056 / T-VALUE: 0.300
74	2/6	24/77*	3/9	2/6	0/0	0/0	0/0	62.00	70.17	62.67	52.00	0.00	0.00	BIS: 0.558 / PBIS: 0.404 / T-VALUE: 2.376
75	28/90*	1/3	1/3	1/3	0/0	0/0	0/0	68.82	70.00	38.00	65.00	0.00	0.00	BIS: 0.510 / PBIS: 0.299 / T-VALUE: 1.687
75	4/12	26/83*	0/0	1/3	0/0	0/0	0/0	52.75	70.65	0.00	52.00	0.00	0.00	BIS: 0.897 / PBIS: 0.606 / T-VALUE: 4.099
76	25/80*	0/0	0/0	6/19	0/0	0/0	0/0	71.44	0.00	0.00	52.33	0.00	0.00	BIS: 0.973 / PBIS: 0.683 / T-VALUE: 5.030
77	0/0	0/0	0/0	0/0	31/100*	0/0	0/0	0.00	0.00	0.00	0.00	67.74	0.00	BIS: 0.000 / PBIS: 0.000 / T-VALUE: 0.000
78	0/0	1/3	1/3	1/3	28/90*	0/0	0/0	0.00	53.00	38.00	52.00	69.89	0.00	BIS: 0.999 / PBIS: 0.585 / T-VALUE: 3.889
79	3/9	2/6	0/0	1/3	25/80*	0/0	0/0	48.33	69.50	0.00	66.00	70.00	0.00	BIS: 0.594 / PBIS: 0.417 / T-VALUE: 2.469

THE UNIVERSITY OF AKRON
COMPUTER CENTER
TEST SCORING SERVICES
INSTRUCTOR'S STATISTIC REPORT FOR
5400-421:080

INSTRUCTOR : B. FRYE
TEST FORM: A
NO. OF STUDENTS: 31
MEAN: 67.742   ST. DEV.: 11.196

ITEM ANALYSIS

QUES. NO.	A NO/%	B NO/%	C NO/%	D NO/%	E NO/%	Omit NO/%	Mult.Resp. NO/%	AVERAGE SCORE BY RESPONSE A	B	C	D	E	Omit	
80	26/83*	0/0	4/12	1/3	0/0	0/0	0/0	70.27	0.00	58.75	38.00	0.00	0.00	BIS: 0.779 PBIS: 0.526 T-VALUE: 3.328
81	0/0	21/67*	9/29	1/3	0/0	0/0	0/0	0.00	70.86	62.33	51.00	0.00	0.00	BIS: 0.526 PBIS: 0.406 T-VALUE: 2.389
82	28/90*	2/6	0/0	1/3	0/0	0/0	0/0	68.18	60.50	0.00	70.00	0.00	0.00	BIS: 0.206 PBIS: 0.121 T-VALUE: 0.656
83	25/80*	5/16	1/3	0/0	0/0	0/0	0/0	69.40	59.00	70.00	0.00	0.00	0.00	BIS: 0.436 PBIS: 0.306 T-VALUE: 1.731
84	23/74*	5/16	1/3	1/3	1/3	0/0	0/0	72.70	56.40	52.00	56.00	38.00	0.00	BIS: 0.999 PBIS: 0.740 T-VALUE: 5.926
85	7/22	16/51*	5/16	3/9	0/0	0/0	0/0	64.14	72.44	58.60	66.33	0.00	0.00	BIS: 0.543 PBIS: 0.433 T-VALUE: 2.589
86	0/0	27/87*	3/9	0/0	0/0	1/3	0/0	0.00	68.00	64.67	0.00	0.00	70.00	BIS: 0.095 PBIS: 0.060 T-VALUE: 0.324
87	1/3	0/0	29/93*	0/0	1/3	0/0	0/0	51.00	0.00	68.38	0.00	66.00	0.00	BIS: 0.427 PBIS: 0.225 T-VALUE: 1.244
88	23/74*	0/0	3/9	5/16	0/0	0/0	0/0	71.78	0.00	46.67	61.80	0.00	0.00	BIS: 0.828 PBIS: 0.613 T-VALUE: 4.183
89	11/35	5/16	1/3	14/45*	0/0	0/0	0/0	72.09	56.00	38.00	70.64	0.00	0.00	BIS: 0.295 PBIS: 0.235 T-VALUE: 1.30

KR-20 REL.: 0.926

FREQUENCY DISTRIBUTION

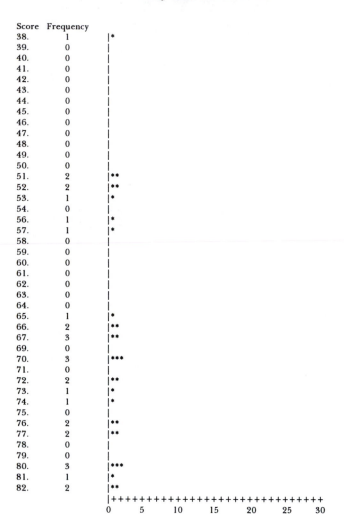

Score	Frequency	
38.	1	|*
39.	0	|
40.	0	|
41.	0	|
42.	0	|
43.	0	|
44.	0	|
45.	0	|
46.	0	|
47.	0	|
48.	0	|
49.	0	|
50.	0	|
51.	2	|**
52.	2	|**
53.	1	|*
54.	0	|
56.	1	|*
57.	1	|*
58.	0	|
59.	0	|
60.	0	|
61.	0	|
62.	0	|
63.	0	|
64.	0	|
65.	1	|*
66.	2	|**
67.	3	|**
69.	0	|
70.	3	|***
71.	0	|
72.	2	|**
73.	1	|*
74.	1	|*
75.	0	|
76.	2	|**
77.	2	|**
78.	0	|
79.	0	|
80.	3	|***
81.	1	|*
82.	2	|**

```
|++++++++++++++++++++++++++++++++
0     5    10    15    20    25    30
```

Appendix 7.6

Chapter 7

Testing and Evaluation

Syllabus

ASHLAND UNIVERSITY
DEPARTMENT OF BUSINESS ADMINISTRATION

BUS 328: Financial Management
Fall 1993

Ms. Sharon Latkovich, Assistant Professor
Office:16D Miller x:5222
Office Hours: MWF 10-11
MW 12-1 1:50 - 2:15
TTH 11:15 - 12:15
If you are unable to meet me at these times, an appointment may be made for a more mutually convenient time.

Prequisites
ECON 231: Principles of Macroeconomics
ECON 232: Principles of Microeconomics
BUS 107: Accounting Principles I
BUS 108: Accounting Principles II
MATH 208: Elementary Statistics

Reading Material
Required:
Campsey and Brigham, *Introduction To Financial Management*, Third Edition, Dryden Press, 1991.
Optional:
Campsey and Brigham, Study Guide - *Introduction To Financial Management*, Third Edition, Dryden Press, 1991.

Course Description
An introduction to the finance function: the obtaining and efficient use of capital in a business setting. Specific topics include risk and return analysis, financial planning decisions involving assets and equities, and the financial structure of the firm.

Course Objectives

The successful student in this course will:

1. Know the basic functions of finance in a corporate or business setting, along with the goals of the firm.

2. Describe the sources of capital and the nature of financial claims exchanged therein.

3. Understand the processes used in the acquisition of capital.

4. Comprehend all elements of good financial planning.

5. Show how financial risk is measured and explain how risk affects rates of return.

6. Use analytical techniques to demonstrate the financial planning process.

7. Explain how managers make capital budgeting decisions.

8. Demonstrate that how a company is financed contributes significantly to the firm's profitability and risk exposure.

Homework

Questions/Problems: Each student is strongly encouraged to work the questions and problems associated with the chapters. Problems will be assigned as homework, to be discussed in class. As the discussion of homework will form the basis for your participation grade, solving the problems during class will be closely monitored.

Project: Each student will be expected to analyze a set of financial statements (which will be provided by the professor) as outlined in Unit 6 (Chapter 6: Interpreting Financial Statements). A separate assignment sheet is appended to this syllabus.

Class Policy

Class attendance and class participation beyond mere physical presence are essential for maximum educational advantage and are strongly encouraged. Responsibility for all course material rests entirely with the student, whether or not he or she attends each class.

I will assume that you have read the text material *before* class. Therefore, lecture will attempt to supplement and expand on the material in the text.

As a rule, I will lecture on a chapter, then we will work some problems as time permits. An optional review session will be held one-half hour before each class, covering the material that was introduced the prior class session.

Cheating of any kind will result in an automatic "F" and dismissal from the class, in accordance with the procedures outlined in the Ashland University Student Handbook.

Test Policy

1. To be officially excused from the exam, your illness or other problem must be reported to me or the department's main office (22 Miller, x:5210) *prior* to the examination by note, letter, or telephone.

2. On all homework, quizzes, and exams, students *must* show all work. Simply giving the "one-figure" answer will result in points deducted from your grade.

3. Use of pencil is required; fully erase any mistakes. Any illegible answers will be graded accordingly.

4. Students must provide their own calculators. No sharing is allowed at test time.

5. All exams will be kept on file in my office where they may be viewed by students.

Student Responsibilities

1. Students will be responsible for completing assigned homework, taking exams, and any notes missed while absent. You are urged to get someone's phone number now as a contact for any missed material.

2. Excessive absences will be noted and the proper authorities notified according to Ashland University policy.

3. If you are having problems with the course, do not hesitate to seek counseling early — failure to do so usually compounds problems later.

4. Don't worry — it's not as bad as it sounds!

Schedule

This course schedule will be followed as closely as possible although occasional adjustments may be necessary.

Week	Topic	Chapters
1 - 2	Unit 1 Primary Functions Goals of the Firm	1
2 - 3	Unit 2 Financial Markets Financial Instruments Capital Formation	2, 17
3 - 5	Unit 3 Short-Term Financial Management	9,10,11
6 - 7	Unit 4 Long-Term Financial Management	16, 17
8 - 9	Unit 5 Measuring Risk Portfolio Capital Asset Pricing Model	12
10 - 11	Unit 6 Ratio Analysis	6
12	Unit 7 Forecasting	7
13	PROJECTS DUE (Monday of Week 13)	
13 - 15	Unit 8 Capital Budgeting Process Target Capital Structure	14, 20

Grading

Evaluating Criteria	Points	Weight
Participation	50	5%
Attendance	50	5%
Project	400	40%
Unit Tests (8)	500	50%
	1000	100%

Students must earn their grades. Students will not be given credit simply so that they can pass, graduate, or earn corporate reimbursement. No curve is anticipated. Letting the professor know "that the student needs a certain grade" will only reinforce rigid adherence to these evaluating criteria.

Scale

A	100 - 92%	B-	81 - 80%	D+	69 - 68%
A-	91 - 90%	C+	79 - 78%	D	67 - 62%
B+	89 - 88%	C	77 - 72%	D-	61 - 60%
B	87 - 82%	C-	71 - 70%	F	59 - 0%

Assignment Sheet - Course Project

Each student will be expected to analyze a set of financial statements (which will be provided by the professor) as outlined in Unit 6: Ratio Analysis. Therefore, this analysis will include:

1. (20) **Outside References:** A minimum of two outside references must be included in your written analysis. These references can be sources of comparative ratios, and/or articles on the company or industry being researched. However, they must be cited and included in a bibliography according to APA writing style.

2. (20) **Calculation:** A minimum of three year's worth of ratios must be calculated with 100% accuracy. The most recent year and the two immediately preceding years should constitute the three years.

3. (240) **Verbal Analysis:** Using the appropriate ratios, explain a given company's liquidity, asset management, debt management, profitability, and market value in your own words. Emphasis will be placed on succinct and thorough explanations: one sentence answers are seriously frowned upon.

4. (40) **Du Pont Analysis:** Calculate all elements of the Du Pont equation for both ROE and ROA for all three years. Assess the trend and comparative performance of the company. Use of graphic aids is looked upon favorably, but not to the exclusion of a written analysis. Refer to handout packet for Unit 6 for an outstanding example of this item.

5. (40) **Comparative Analysis:** Given any source of comparative ratios as discussed during the Unit 6 lecture (and listed in the text), compare the various ratios to the industry average. Use of graphic aids is looked upon favorably, but not to the exclusion of a written analysis.

6. (40) **Trend Analysis:** From the calculations #2 above, verbally analyze the trends of the various ratios. Use of graphic aids is looked upon favorably, but not to the exclusion of a written analysis.

Appendix 7.7

Chapter 7

Testing and Evaluation

Syllabus

COMMUNITY COLLEGE
PHYSICS FOR RESPIRATORY CARE

RESP 119

Fall - 1993

Instructor: Bonnie Lusardo, RRT, RPFT

Dept. Phone Number — 4706

Textbooks:

> *Physics for the Health Sciences,* Nave and Nave, W.B. Saunders, 3rd. Ed., 1985

> *Respiratory Therapy Equipment,* S. McPherson, C.V. Mosby, 4th. Ed., 1990.

Reading Assignments and Exam Dates:

1st wk.	Nave (chap. 1 & pg 169) McPherson (pp. 89-93)
2nd wk. 09/28	Nave (chap. 2 & 3) McPherson (pp. 18-22)
3rd wk. 10/05	TUESDAY — 10/6 — EXAM Nave (chap. 4)
4th wk. 10/12	Nave (pp. 265-272) McPherson (chap. 9)
5th wk. 10/19	Nave (chap. 5) McPherson (pp. 27-31)
6th wk. 10/26	THURSDAY — 10/28 — EXAM Nave (pp. 192-207) McPherson (chap. 2)
7th wk. 11/02	Nave (chap. 6) Handout
8th wk. 11/09	Nave (chap. 7) McPherson (chap. 3)
9th wk. 11/16	THURSDAY — 11/18 — EXAM
10th wk.	Thanksgiving Week — No Class
11th wk.	TUESDAY — 11/29 — LAB FINAL THURSDAY — 12/02 — FINAL EXAM

Grading Plan

Lecture:

Unit exams (3) @ 40 points/exam		120	40%
Comprehensive Final		102	34%
Subjective		21	7%
Class participation	7		
Attendance	7		
Professionalism	7		
Total:	21		

Lab:

Weekly assignments (9)	27	9%
Comprehensive Lab Final	30	10%
Total:	300	100%

A = 100-93%   B = 92-84%   C = 83-75%   D = 74-68%

Attendance: College policy will be followed.

Missed Exams: If you must miss an exam date, please call prior to the scheduled hour of examination. Failure to do so will result in an F on the exam.

Tutors: Will be licensed RRTs who have completed this program and are employed by health care institutions. They are available by schedule or appointment. Their schedules will be posted outside of the lab.

Lab Assignments: Will be discussed in the lab and completed and turned in by beginning of the next scheduled lab.

New Unit Objectives: Will be passed out one week before starting the unit.

Holidays: Classes will not be in session:
        Wed. 11/11/93 - Veteran's Day
        Mon. 11/22/93 - 11/29/93 (classes resume)

Unit 1 Objectives

1. Define **Physics** as stated in class.

2. List, as stated in class and in order, the phases of the scientific method.

3. Given four written statements, identify, without error, the phase of scientific method used.

4. Given specific problems or scenarios and without conversion charts, be able to correctly convert and calculate areas of length, weight and volume by employing the English and Metric systems.

5. Given numerical values, select the correct scientific notation for each; no errors.

6. Given specific problems and without conversion charts, correctly convert temperatures between the Fahrenheit, Celsius, Rankine and Kelvin scales.

7. Define, as stated in class, absolute temperature.

8. Given a diagram based on a typical spirogram, correctly label all lung compartments with their titles and normal values, as stated in class.

9. Recognize, without error, the lung volume or capacity by the technique used to measure it.

10. Identify all lung volume alterations in obstructive and restrictive patterns.

11. Given a scenario, correctly distinguish between indicated PFTs and those PFTs that are not indicated.

12. Define, as stated in class, each of the properties related to Kinematics with 100% accuracy.

13. Explain, without error, Newton's three laws of motion by citing examples of each.

14. Define a vector quantity as state by NAVE and give one example of a vector that was mentioned in lecture.

15. Define the terms: equilibrium, static equilibrium and torque as stated by NAVE.

16. Define, according to NAVE, surface tension and its relationship to the terms cohesive and adhesive in respiration.

17. Define surfactant as to its composition, including the ratio; when it first appears in gestation and when it matures and stabilizes.

18. Given information and a set of values and in accordance to lecture notes, be able to interpret the stability of a patient's respiratory status with 100% accuracy.

Index